Kalliopi (Popi) Sotiriadou

Sport Development Processes and Practices in Australia

The Attraction, Retention/Transition, and Nurturing of Sport Participants and Athletes

Lambert Academic Publishing

Impressum/Imprint (nur für Deutschland/ only for Germany)
Bibliografische Information der Deutschen Nationalbibliothek: Die Deutsche Nationalbibliothek verzeichnet diese Publikation in der Deutschen Nationalbibliografie; detaillierte bibliografische Daten sind im Internet über http://dnb.d-nb.de abrufbar.
Alle in diesem Buch genannten Marken und Produktnamen unterliegen warenzeichen-, marken- oder patentrechtlichem Schutz bzw. sind Warenzeichen oder eingetragene Warenzeichen der jeweiligen Inhaber. Die Wiedergabe von Marken, Produktnamen, Gebrauchsnamen, Handelsnamen, Warenbezeichnungen u.s.w. in diesem Werk berechtigt auch ohne besondere Kennzeichnung nicht zu der Annahme, dass solche Namen im Sinne der Warenzeichen- und Markenschutzgesetzgebung als frei zu betrachten wären und daher von jedermann benutzt werden dürften.

Verlag: Lambert Academic Publishing AG & Co. KG
Dudweiler Landstr. 99, 66123 Saarbrücken, Deutschland
Telefon +49 681 3720-310, Telefax +49 681 3720-3109, Email: info@lap-publishing.com

Herstellung in Deutschland:
Schaltungsdienst Lange o.H.G., Berlin
Books on Demand GmbH, Norderstedt
Reha GmbH, Saarbrücken
Amazon Distribution GmbH, Leipzig
ISBN: 978-3-8383-3860-6

Imprint (only for USA, GB)
Bibliographic information published by the Deutsche Nationalbibliothek: The Deutsche Nationalbibliothek lists this publication in the Deutsche Nationalbibliografie; detailed bibliographic data are available in the Internet at http://dnb.d-nb.de.
Any brand names and product names mentioned in this book are subject to trademark, brand or patent protection and are trademarks or registered trademarks of their respective holders. The use of brand names, product names, common names, trade names, product descriptions etc. even without a particular marking in this works is in no way to be construed to mean that such names may be regarded as unrestricted in respect of trademark and brand protection legislation and could thus be used by anyone.

Publisher:
Lambert Academic Publishing AG & Co. KG
Dudweiler Landstr. 99, 66123 Saarbrücken, Germany
Phone +49 681 3720-310, Fax +49 681 3720-3109, Email: info@lap-publishing.com

Printed in the U.S.A.
Printed in the U.K. by (see last page)
ISBN: 978-3-8383-3860-6

The Sport Development Processes in Australia: The ARTN Model

Popi Sotiriadou

Supervisors

Professor Shayne Quick, Bond University

Professor David Shilbury, Deakin University

A book submitted for the Degree of Doctor of Philosophy in Sport Management in 2005 at the University of Technology, Sydney, Australia

Dedication

I cannot find words good enough to express my gratitude to mother for her role and anticipation in my starting and finishing this book. For all the things I could not share with or offer her all these years of my devoted studies, for all the agony that my absenteeism has caused her and in appreciation of her contribution, I dedicate this book to my dearly loved mother, Elli.

Acknowledgements

My name on the cover of this book might make it look like I did all the work in this project. It would be so unfair to take all the credit. Several people and institutions deserve my sincere acknowledgements for their most precious contributions. I present this page to thank *the Greek Institute of Scholarships* that granted me with a scholarship to conduct the study. I wish to thank *Professor Shayne Quick* for giving me the opportunity to 'achieve the impossible' and always believed in me. *Professor David Shilbury* for his guidance has been invaluable in terms of conceptualising this book. The quality of this project would have not been the same had it not been for David. I would like to thank *Scott Porman*, my beloved partner, for his affectionate and caring nature who nourishes me with optimism, support and happiness. I must also thank some special friends; I thank *Linda*, *Diane* and *John* for being there for me when I was a stranger in this country and for their unconditional friendship.

Table of Contents

iv

List of Figures

List of Tables

List of Abbreviations

Australian Baseball Federation	ABF
Australian Capital Territory	ACT
Australian Cricket Board	ACB
Australian Football League	AFL
Australian Institute of Sport	AIS
Australian Labor Party	ALP
Australian Rugby Union	ARU
Australian Sports Commission	ASC
Australian Weightlifting Federation	AWF
Australian Yachting Federation	AYF
Bocce Federation of Australia	BFA
Business Operations Group	BOG
Confederation of Australian Motor Sport Limited	CAMS
Confederation of Australian Sport	CAS
Department of Industry Science and Resources	DISR
Federation of Judo Australia	FJA
Key Performance Indicators	KPIs
National Sporting Organisations	NSOs
New South Wales	NSW
Olympic Athlete Program	OAP
Roller Sports Australia	RSA
Sport Development Group	SDG
Sport Development Officers	SDOs
State Sporting Organisations	SSOs
Surf Life Saving Australia	SLSA
United States of America	USA
United States Olympic Committee	USOC

CHAPTER 1: INTRODUCTION

1 INTRODUCTION

The distribution of resources to mass participation versus the few elite athletes has, since the instigation of Federal Government involvement with sport in Australia in the mid-1970s, been a major concern for both the Federal Government and the public. This book provides an analysis of the sport development processes as they occur in the Australian sports environment. In particular, it focuses on one aspect of Australian Federal Government sport policy, the debate surrounding elite versus mass participation. The significance of this policy issue lies within the increased role and involvement of the Federal Government in sport development in Australia. This long-established involvement results in the provision of policy, funding and delivery programs at all levels of sport development.

1.1 PUBLIC POLICY ANALYSIS AND POLITICAL IDEOLOGIES

While *public policy* by definition is "whatever governments choose to do or not to do" (Forward, 1974, p. 1), *public policy analysis* is the "policy-orientated research, which aims to improve public decision-making" (John, 1998, p. 204). The theoretical origins of this book lie within the political science framework, since according to Heclo (1983) the analysis of public policy is one of the most important fields of political science. John (1998) explained that public policy's main contribution to political science is that it seeks to explicate the operation of the political system. However, he continued, political systems may vary depending on the ideology governments espouse. Hence, regardless of the results of the analysis, the public policy approaches adopted by governments differ according to their *political ideologies*.

Burden (1998) highlighted the importance of being able to identify and make sense of the ideological and political positions taken by governments in understanding the literature on public policy. He explained that ideologies are "relatively systematic theories of the relationship between needs, welfare, the state and policy" (p. 10), and identified three approaches under the headings of *"right"*, *"centre"* and *"left"* (p. xiii).

1

Leach (1993) provided the *political spectrum model*, which illustrates the ideological approach (see Figure 1.1).

Figure 1.1: The Political Spectrum Model

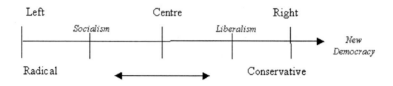

Source: Leach, 1993, p. 1

Leach (1993) explained that the left side of the ideological spectrum identifies the most radical political ideologies of anarchism and communism, with the latter being a step closer to the centre. At the right end of the model fascism and conservatism find their place (with the latter closer to the centre). Additionally, Leach (1993) indicated that by the middle of the twentieth century, the world was largely divided between two contesting major ideologies, liberalism (to the centre right side of the continuum) and socialism (to the centre left side of the model).

Conceptualising political ideologies is important as it aids the understanding of the way governments approach public policy issues. Burden (1998) claimed that liberalistic ideology advocates minimum government as well as individual and market freedom. In this view, extensive state welfare provision is generally seen as undesirable, although it may be required to maintain social order by improving the conditions faced by the most hard-pressed members of society. In contrast, Burden (1998) explained, socialist states view state welfare provision as a form of collective intervention which is designed to meet a range of social needs and solve important social problems in the general interest. Proponents of this view normally support public policies.

In addition to political ideologies, a factor that contributes to the importance of carrying out policy analysis is that public policy may also deal with a variety of substantive areas/issues such as defence, energy, environment, education, health, taxation, inflation, sport and so on (Dye, 1987). Dubnick and Bardes (1983) argued that public policies deal with problems ranging from what is necessary for survival (e.g. provision of food) to demands for some of the amenities of life that only an affluent society can afford (e.g. public swimming pools).

Scholars such as Armstrong (1985; 1987), Bramham, Hylton, Jackson and Nesti (2001) and Johnson and Frey (1985) have argued about the integrated nature of sport policy within the public policy domain. For example, Armstrong (1987) contended that sport policy is a variant of public policy. Furthermore, Johnson and Frey (1985) explained that with respect to "the relationship between government and sport … many issues in the world of sport are also issues of public policy" (p. 1). Therefore, public policy affects the structure, operations, and future of sport. Sport development, as one of sport policy concerns, is also incorporated into the public policy sphere. For example, Bramham et al. (2001) argued that "sports development lies at the heart of public policy" (p. 6).

1.2 THE SPORT POLICY DEBATE

Public policy analysis has been the focus of considerable research since the 1950s. Consequently, there is no shortage of literature addressing public policy issues (John, 1998). However, Chalip (1996b) believed that although policy journals are awash with studies on "education, welfare, military, environmental, tax, health, and criminal justice policies, studies of national sport policies are relatively rare" (p. xiii). According to Chalip (1996b), the study of sport policy can reveal a great deal about the most instrumental policy concerns such as sport development policies. Finally, he asserted that sport development policies have been the focus of considerable policy debate over the last three decades.

Sport development as defined by Eady (1993) is the "promotion and implementation of positive change" (p. 8). Moreover, in a more extensive definition, he states that:

> Sport development is a process whereby effective opportunities, processes, systems, and structures are set up to enable and encourage people in all or particular groups and areas to take part in sport and recreation or to improve their performance to whatever level they desire. (p. 8)

3

An "important and contentious area facing sports development has been the need to work at both grassroots levels and in elite sport" (Bramham et al., 2001, p. 2). Disagreements as to where the focus should be, and disputes about the importance of each level, have bedevilled this area (Bramham et al., 2001).

Sport policies, as they relate to sport development, have been approached differently internationally and intranationally at various times, by different governments (Chalip, Johnson & Stachura, 1996). First at the international level, the literature on national sport policies (e.g. Chalip et al., 1996; Houlihan, 1997a; Landry, Landry & Yerles, 1991; Shin-pyo, MacAloon & DaMatta, 1988) demonstrates how different countries have approached sport development. For example, in socialist countries, such as China, the former Soviet Union and Cuba, sport does not exist independent of the state (Donnelly, 1991). Chalip (1991) argued that the differences in legitimation for sport policy explain, in part, the different focus resultant policies have had. Chalip (1991) has also suggested that "one reason that the degree of government involvement differs cross-nationally" (p. 249) is their differing ideological bases.

Indicatively, the Cuban government appears to have initiated a successful policy on national fitness and *Sport for All* programs. Donnelly (1991) suggested that "a broadly based system of participation can form the base of a pyramid out of which the elite athletes will emerge" (p. 305). This has not been the case in Cuba. Rather, the Cuban government has modelled a system of early identification and specialised training for those with the potential to be high performance athletes (Donnelly, 1991). Cuba has achieved international success in elite sport. However, elite athletes cannot be considered as the first political priority (Rodichenko, 1991). According to Pettavino and Pye (1996) the Cuban government is dedicated to seeking egalitarianism in all areas of society, including sport.

By comparison, under governments that strongly conform to liberal ideologies, such as the United States, policies that cater for mass participation development, such as Sport for All programs, have not been asserted. Rather, in the American political context "sport policies have been legitimised in elite terms as matters of national representation" (Chalip, 1991, p. 249). The rhetoric of American public policy

4

historically has been that sport is independent of government, and does not attain the level of policy significance that it has acquired in other counties, including Australia (Chalip & Johnson, 1996). Evidently, different countries approach the same public policy issue/problem (i.e. sport development) from a different perspective, depending on the ideology they espouse.

Second at the intranational level, change in the approach to sport policy may also occur in countries over time. This becomes clear by examining Australian sport policy. Stewart-Weeks (1997) identified three *policy waves*.

> The first wave lasted from the beginning of the century to the mid-1970s and saw a fairly distant relationship between the government and sport. The second wave started with the first Whitlam Government sports budget and will culminate in the Sydney 2000 Games. The third wave is a convenient way to describe the post-2000 environment. (p. 6)

Studies examining Federal Government sport policy during the second wave indicate that it has only been since the mid-1980s that Australian sport policy "has come of age and been recognized as a legitimate area of public expenditure" (Farmer & Arnaudon, 1996, p. 2). This era coincided with a period of extended governance by the Australian Labor Party (ALP), and is consistent with leftist ideology and equality of sporting opportunities.

According to Veal's (2002) rationales for government intervention, many publicly provided services are maintained because of tradition, as it is politically difficult to introduce changes, especially when there is a lobby group that may be offended. By the time the Liberal Party was elected in 1996, sport had established itself within the Federal Government as a legitimate policy concern. Hence, despite preferences for minimal government, the Liberal Party in Australia not only supported and promoted sport, it increased its involvement following its election in 1996 (Shilbury & Deane, 1995). Various programs and resource allocations supported the development of Australian athletes and their successful performances at the Sydney 2000 Olympic Games. Veal (1994) added to the justification for increased Federal Government involvement with sport arguing that certain projects are too large to be taken on by the private sector. Hence, with the 2000 Olympic Games looming in Sydney, the Liberal

Government increased and confirmed its involvement with sport. This was achieved mainly through the implementation of the Olympic Athlete Program (OAP) and the support for constructing the Olympic sporting facilities.

1.3 FEDERAL GOVERNMENT INVOLVEMENT WITH SPORT

Hogwood and Gunn (1984) argued that sport policy does not occur in a vacuum, rather within a government's sport *"policy space"* (p. 13). Webb, Rowland and Fascano (1990) explained that policy space is the area of activity "for which government takes responsibility, regulates and provides support for sport" (p. 6). As far as the organisations involved within the policy space are concerned, they form the policy arena, or they are the *"policy players"*. Sport policy players are the sport organisations within the sport policy space responsible for the formulation and implementation of sport policy (Webb et al., 1990). An overview of the existing literature on Australian sport policy since the mid-1970s is useful in illustrating the increasing Federal Government involvement with sport (Shilbury & Deane, 1995) and the expansion of policy space and players (Armstrong, 1987).

A number of developments occurred in the Australian sport system post 1975 with the most influential being the establishment of the Australian Sport Commission (ASC), a statutory authority responsible for sport policy. According to the Department of Industry Science and Resources (DISR) and the Sport 2000 Taskforce Report (DISR, 1999), from the great number of people and organisations involved in delivering sport in Australia, the Federal Government through the ASC plays the most important role in relation to sport policy and the provision of finance. The ASC is responsible for implementing the government's national sports policy. Working with sporting organisations at all levels (i.e. national, state, and local), the two delivery arms of the ASC – the Australian Institute of Sport (AIS) and the Sport Development Group - promote the basic sports philosophy of the Australian government: participation and excellence (ASC, 2003d).

Hierarchically, the closest sport policy players to the ASC are the sporting organisations at the national level, namely the National Sporting Organisations (NSOs). NSOs manage and co-ordinate the participation and development of individual organised sports through a network of delivery agents (i.e. clubs) and registered participants. The Federal Government, through the ASC, funds NSOs, which then channel funds to the state, regional and local clubs (Westerbeek, Shilbury & Deane, 1995). The nature of the NSOs recognised by the Federal Government (i.e. those NSOs that receive funding from the ASC) varies according to their Olympic or non-Olympic status and the levels of funding they receive from the ASC.

Chalip (1995) contended that the increase in government involvement with sport necessitates sport policy analysis being an area of study. Interestingly, the existing body of literature on Australian sport policy studies appears to be attributed to a limited number of scholars, such as Farmer and Arnaudon (1996), Houlihan (1997a), Jobling (1991), Semotiuk (1981, 1987), Shilbury and Deane (2001) and Stewart-Weeks (1997). Jarvie (1987) explained that the lack of sport policy studies and research in the area from a political science perspective, at least up until 1987, was due to ambivalence towards becoming involved in political debates concerning leisure and sport. The available literature covers the initial expansion in the Federal Government's involvement with sport from the mid-1970s until the early 1990s. Yet, since the early 1990s, there has been a remarkable increase in government involvement in sport. This increased involvement has not been followed by equivalent scholarly interest, leaving a void in the literature pertaining to sport policy in Australia since the early 1990s.

In addition, the focus of the existing research in the area of sport policy in Australia has been largely descriptive rather than hermeneutic (i.e. interpretive and critical). Chalip (1995) argued that the nature of sport policy debates requires the development and application of hermeneutic methods for policy analysis. He further suggested that there are five necessary elements for sport policy analysis to proceed. They are operative limitations, focusing event(s), problem definitions, problem attributions and decision frames, and each must be identified. These five elements comprise the *Model of Sport Policy Analysis,* which was introduced and used by Chalip (1995) to analyse the formulation of PL 95-606, the Amateur Sports Act in the United States.

Chalip (1995) described these five elements and the way they interrelate as follows. *Legitimations* reflect the political ideologies espoused by governments, and set the

7

government space for policymakers (i.e., the boundaries for policy making). However, Chalip (1995) argued that "legitimations are insufficient to generate policy action" (p. 5). Therefore, it takes an event of national significance, for example failure to meet expectations to substantially increase mass participation numbers after the 2000 Sydney Olympic Games, to "symbolize a policy issue and focus policymakers' attention on proposals to redress the issue" (p. 5). Hence, *focusing events*, as described by Chalip (1995), are "symbolic representations of policy concern" and "give momentum to policy making" (p. 5).

Legitimations and focusing events generate (a) *problem definition* and (b) *attributions*. Problem definitions specify what it is that policies within the given government space "must do" (Chalip, 1995, p. 5) and indicate the aspects of a situation that require redress. Weimer (1993) argued that problem definition involves three parts: a) investigation of the nature and probable causes of the problem, b) justification of public policy intervention to amend the problem, and c) specification of the relevant goals for evaluating sport policy solutions. Problem definitions give rise to decision *frames*, the parts of the analysis that provide and determine what information or generalisations are pertinent to redress the policy debate and support the decision making (Chalip, 1991). Finally, the problem attributions are the causes/origins of the event. Therefore, they indicate the areas where policymakers need to focus if they are to resolve an issue.

With reference to the formulation of the Amateur Sport Act 1978 in the United States of America (USA), Chalip (1995) illustrated the applicability and significance of his model by analysing the framing and implementation of American policies on Olympic sports. Chalip (1995) first examined the focusing event(s) (USA Olympic Failures, pre-1978); second, the legitimations (National Prestige) and problem definition (desire to Beat Soviet Athletes); third, the attribution (Administrative Incompetence); and finally, the decision frame (Administrative Rationalisation - without government control), and then discussed the outcomes of the policy discourse.

Chalip's (1995) approach to policy analysis represents a post-hoc examination of a sport policy issue. He analysed a case after the focusing event was resolved. This represents a limitation of the applicability of the Chalip (1995) model to a real life

8

examination of sport development when the actual sport development processes (i.e., the focusing event) are under examination, are not given. Real life situations necessitate an empirical examination of the attributions of the event rather than taking them for granted. As there is no evidence on how the model fits the results of the book, its use may set up false expectations regarding the results on sport development processes.

A further limitation of the Chalip's (1995) model and its applicability to this book is its one-way causal relationship representation of the policy issue under examination, when a main characteristic of sport development is the two-way causal relationships of its building blocks. For example, Australia's elite athletes' failure to win any gold medals at the 1976 Montreal Olympic Games gave momentum to policy making in Australia which resulted in fundamental sport development changes and improvement of athletes' international performances. In addition, even though Chalip (1995) suggested the relationships between the variables and the order of examining the five elements of the model, there is no obvious starting point directing the analysis. In conclusion, the Chalip (1995) model on sport policy, however useful in studying the Amateur Sports Act in the United States, does not lend itself as a theoretical driver for the book.

1.4 ELITE VERSUS MASS PARTICIPATION AND THE SPORT DEVELOPMENT CONTINUUM

Support and services to organised sport and their NSOs through the ASC ranges from increasing mass participation to identifying talented athletes at the elite level. This reflects the two-fold aim of Federal Government sport policy, (a) to promote and encourage community participation in sports, and (b) to significantly improve Australia's sporting performance at the elite level (ASC, 2002a).

Farmer and Arnaudon (1996) argued that:

> The balance between elite- and mass-sport is always unstable in that, with limited funds, there is always a tension between funding for international competitors to produce world champions, and funding participation in programs to deliver national health and socioeconomic benefits. (pp. 20- 21)

However, they claimed that there was no longer a debate in Australian sporting circles as to whether funding sport was a government priority. The sports policy debate shifted to the key issues concerning "distribution of funding, namely selective versus broad based; centralized versus decentralized; elite versus participation" (p. 20). Farmer and Arnaudon (1996) further argued that since the mid-1980s, when the Federal Government's involvement with sport increased, questions of elite versus mass participation "became the central themes in Australian sport policy" (p. 10).

Traditionally, three s*port development continuum* models have illustrated the relationship between mass and elite participation (Eady, 1993; Shilbury & Deane, 2001). Eady (1993) explained that the term *continuum* in diagrammatic form is an attempt to illustrate the way in which the sports development continuums provide pathways for individuals "to progress to the level of performance which is appropriate/available to them" (p. 14).

There are four levels in the continuum (see Figure 1.2). Cooke (1986) argued that these are (a) awareness, (b) participation, (c) enjoyment and (d) excellence. Bramham et al. (2001) and Houlihan (2000) recognised the following four levels:

Figure 1.2: Model 1, The Traditional Sport Development Continuum/Pyramid

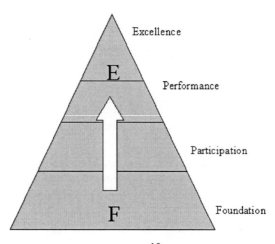

Source: Bramham et al., 2001, p. 3

(a) *Foundation* is the base of the pyramid/continuum, and involves the vital first steps of learning basic movement skills.

(b) *Participation* is one level up from the foundation, and involves exercising one's leisure option, taking part in sport for health, fitness, friends and fun.

(c) *Performance* is one level higher than participation, and involves the challenge of increasing proficiency by striving to improve personal standards of participation.

(d) *Excellence* is reaching the top of the continuum and involves accomplishing nationally and publicly recognised standards of performance.

While these levels appear to be common in all existing sport development model variations, Eady (1993) provided an interpretation of the remaining attributes of the three sport development models. Traditionally in Australia, sport development has been theoretically aligned with the *sports pyramid* (Bloomfield, 1974). In the sports pyramid model, which represents the first effort to graphically reflect on sport development processes, the goal is to increase the number of participants at each level to increase the number of potential elite athletes flowing through to the apex or top of the pyramid. Theoretically, the wider the base, the greater the number of participants at each level above (Donnelly, 1991; Eady, 1993). Hence, governments inject resources at the bottom of the sport development continuum, expecting that a broad base will produce many champions (Veal, 1994). According to Hogan and Norton (2000), this process is referred to as the *bottom-up* or *trickle-up* effect, and "was essentially the basis of the Whitlam Government's sports budget" (p. 205).

The pyramid framework can be examined from another perspective, when government resources are allocated directly at the top of the pyramid and a *top-down* or *trickle-down* effect is expected (ASC, 1994). The top-down process asserts that successful performances by elite athletes encourage people to take part in physical activity and lead to an increase in mass participation numbers at the base of the pyramid. However, there is no evidence to suggest that either of the above relationships is accurate.

11

Moreover, it allows governments, depending on their political agenda, to claim and argue any relationship, to justify funding allocations accordingly (Hogan & Norton, 2000). Hogan and Norton (2000) argued that "since the establishment of the AIS, the Australian government, through the ASC, has clearly adopted the second philosophy as its basis for sports funding. That is, a large amount of the ASC's budget is directed towards high-performance athletes in a decreasing number of sports" (p. 205).

Shilbury and Deane (2001) claimed that the sports pyramid model assumes that people progress logically to the next level of sport participation without any movement between recreational competitions and semi-elite or elite competitions. Hence, the sporting pyramid is considered to be "static" (p. 189). A second model, to illustrate the above mobility, resulted in a variation of the sport development continuum, which with the addition of arrows shows the different directions individuals can take within the continuum (see Figure 1.3). This model simply illustrates how individuals can move up and down the continuum whenever they choose or are ready to.

Figure 1.3: Model 2, The Sport Development Continuum

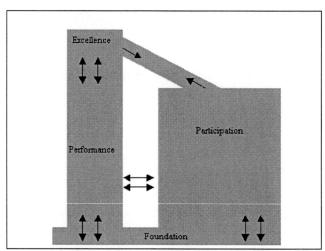

Source: Eady, 1993, p. 14

A third effort to better encapsulate this mobility resulted in a more dynamic model which incorporates the concept of a *performance decision* point when "a conscious decision is made to remain at a particular level of performance for the time being" (Eady, 1993, p. 15). This model as shown in Figure 1.4 returns to the initial graphical representation of a pyramid and allows for the possibility of the individual leaving and re-entering the sport and altering the level at which they aspire to take part over time. Overall, these frameworks present a very simplistic approach to sport development and do not explain the actual sport development processes and pathways that take place.

Eady (1993) explained that the term *sport development continuum* is slightly misleading when used to describe the route that an individual might take when progressing through the defined different levels of sport participation. Eady (1993) argued that:

> Both the term continuum - which implies an imperceptible transition - and the 'levels' of participation are over-simplifications but they do allow practitioners and academics to rationalise and describe in simple terms the process to which the SDO [Sport Development Officer] and others involved in sport and recreation are contributing. (p. iv)

Additionally, McDonald and Tungatt (1992) argued that the relationship between mass participation and elite performance is a far more complex interaction than the simple pyramid model would suggest.

Figure 1.4: Model 3, The Sport Development Continuum

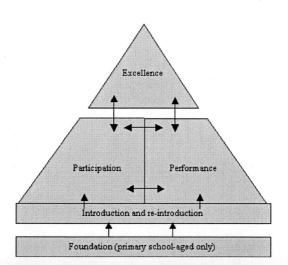

Excellence

Participation · Performance

Introduction and re-introduction

Foundation (primary school-aged only)

Source: Eady, 1993, p. 15

The existing conflict of perceptions identified in relation to the sport development continuum implies the recognition of two opposing strategies, (a) top-down (trickle-down), and (b) bottom-up (trickle-up) processes. These two concepts reflect diverse sport policy approaches. Chalip (1996a) argued that the conflict of theories is legitimised since different governments may have grounded their policies in very different understandings/presuppositions, which may generate subtle yet telling differences in policy implementation.

Collectively, the existing sport development frameworks only depict people's mobility from one level to another and not the trickle effects purportedly driving sport policies, programs, and their exceptions of outcomes. Additionally, no framework exists to explicitly illustrate and justify the trickle-up and down-effects. Moreover, there is no model or theory describing the interrelationship between sport policy and sport development processes. Hence, the existing models are inadequate to show how sport policy influences and shapes sport development processes. These issues led to the rejection of the existing sport development continuum as a viable theoretical framework to explain interrelationships between sport development processes and government sport policy. This rejection left no existing theoretical framework to underpin the study, which in turn suggested the need for a grounded theory approach as will be discussed in Chapter 3.

1.5 STATEMENT OF THE PROBLEM

The research problem that this book will address is the following:

How does Federal Government sport policy impact on elite and mass participation in terms of national sport development processes?

Essentially, this book aims to examine how the Federal Government's sport policy impacts on sport development processes at a national level in order to understand the role of sport policies in providing the required pathways for sport development in Australia. This is achieved by empirically building a theory of sport development relevant to the Australian sport system. The author argues that the current sport development pyramids/continuum (see models 1, 2 and 3) do not address the question of the way the trickle-down and trickle-up processes operate in Australia. More specifically, this book will demonstrate that sport development does not operate in a vacuum and that the sport policy players have a significant role in the process.

Then author of this book argues that there are sport development stakeholders, practices and pathways which are essential for successful development processes. These need to be empirically studied and identified. In essence, this study is the first effort to provide a means "of identifying the different roles and responsibilities for those involved in sports development, from the lowest to the higher levels of achievement" (Bramham et al., 2001, p. 3). The research areas of inquiry are summarised below:

(a) What is the role of the key sport development players in sport development?
(b) How do sport policies affect or shape sport development processes?
(c) What are the available sport development pathways and how do they take place/function?
(d) What are the relationships between sport policy players, policies and sport development processes?

1.6 JUSTIFICATION OF CURRENT STUDY

The existing research on Australian sport policies is limited to the work of Houlihan (1997a), Jobling (1991), Farmer and Arnaudon (1996), Semotiuk (1981, 1987), Shilbury and Deane (2001) and Stewart-Weeks (1997). Even though some of this work was published in the late 1990s, it nevertheless only reflects the sport policy development up until the very early 1990s. Therefore, these studies do not examine the current impact of sport policy in Australia. This book will fill a void in the literature of Australian studies on sport policy. Additionally, it will accomplish the above in a

15

hermeneutic, analytic approach, to provide the first empirical sport policy analysis in Australia in relation to sport development.

Most importantly, the theoretical significance of this book lies in its contribution towards building theory on sport development processes, in clarifying the conflict between opposing assumptions on elite versus mass participation development and by critically evaluating Australian practices. According to Eady (1993), the current sport development pyramids/continuum do not offer a description or rationalisation of the policy players involved. This book incorporates sport policy players and their perception of the sport development process to demonstrate the relationship between policy players and sport development processes.

The book provides a theoretical framework that incorporates all the aforementioned factors (i.e. stakeholders, practices and pathways) which determine sport development processes in Australia. Furthermore, it aims to construct a theory on sport development processes which will be available for further research and testing of hypotheses. By utilising inductive reasoning, grounded theory allows a substantive theory to emerge which fits the situation being researched, deals with the specific area of inquiry and explains the processes and interactions under study. The results of this study indicate the effects of national sport policy on organisations of the Australian sport industry operating at a state or local level, hence offering a comprehensive depiction of the Australian sport industry.

Weimer (1993) argued that the policy analyst seeks to establish the presuppositions of policy makers. Chalip (1995) summarised Weimer's work by maintaining that the objective is not merely to describe the logic of policy debates but rather "to identify points of poor logic, to facilitate criticism of the driving assumptions, and to locate significant considerations that have been excluded from policy deliberations" (p. 5). Analysis of this kind can serve the traditional aims of policy analysis – to enhance the quality of policy design (Chalip, 1995; Weimer, 1993). However, these same analyses "provide the requisite tools for identifying research needs and formulating argument strategies to be applied to lobbying efforts and public opinion campaigns. In this sense policy analysis is an essential tool for sport management" (Chalip, 1995, p. 5).

This book explores the dynamics of sports development policy in Australia, and provides an advanced understanding of government involvement with sport and sport policies for sport managers. It also provides a framework to assist understanding of successful sport development from elite to mass participation and vice versa. Additionally, this book offers a theoretical framework with considerable potential to future scholars for further research. Additional research could test the model using a quantitative empirical study and extend the boundaries of knowledge on sport development in Australia and internationally.

1.7 METHODOLOGY AND DATA ANALYSIS

Chapter 2 reinforces the argument that there is minimal conceptual work in the area of sport development and a lack of cohesive theory in the field. Hence, there is little theory to postulate and test hypotheses. Therefore, the study has an *explorative nature* and aims to better understand the area of sport policy and sport development. The explorative nature of the research problem and the recognition of the theoretical vacuum as it pertains to the sport development process in Australia indicate that a qualitative methodological approach is the most appropriate. According to Strauss and Corbin (1998), social processes can be best explored by using grounded theory which has come to rank among the most influential and widely used modes of qualitative research.

The *cases* pertinent to this study are the Australian NSOs, which represent sports at a national level and liaise directly with the Federal Government statutory authority, the ASC, regarding sport policy and development issues. From the variety of surveying options available, this study used public documents as its primary source of data generation, and more specifically NSOs' annual reports. The justification for examining NSO annual reports lies in the nature of these documents and the fact that they constitute the formal written source of information that reflects both NSOs' operations with regard to sport development policy and practice, and interactions with the Federal Government and other key players. Additionally, these reports constitute the annual contributions of all State Sporting Organisations (SSOs), staff and members of the board of directors collectively in a reliable publicly available form.

Data was collected from the annual reports of 35 NSOs covering both Olympic and non-Olympic sports and varying from high to low profile. From the 35 NSOs 13 sports received more than $1 million each from the ASC during the financial year 2001/02, while the other 22 sports received less than $1 million each in total grants. The data collection process involved gathering information, analysing the data, back to gathering more information, analysing the data, and so forth (Glaser, 1978). This process allows for theoretical sampling, that is, the process of data collection where "the analyst jointly collects, codes, and analyzes his data and decides what data to collect next and where to find them, in order to develop his theory as it emerges" (Glaser, 1978, p. 36). As concepts emerged, further sampling was guided by the need to test assumptions about emerging analytic concepts and their properties.

The constant comparison of incident to incident, a concept to more incidents, and concept to concept with the purpose of finding the best fit of concepts to a hypothesis, as suggested by Glaser (1978), was employed in this study. Ultimately, similarities and differences indicated patterns that were utilised as part of the theory development. The constant comparison of 'cases' facilitates the coding processes that involved a) Substantive (Open) Coding, which unravels substantive codes, their properties and the core category; b) Theoretical Coding that links substantive codes and their properties, and developing hypotheses – or building a 'story' that connects the categories; and c) Writing and Theory Advancement. During this stage, and after the coding is finished, the analyst goes beyond the descriptive story by elaborating an analytical story and finally the second body of literature is incorporated in the story line for similar and dissimilar theories to be integrated.

1.8 LIMITATIONS

This book is concerned with one aspect of Australian Federal Government sport policy, that is, policy formulation and implementation in relation to elite and mass participation development. It investigates sport development processes from a particular angle, that of the NSOs, and explores the phenomenon as it is represented at the national level. Even though NSOs report on how sport development processes occur at all levels, the fact that this study did not explore all levels of sporting organisations represents a limitation. Additionally, the study excludes sports that are not represented by a national body or funded by the Federal Government via the ASC. The justification for excluding NSOs that are not recognised by the ASC lies in the fact that ASC policies are only applicable to those NSOs that are recognised, receive funding, interact with the ASC on a regular basis and apply the ASC policies in practice. From all the funded NSOs, those that catered for the development of sport at only one end of the sport continuum (elite or mass participation) were also excluded.

The period of examination comprised from 1999 to 2002. This timeframe covers a four-year funding cycle that the Federal Government espouses. This pertains to the era between the lead up to the Sydney Olympic Games and the post-Olympic Federal Government sport policy plan announced in 2001. According to Stewart-Weeks (1997) this era marks the transition period from the second to the third wave of sport policy in Australia. Even though annual reports are documents with public accountability, it is impractical to verify that their content depicts the reality. Nevertheless, qualitative research techniques such as interviews have also been criticised for not being accurate accounts of reality. Regarding the generalisability of the findings deriving from NSOs documents, as each case was selected for its contribution towards the emerging theory, it was this selecting that ensured that the theory is "comprehensive, complete, saturated, and accounts for negative cases" (Morse, 1999, p. 5).

1.9 BOOK OUTLINE

Chapter 2 provides a review of the literature and the empirical and theoretical background relevant to this book. It also illustrates the gap in the relevant body of knowledge. Chapter 2 explores the existing body of knowledge and, more specifically, the sport policy experience, its major players, and the Australian policy approach in relation to the problem. Additionally, the literature provides comparative studies to present different approaches other countries have initiated in response to similar situations.

Following the literature review, Chapter 3 provides an analysis of the existing controversy over the different approaches to grounded theory and justifies the methodological choices made for this study. It explains the coding processes used and supports them with illustrative examples of the different coding stages. The chapter concludes with a presentation of the limitations of the study and the ways they were addressed by the researcher.

Chapters 4, 5 and 6 offer a comprehensive description and analysis of the results on *Sport Development Processes* as they take place in Australia. This discussion is supported by reference to existing literature that reinforces or contradicts the results of this book. These chapters represent the three main codes of this study. Chapter 4 provides a stakeholder analysis by discussing the Australian *Sport Development Stakeholders*, the Federal Government policies and the ways the sport development stakeholders are involved with sport development. Chapter 5 explains what *Sport Development Practices* the Sport Development Stakeholders are involved with. In addition, it illustrates the role these practices play in sport development. Finally, Chapter 6 provides an analysis of the *Sport Development Pathways* that are in place to facilitate the Sport Development Processes in Australia. This chapter concludes with the presentation of the *Australian Sport Development Processes Model*.

Chapter 7 is the concluding chapter of this book and summarises the theory on Sport Development Processes in Australia. It discusses the fundamental contribution of the theory developed in this field in terms of its theoretical input and practical applications by sport policy and development practitioners. The book concludes with suggestions for further verification research in order to advance the generalisability and testability of the developed theory.

1.10 SUMMARY

In summary, this chapter has laid the foundation for this book. This book aims to offer an understanding of the impact of the Federal Government's sport policy on national sport development processes in order to understand how the variables that determine the trickle-up and trickle-down effects influence such processes in Australia. This is achieved by empirically building a theory of sport development relevant to the Australian sport system. The research has been justified on the grounds of theoretical and practical significance. This chapter presented a brief overview of the justification and the methods used for this research. Limitations were acknowledged and the book structure outlined. On these foundations, the book can proceed with a detailed description of the research.

CHAPTER 2: SPORT POLICY AND DEVELOPMENT

2 INTRODUCTION

Chapter 2 is organised as follows: initially, section 2.1 is a discourse on (a) public policy and policy analysis, (b) political ideologies, (c) sport policy in the public policy sphere, and (d) the boundaries for policymaking. Then, section 2.2 is an introduction to the research problem with which this book is concerned. More specifically, the sport development debate on elite and mass participation in relation to Federal Government sport policies. The debate unfolds by means of the sport development continuum, which is utilised by the sport policy makers in Australia.

Next, section 2.3 is a review of (a) the historical developments of the sport system and policy in Australia, (b) main attributes of sport policy, and (c) what sport policies are set out to do. Following this, section 2.4 is a representation of sport development practices across a range of countries (as well as within countries over time) as a comparative study to allow the examination of different approaches to the same problem and enable a better focus in an effort to correct it. The last part of this chapter (section 2.5) summarises the research questions, and stresses the potential theoretical and practical importance of this study.

2.1 POLITICAL IDEOLOGIES AND SPORT POLICIES

Australian politics holds that government minimises interference in the daily lives of its constituents and maximises individual and private sector initiatives. The consequent legitimations for government interventions "establish the boundaries for policymaking" (Chalip, 1995, p. 5). According to Chalip (1995), legitimations should be explicit and be agreed early on in the process of policy analysis. Hence, they should emerge in advance as a reflection of policy. In order to locate the argument for the justification for government intervention in sport development, a description of the context in which it takes place, its history and origin, as well as the rationales and boundaries of Federal Government involvement with sport policy in Australia follows.

2.1.1 SPORT AS PUBLIC POLICY

Sport policy studies lie in the discourse of public policy (Armstrong 1987; Nixon & Frey, 1996; Olafson & Brown-John, 1986; Olin, 1981; Riess, 1998). Interest in public policy analysis commenced in the 1960s, when policy studies emerged as a sub-discipline of political science. The literature offers a variety of definitions for public policy. From the great number of authors who studied the discipline (e.g. Burden, 1998; Davis, Wanna, Warhurst & Weller, 1988; Dubnick & Bardes, 1983; Dye, 1976, 1987; Edwards, 2000; Forward, 1974; Ham & Hill, 1984; Heclo, 1983; Hill, 2000; John, 1998; Seiter, 1983; VanderZwaag, 1998) *policy* is a term for which there seems to be a certain amount of definitional agreement (Heclo, 1983). However, there is often little consistency in the definitions to describe *public policy* and *public policy analysis* employed by different writers, such as Dubnick and Bardes (1983), Dye (1976), Ham and Hill (1984), and Hill (2000).

Dye (1976) argued that "policy analysis is finding out what governments do, why they do it, and what difference it makes" (p. 1). However, it appears that the most commonly accepted definition of public policy is from Forward (1974) who argued that:

> Public policy equals actions taken by governments. Strictly speaking though, public policy must be policy which affects the public…this includes the actions of private citizens and corporations, for even when an area of activity is left entirely in private hands the very act of leaving it alone can be a deliberate policy by authorities. (p. 2)

Thus "any serious analysis of questions about public policy quickly expands into a discussion about politics in general and society as a whole" (Forward, 1974, p. 5).

Nixon and Frey (1996) maintained that public issues "are matters that are beyond the individual's immediate experience, local environment, and personal awareness; they reflect the larger social forces in a society" (p. 2). Faced with public problems, governments respond with statements and actions. Those statements and actions are the heart of public policies. The statements express the intentions of government actors, while the actions reflect the steps taken to fulfil those intentions. However, public policies are not solutions to problems but, as Dubnick and Bardes (1983) argued, they are responses to public problems. Therefore, to understand public policies we must understand first what makes a problem public. Dubnick and Bardes (1983) suggested "a problem becomes public when it calls for the use of government resources or involves groups so large in number or politically significant that government policymakers cannot ignore them" (p. 6). It is in this sense that public policies are established as possible solutions to public problems.

Hence, Dubnick and Bardes (1983) agreed on a problem-based definition that sees public policies as "the expressed intentions of government actors relative to a public problem and the activities related to those intentions" (p. 8). They concluded that "public policy analysis is the application of problem-solving techniques to questions concerning (1) the expressed intentions of government relative to a public problem and (2) those actions government officials take (or avoid) in attaining those objectives" (p. 11).

Dye (1987) further explored the term *policy analysis* and along with the concepts of intentions and actions (or inaction) by governments he added the notion that policy analysis assists in explaining the cause and consequences of various policies. He argued that public analysis involves:

> (1) a primary concern with explanation rather prescription, (2) a rigorous search for the causes and consequences of public policies, [and] (3) an effort to develop and test general propositions about the causes and consequences of public policy and to accumulate reliable research findings of general relevance. (p. 7)

As such, policy analysis encourages scholars "to attack critical policy issues with the tools of systematic inquiry" (Dye, 1987, p. 7).

Even though there is some disagreement on the definition of public policy and policy analysis, there is agreement between scholars, such as Heclo (1983) and O'Faircheallaigh, Wann and Weller (1999), that public policy is necessarily at the heart of the political scientist's concern. While the analysis of public policy was "one of the most rapidly expanding and least well-mapped areas of political science" (Heclo, 1983 p. 83) during the 1950s, it was not until 1960 that the new field within the discipline of political science emerged. With the social and economic problems of the inter-war period, "there was an upsurge of interest by British and American scholars in the study of particular government policies" (Heclo, 1983, p. 86). This in turn enriched political science research with another perspective, that of policy analysis in the 1960s in the USA (you have already introduced the acronym) (Hill, 2000; John, 1998), and research/interest in the United Kingdom (UK) followed not far behind.

The pervasiveness of public policies is explicated by a number of authors including Dubnick and Bardes (1983) and Dye (1987). They argued that public policies deal with problems that traverse a wide variety of substantial areas. For example, Hylton, Bramham, Jackson and Nesti (2001) confirmed the integration of sport policy into the discipline of public policy. Houlihan (1990) maintained that while some areas of public policy such as housing, transport and education afford a healthy literature concerning the processes by which policy is made, sport policy studies are sparse. He explained that this derives in part from the failure to recognise sport as a legitimate or core area of government involvement. Nevertheless, trends towards increased government involvement in sport suggest that "closer consideration" (p. 55) to sport policy should be given.

A number of authors who studied sport policy as a variant of public policy (e.g. Armstrong, 1985, 1987, 1988; Douglas, 1978; Houlihan, 1990, 1991, 1997b, 2000; Johnson, 1978; Johnson & Frey 1985; Ogle, 1997; Olafson & Brown-John, 1986; Olin, 1981; Veal, 1987, 1998; Webb et al., 1990) reinforce the breadth of public policy discourse. While authors such as Armstrong (1987) agreed that sport policy is a variant of public policy, Johnson and Frey (1985) maintained that the relationship between government and sport "and many issues in the world of sport also are [sic] issues of public policy" (p. 1). Armstrong (1988) in his thesis on *Gold Lust: Federal Sport Policy since 1975* argued that sport is a legitimate area of public policy and since "public policy cannot be neutral, policies affecting sport are no exception" (p. 362).

2.1.2 POLITICAL IDEOLOGIES

While the literature verifies the integration of sport into public policy, scholars studying public policy in Australia, such as Davis et al. (1988) and O'Faircheallaigh et al. (1999), claimed that there is much debate about its legitimate boundaries. According to Davis et al. (1988), there appear to be two main approaches adopted by governments: "[t]hose who oppose an extensive public sector" (p. 2) assuming that "government intervention is inherently inefficient and usually ineffective" (p. 2), and those committed to "maintaining or extending the activities of government" (p. 3). These approaches are important "when we consider the different interpretations" (Burden, 1998, p. xiii) by governments, as different interpretations have immediate implications for sport (Henry, 2001; Leach, 1993; Veal, 2002).

Bramham (2001) argued that to understand the policy process "it is essential to start at the policy studies end of the continuum by examining the broad ideological assumptions that not only direct policy but also underpin the very institutions that shape and deliver policy" (p. 9). Burden (1998) contended that to understand public policy, hence sport policy, it is essential to be able to identify and make sense of the ideological and political positions adopted by governments. By examining political positions, Brown (1973) suggested that political ideologies can be defined as follows:

> Any systematic set of attitudes and beliefs, whether about the nature of the universe, political policy, family structure and patterns or family planning, can be 'explained' with reference to a wider ideological context which may in its turn be related to a deeper ideological structure that uses for its terms an appeal to economic factors, reasons or emotion, or an appeal to a personality-based process of which the subject may be unaware. (p. 10)

In identifying additional functions that political ideology encompass, Bramham (2001) observed that political ideologies:

> offer a prescription of how the world ought to be and subsequently a guide or mandate for political policies and action. One of the major functions of political ideology is to provide a particular perspective on the world and to highlight the key issues, debates and problems that need to be tackled. Ideologies therefore provide understanding of how the world works as well as mapping out mission statements as to how the world needs to change and be managed. In the 'restricted' view, ideology refers to different political ideas debated and contested between and within political parties and party activists. (p. 9)

In simple terms, ideologies are "relatively systematic theories of the relationship between needs, welfare, the state and policy. They link abstract analyses of welfare concepts such as need, justice, equality and freedom with concrete political programmes of welfare reform" (Burden, 1998, p. 10) or, as Veal (1994) succinctly noted, political ideology consists of sets of "political ideas about how society should be run" (p. 20).

Burden (1998) claimed that in making sense of both political thought and public policy it is useful to distinguish the main ideological approaches. These are most commonly understood under the headings *right*, *centre* and *left*. The underlying model for the description of the political ideologies is the *Political Spectrum* model shown in Figure 1.1. According to Wilson (1988) the left-wing forces favour intervention with sport, while the right-wing forces support reliance on individual initiative and private entrepreneurship.

Located from the left to the right end of the continuum are Communism, Democratic Socialism, Social Democracy, Conservatism and Liberalism. The ideologies of each of these and their main attributes and implications for sport will be discussed in the following section. [NB Since the main difference between Democratic Socialism and Social Democracy is the tolerance of private enterprise and capitalism (Veal, 2002) only Social Democracy will be explored.]

Conservatism

Wilson (1988) argued that since the Industrial Revolution, the dominant ideologies in Western capitalist countries have been conservatism or liberalism. Both ideologies locate leisure and sport within the "private sphere" (Wilson, 1988, p. 9). Wilson (1988) continued that while the private sphere "connotes freedom and autonomy" (p. 9), the public sphere means "constraint and alienation" (p. 9). Conservatism emerged as a political ideology of the aristocracy to resist the French Revolution in the late 1780s (Bramham, 2001). As its name implies, conservatism emphasises the maintenance of the status quo and the preservation of all the pieces that proved to be successful in the past. According to Bramham (2001) and Veal (2002), what distinguishes conservatism from leftist ideologies is the belief that inequality is part of the natural order of things, hence inevitable. In relation to sport, conservative tenets favour elitism as a concept. Veal (1994) maintained that the use of public funds to support elite activity and excellence in sport "presents no problem" (p. 22) to conservatives.

Liberalism

Chronologically, liberalism was formed by the emerging middle class, the bourgeoisie, as a protest to the aristocrats' conservative, anti-individualistic creed (Bramham, 2001). According to Brett (1997) liberalism is a political philosophy which "places the rights and interests of the individual at the centre of its political thinking" (p. 149). Veal (2002) added that liberalism emphasises the freedom of the individual, the supremacy of the market, minimal state interference, low taxes and minimal controls on industries. The implications of such an ideology for sport are characterised by minimal state involvement, user-pays systems, privatisation of services, sponsorship, minimal to no state support of industry and finally, but least important, support of elitism and excellence in sport (Henry, 2001). As with the conservatives, the support of elitists and excellence is welcomed, yet private sector sponsorship would be preferable (Veal, 2002).

Social Democracy/Social Reformism

While liberalism thrived in the industrialist capitalism of the nineteenth century, social reformism "is very much the product of the twentieth century... it grew out of a range of working-class movements which sought government intervention to mitigate the intended and unintended consequences of market forces" (Bramham, 2001, p. 12). In contrast to the radical Communist/Marxist ideologies of overthrowing capitalism and establishing communist states and the liberal ideology stressing individualism, social reformism stresses the need for equality and the importance of a large government in order to redistribute resources through taxation, to protect the disadvantaged groups of society and provide a welfare state (Bramham, 2001; Veal, 2002). Moreover, and in contrast with conservative and liberalistic doctrines, it views government provision for mass sport participation, equality of opportunity in sport, and access and democratisation of institutions as highly important.

Communism/Marxism

According to Karl Marx's radical ideology, the relationship between employer and employee in capitalist societies is exploitative. He predicted that since investment opportunities for capitalists will eventually be exhausted and profit margins will decrease unless further exploitation of the working class takes place, those same workers should transform society into a socialist state controlled solely by them (Veal, 2002). However, with capitalism blooming, neo-Marxist alternatives arose seeking to interpret the survival of capitalism. Countries under a communist regime viewed sport as a means to promote the building of a strong nation, improve health and productivity, foster national integration, enhance military training and defence and combat crime (Xiangjun & Brownell, 1996).

As the investigation of the political ideologies indicates, different government approaches to public policy have different implications for one aspect of public policy concern, that of sport development (Henry, 2001). Pitter (1996) reinforced the argument that the state's role in sport policy development "is shaped by the organisational structure of governments and the political ideology of governing parties" (p. 48). Hence, while social reformists see the development of sport and leisure as a social service, stand for democratisation and support the right of access for all, the implication for sport development of liberal ideologies is the support of elitism and excellence (Henry, 2001). Bedecki (1979) argued that the degree to which governments are involved with sport appears to be directly related to an expressed political ideology.

Australian Ideological Phases

The Australian Labor Party (ALP) and the Liberal Party respectively represent the two main ideological approaches of social democracy and liberalism in Australia. While the ALP is Australia's oldest political party with its origins at the first Federal elections of 1901, its post-World War II term in government has been limited to the Whitlam years 1972-1975, the three consecutive Hawke governments from 1983 to 1990 and finally the Keating government in 1991 to 1996 (Australian Labor Party, 2003). Warhurst (1997) argued that the Labor Party has been notably unsuccessful in national elections. Conversely, since its introduction in 1944, the Liberal Party that has been the major policy player in Australia.

The Liberal Party of Australia was formed on the initiative of Robert Menzies. Menzies believed the non-Labor parties should unite to present an alternative government with greater personal freedom than that offered under Labor's socialist plans. Since its formation in 1944, the Liberal Party has become Australia's most successful political party. It was elected to government for 23 years from 1949 to 1972, and for another term of 7 years from 1975 to 1983. In 1996, 1998 and 2001 it was re-elected in coalition with the National Party of Australia (Liberal Party of Australia, 2003).

The major ideological standpoint of the party is a lean government that minimises interference in people's daily lives and maximises individual freedom and private sector initiative. Hence, the Liberal Party is a party of individual freedom and private enterprise (Liberal Party of Australia, 2003). Veal (2002) argued the distinct role that liberal governments play in promoting elitism as a symbol of individual success. Sport policy in Australian has been a reflection of the political stances of the government in power.

2.1.3 SPORT POLICY IN AUSTRALIA

Sport policy studies have generated worldwide attention from a great number of authors such as Baka (1976; 1986), Booth (1995), Bramham (2001), Chalip (1996a), DaCosta (1996), Farmer and Arnaudon (1996), Girginou (2001), Gittins (2000), Green and Oakley (2001), Haynes (1998), Henry and Nassis (1999), Hogan and Norton (2000), Houlihan (1990, 1991, 1997a, 1997b), Johnson (1978); Johnson and Frey (1985), Macintosh, Bedecki and Franks (1987), Mishra (1990), Oakley and Green (2001), Ogle (1997), Olafson and Brown-John (1986), Olin (1981), Puig (1996), Riordan (1993; 1995), Semotiuk (1987), Shilbury (2000), Shilbury and Deane (2001), Stewart-Weeks (1997), Thoma and Chalip (1996), Webb et al. (1990), Woodman (1988) and Zilberman (1996). However, while the extension of the ideological and political legitimations for Australian Federal Government involvement with sport development has existed for some time, sport policy in Australia has been studied by a small number of scholars (e.g. Armstrong, 1985, 1987, 1988; Booth, 1995; Farmer & Arnaudon, 1996; Hogan & Norton, 2000; Mishra, 1990; Semotiuk, 1987; Shilbury, 2000; Shilbury & Deane, 2001; Stewart-Weeks, 1997; Webb et al., 1990; Woodman, 1988).

Moreover, though some of this work was published in the late 1990s, it only addresses the sport policy development up until the very early 1990s. Therefore, the majority of these studies do not reflect the current sport policy issues in Australia. Additionally, the nature of the studies appears descriptive and not supported theoretically by a

30

framework resulting from an empirical study. Nevertheless, a description of sport policies provides a good starting point when establishing the policy boundaries and their context to better understand current situations (Chalip, 1995). Hence, the examination of the history of sport policy is necessary to locate arguments for the legitimacy of government action.

Lynch and Veal (1996) asserted that the Australian Federal Government's level of involvement with sport varies according to the political ideology and the policies of the government in power. As noted by Veal (2002), generally Labor governments tend to be more actively involved than Liberal governments, the latter believing in less government involvement in the community and minimum government generally. Previous research, such as Armstrong's (1988) thesis on sport policy in Australia, Farmer and Arnaudon (1996) and Jobling's (1991) studies on Australian sport policy, and the Sport 2000 Task Force (DISR, 1999) report, support Veal's (2002) statement. They all present a historical overview of sport policy in Australia and illustrate the fluctuating levels of Federal Government involvement with sport policy.

More specifically, Armstrong (1988) identified five periods of differing Federal Government approaches and involvement in sport policy: (a) the politics of neglect (Menzies, 1949-1972), (b) the politics of reform (Whitlam, 1972-1975), (c) the politics of managed decline (Fraser, 1975-1983), (d) the politics of elite sport, and (e) the politics of consensus (Hawke, re-elected in 1983, 1984, 1987-1990 successive terms). An examination of Federal Government sport policies within these five periods as well as the policy waves of the 1990s and 2000s follows.

(a) The politics of neglect

Jobling (1991) stated that it was not until 1939 that the Federal Government established the National Fitness movement by providing funds to set up councils in each state. Baka (1986) maintained that there was some assistance for team travel and accommodation to Commonwealth and Olympic Games and for costs associated with hosting such events. However, "financial support was meagre and even in 1968-69 the amount allocated for National Fitness Council purposes was only 416 000 $ [sic] for the six states and the Australian Capital Territory" (Jobling, 1991, p. 252).

31

At the Federal level, Robert Menzies, Liberal Prime Minister for 16 years, opposed any form of Federal sport policy. He argued that sport was ideologically and financially an issue of free choice for the individual, hence outside the realm of Federal Government responsibility (Armstrong, 1988). His successor, John Gorton, maintained much of this philosophy long after Menzies' retirement. In summing up the reason for the government's non-support of sport he noted: "On the question of sporting activities...the government does not believe it should enter into these matters but that the running of sporting activities should be done by the sporting bodies concerned" (House of Representatives, 1989, p. 56).

(b) The politics of reform

With the election of the ALP and its Prime Minister, Gough Whitlam, in December 1972, the Federal Government recognised sport as a legitimate area of involvement and expenditure during its term of office from 1972 to 1975 (Armstrong, 1988; Confederation of Australian Sport, 1999). In fact, the 1970s "turned out to be a watershed in the way Governments thought of sport" (Cooke, 1996, p. 17). In order to provide Australian citizens with mass sport participation opportunities, the first formal Federal Government support for sport was established through the formation of the Department of Sport and Recreation and the Ministry of Tourism and Recreation in 1972 (Farmer & Arnaudon, 1996; Jobling, 1991). According to Cashman (1995) the year 1972 marked a turning point in Federal Government involvement in sport. The mid-1970s witnessed an Urban Development Strategy whereby new leisure and sports facilities were provided as a means of improving the quality of life in urban and suburban areas (Confederation of Australian Sport, 1999).

> By working through local government, the Commonwealth upgraded and improved a range of existing facilities, or built new ones. Most significantly, it involved the Commonwealth in the planning process. The goal was to use sport to help overcome the very real inequalities resulting from the way in which facilities and services in our towns and cities are provided. The strategy was to develop a function available to all, rather than isolating groups for specific attention. Projects were funded in association with authorities grouped into regional associations ... The benefits were immediately accessible to all. (Armstrong, 1988, pp. 371-2)

The then Minister, Frank Stewart, commissioned John Bloomfield of the University of Western Australia to prepare the first detailed report on sport development. Thus, a document entitled *The Role Scope and Development of Recreation in Australia* was tabled in Parliament (Confederation of Australian Sport, 1999; Woodman, 1988). For the first time in the history of Australia, sport was politically recognised as an integral part of Australians' lives and received Federal Government attention (Jobling, 1991). The importance of the report was the framework it established for Federal Government support and assistance to National Sporting Organisations (NSOs) (Confederation of Australian Sport, 1999). The report produced recommendations pertaining to mass and elite participation development and it was then for the first time that questions of elite versus mass participation development were raised. The issue has since become a central theme in Australian sport policy debate (Farmer & Arnaudon, 1996).

Soon after Bloomfield's report, Allan Coles chaired an additional Task Force that considered a crucial aspect of Australian sport, specific support for elite athletes. This report identified the need to develop a centre of excellence, the AIS, to cater to Australia's elite athletic community (Australian Sports Institute Study Group, 1975; Farmer & Arnaudon, 1996). Armstrong (1988) contended that whilst the recommendations to develop the AIS were not implemented immediately, the report certainly laid the foundation plans for the establishment of the AIS in 1981. Shilbury (1999) argued that the establishment of the AIS "signalled a change in government policy that has seen a steady increase in government funding to sport" (p. 109). Additionally, McKay, Lawrence, Miller and Rowe (1993) argued that since 1985 the government "has embarked on an ambitious path of intervention in sport" (p. 19).

Even though the Australian Labor Party lost office before official progress could be made, Armstrong (1987) pointed out two major 'unofficial' trends: (a) the increase in sports accessibility to the public; and (b) the need by sports organisations for improved long-term planning. Politicians such as Whitlam, Cohen and Stewart recognised the importance of sport in implementing a program to translate Australians' sporting passion into universal political outcomes (House of Representatives, 1989).

(c) The politics of managed decline

The Labor government was replaced at the subsequent election by Malcolm Fraser's ideologically conservative Liberal-Country Party coalition (1975-1983). During the course of this government, funding and services were cut back dramatically (Baka, 1986). For example, Jobling (1991) stated that from 1975 to 1979, spending on sport dropped from $7.4m to $5.8m. Additionally, the Ministry of Tourism and Recreation was dissolved, its responsibilities absorbed first by the Department of Environment, Housing and Community Developments and then in 1977 by the Department of Home Affairs (Armstrong, 1988; Jobling, 1991).

Whereas Whitlam's Labor government sought ways to engage itself, "unquestioningly accepting sport as part of fulfilling its urban responsibilities, the Coalition sought ways to disengage itself as a cost-saving measure. The result was an insubstantial inroad into the size of government, and a substantial growth in inequality" (Armstrong, 1988, pp. 374-375). However, as Armstrong (1988) claimed:

> The difference between the Coalition and Labor was more than one party emphasising the individual, while the other emphasised community, although this was its patent manifestation. The key difference between the two was the realisation by Whitlam and his colleagues that sport and recreation constitute a legitimate area of social policy, having a role to play in addressing issues of social inequality. It was the Fraser Government's denial of the social implications of sport and recreation that led to that government's abdication from this area of planning. (p. 56)

Therefore, it is argued that the Liberal government involvement with sport was not characterised by total lack of interest in sport, rather a more conservative approach (Baka, 1986).

(d) The politics of elite sport

The waning of the international reputation that Australians had enjoyed in sports reflected the government's budget decline. In 1956 Melbourne Olympics Australia won 36 medals, 13 of which were gold. In Rome in 1960 Australian athletes won 8 gold. In Tokyo in 1964 the tally of gold medals won went down to 6, in the Mexico 1968 Olympic Games 5 and in Munich in 1972 Australia won 8 gold. In Montreal in 1976 Australia failed to win one gold medal (Jobling, 1991). Thus, "the Montreal 'debacle' served notice that Australia's sport had declined and was in need of repair" (Farmer & Arnaudon, 1996, p. 9).

The government waited four years before implementing the 1975 Task Force recommendations to establish the AIS (Vamplew, Moore, O'Hara, Cashman & Jobling, 1994). Prime Minister Fraser officially opened the AIS in Canberra on 26 January (Australia Day) 1981. This initiative was born out of a \$2.7 million Federal Government grant (Farmer & Arnaudon, 1996). However, the initiative was not simply a response to the public outcry that followed the Montreal Olympic performances. Critics of the introduction of the AIS, such as Armstrong (1987), claimed that the initiative was intended primarily as a means of controlling elite sport by *throwing money* at it. Armstrong (1988) provided further insight into the reasons for the government's u-turn in politics in relation to sport:

> Tightfisted [sic] attitude towards publicly assisting Olympic athletes evident in 1976 gave way to an effusive generosity. The reason was politics. It took four years for the Fraser Government to realise that in sport lay a wealth of populist opportunity ... The outcry over Australian performances was not the motive for the establishment of state sponsorship, but [it] did become the justification for its maintenance. This was especially the case as the Institute developed at a frenetic pace... The real motive for the policy tells us something about politics inside the Liberal Party. (pp. 375-376)

Fraser's connection to sport helped him restore and even build a new popular image that facilitated his pursuit of foreign policy goals (Armstrong, 1987). Once he realised the importance of sport, "Malcolm Fraser was only too willing to approve any request from the Institute for money" (Armstrong, 1988, p. 376). When comparing Fraser's policy to the Menzies' Liberal government, Armstrong (1987) argued that the Liberals "did not revive the Whitlam Government's initiatives to make sport more accessible in the suburbs of Australia's cities. Supporting the urban and social elements of sport was not as important as giving the Institute the support it wanted" (p. 377).

The early 1980s did not give rise to any significant programs to promote mass participation or develop an integrated approach involving NSOs and state authorities (Farmer & Arnaudon, 1996). Hence, while Federal Government sport policy focused on promoting the elite for political reasons, mass participation numbers started to decline.

As Westerbeek et al. (1995) noted, up until the mid 1980s at the junior and youth (until the age of 18 years) sport levels, the Australian sport system predominantly focussed on identifying elite performers. A high 'drop-out' rate in the adolescent years was the result.

Stewart (1985) explained that whereas the early government allocations emphasised the recreation and fitness needs of mass participation, the 1980s policies highlighted the desire to improve elite athlete performances. Another development in the 1980s was the trend towards professionalism (Cashman, 1995). Westerbeek et al. (1995) observed that more government funding marked the growing recognition of the importance of professionally played sport in Australian society. This led to increasing professionalism in the management of sport organisations.

(e) The politics of consensus

When the ALP returned to power with the Hawke government in 1983, it espoused social democratic tenets which acknowledge capitalism and private enterprise (Veal, 2002). While retaining the AIS, this government "proposed that an Australian Sports Commission function as a statutory authority" (Jobling, 1991, p. 254). The ASC was established in September 1984 and had three main objectives: (a) "to sustain and improve Australia's level of achievement in international sporting competition", (b) "to increase the level of participation in sport by all Australians", and (c) "to increase the level of assistance from [the] private sector" (Jobling, 1991, p. 254).

The institutional base of Federal support changed in May 1989 with the amalgamation of the AIS and the ASC to form a new commission under the ASC Act 1989 (Farmer & Arnaudon, 1996; Jobling, 1991; Shilbury & Deane, 2001). In this way, sport policy found itself administered through a government department (the Department for Sport, Recreation and Tourism) and a statutory authority (the ASC) (Armstrong, 1988). In practice the amalgamation of the ASC and the AIS gave the government "the economic and political room to manoeuvre, elements essential to the firm control of policy" (Armstrong, 1988, p. 380).

The declining level of Federal Government funding for sport changed the same year. However, Armstrong (1988) argued that despite the funding increase the election promise of community leisure and sport facilities and centres was unfulfilled. The approach to policy was more reflective of conservative ideologies by means of reducing conflict, maintaining stability and preserving the political system itself (Armstrong, 1988).

Armstrong (1988) summarised the Hawke government's politically cautious nature by stating: "Sport may indicate the extent to which the Hawke Government is frightened to risk its popularity with the electorate by experimenting with policy" (p. 385). So it maintained what has been in train since 1975, effecting incremental changes to a policy established by the Coalition after the fall of Whitlam Labor Government. Armstrong (1988) continued that sport fulfilled an important political function for the Hawke government. It contributed to "an image of political stability, as well as generating nationalistic fervour during times of international competition. It is not intended to be a facilitator of change, serving instead as a contributor to political stability, economic growth, and national unity" (p. 388).

Farmer and Arnaudon (1996) perceived the Hawke era of the late 1980s as an age of sports policy that was "spurred by the activities of the Confederation of Australian Sport [a sports lobbying group] and the Australian Olympic Committee" (p. 18). Moreover, there was an "emerging sophistication of the sports movement itself, through the numerous national sporting bodies and their constituents" (p. 18).

(f) The policy towards the Sydney 2000 Olympic Games

Armstrong's (1988) and Farmer and Arnaudon's (1996) contributions to classifying sport policy analysis in Australia according to different policy approaches come to an end with the late 1980s. The existing scholarship on sport policy analysis as a public policy issue in Australia does not include the late Hawke government, the two consecutive Labor governments of Paul Keating (1991, 1993–1996) and the three consecutive Liberal governments of John Howard since 1997.

A number of ASC and Task Force reports (e.g. ASC annual reports and the Sport 2000 Task Force report from the DISR in 1999), as well as scholarship on Australian sport policy (e.g. Farmer & Arnaudon, 1996), clearly indicate that since 1989 the Federal

Government has allocated money to the development of elite sport in discrete packages every four years. Examples include the *Next Step* initiative from 1989 to 1992, the first comprehensive sport policy in the nation's history, which poured $217 million into sport over the four-year cycle (Cooke, 1996). The *Maintain the Momentum* program from 1992 to 1996 injected another $293 million over its four-year cycle and shed the notion of decentralisation handing more power to NSOs (Cooke, 1996). Under normal circumstances this four-year cycle would have run its course in 1996, the year of the Atlanta Olympic Games. However, circumstances changed on 23 September 1993 when the International Olympic Committee awarded the 2000 Olympic Games to Sydney (ASC, 1996; Confederation of Australian Sport, 1999).

In response to hosting the 2000 Olympic Games, the Federal Government, through the ASC (1996), decided to continue with the *Maintain the Momentum* funding cycle and in 1994 announced the *Olympic Athlete Program* (OAP), a new $135 million six-year package. In addition, in 1995 the ASC formally established a Sport Development Division. Its goal was to foster a culture in which all Australians had access and opportunities to participate in sport and/or physical activity (ASC, 1999a). Evidently, the pattern of four-year funding cycles of sport, "set against strategic plans of organizations such as the Australian Sports Commission and accompanied by a regular evaluation process and review" (Farmer & Arnaudon, 1996, p. 20), became part of the ongoing scene for Australian sports.

As a response to the lack of sport policy analysis in Australia during the 1990s, Stewart-Weeks (1997) undertook the task of framing the Australian sport policy eras. In his examination he explored the ways sport policy changed over time by identifying three *policy waves*. He identified the period from 1900 to the mid 1970s where sport was largely independent from government as the first wave. His second wave ran from the first Whitlam Government budget to the 2000 Games. The third covers the period since then.

The limited number of studies examining the Federal Government sport policy during the second wave suggest that it has only been since the mid-1980s that Australian sport policy has come of age and been "recognized as a legitimate area of public expenditure" (Farmer & Arnaudon, 1996, p. 2). This era coincided with a period of extended governance by the ALP, and its policy is consistent with the social democratic tenets of equality that put an emphasis on mass participation in sport development.

According to Veal's (1994) rationales for government intervention, many publicly provided services are maintained because of *tradition*, as it is politically difficult to introduce changes, especially when there is a lobby group that may be offended. By the time the Liberal Party was re-elected in 1996, sport had established itself within the Federal Government as a legitimate policy concern. Despite its preferences for minimal government, the Liberal Party in Australia not only supported and promoted sport; it increased its involvement following its re-election in 1996 (Shilbury & Deane, 2001).

Various programs and resource allocations supported the development of Australian athletes and their successful performances at the Sydney 2000 Olympic Games. Veal (1994) added to the justification of increased Federal Government involvement with sport arguing that certain projects are too large to be taken on by the private sector. Hence, with the 2000 Olympic Games looming in Sydney, the Liberal government increased and confirmed its involvement in sport. This was clearly felt at the elite level by means of programs such as the OAP.

In relation to the adequacy of the sport system, the Sport 2000 Task Force (constituted on 1 June 1999 by the then Minister for Sport and Tourism, Jackie Kelly) declared that while Australia's results in international sporting competitions were exceptionally good and showed that "elite sport has been served well by the ASC" (DISR, 1999, p. 73), the lack of real growth in the membership levels of sporting organisations and the decline of numbers participating in organised sport during the previous 25 years suggested that "strategies have not achieved increased participation in organised sport" (DISR, 1999, p. 73).

(g) The third wave

The second wave of sport policy ended with the elite athletes' success at the Sydney 2000 Olympic Games, winning 58 medals 16 of which were gold, and the 2000 Olympic Games closing ceremony. Technically, the end of the era was marked by a series of events. These included the termination of the OAP, major restructuring within

39

the ASC itself and warnings by the ASC that post-2000 Olympic Games funding and allocation of resources by the government would be drastically reduced. It was argued that these extreme levels of funding could no longer be maintained. What followed was a period of great insecurity and ambiguity at the national level on the future of sport in Australia (Shilbury, 2000).

Brown (2000) argued that no one was certain what direction the government would take, whether there was going to be a continuation of elite funding at the same levels or whether more emphasis should be placed on mass participant sports. According to Stewart-Weeks (1997), Australia would face a *third wave* of sports policy in the post-Olympic era, a wave of policy with the main trend towards less public funding at all levels of sport. According to Shilbury (2000), the most relevant implication of this trend for NSOs was the reduced levels of reliance on Federal Government funding and the need to establish greater independence as a necessity for financial survival post-2000.

The end to this ambiguity and the instigation of the third wave of Australian sport policy came in the form of a Federal Government sport policy announcement on 24 April 2001, the new 10-year *Backing Australia's Sporting Ability – A More Active Australia* plan. ASC Chairman Peter Bartels (ASC, 2001) perceived 2001 as a transition year that evidenced a restructuring within the ASC to respond to the post-Olympic era.

As Sweany (2001) reported, while the government had indicated that it would reduce sport funding after the Olympics, Australia's success at the Olympic Games forced the government to change its policy direction. This is in line with Hogan and Norton's (2000) prediction that despite talks of a redirection and redistribution of government funding in favour of mass participation sport, the government would be forced to maintain the levels of elite funding. The new plan included $408 million funding for the new *Sport Excellence Program*, which was introduced to build upon the achievements of the elite athletes at the international and national levels (DISR, 2001). There was also a provision for an $82 million infusion of funding (over a four-year period starting

40

2001-2002) through *Active Australia* to increase mass participation in sport at the club level (Grattan, 2001).

The 2002 Federal election saw the third consecutive John Howard Liberal government in power. The strategies were already set, monies were allocated, the path was already clear and the third wave of sport policy was on the way. One element of the new policy was certainly evident: the realisation that grass roots development was in need of greater attention than previously had been the case. According to the Department of Industry, Science and Resources (DISR, 2001) there has been a slight shift towards participation programs with the ultimate aim of increasing the pool of elite athletes. So, while catering for the elite level remained a policy priority, the four-year plan announced in 2001 saw participation as a means of increasing the pool of talented athletes and not as an end itself. Smith (2000) perceived this increase in community sport as a possible response to one of the key findings of the Sport 2000 Taskforce's *Shaping Up* report, that too many Australians are too inactive and that more resources need to go to participation programs and campaigns.

2.1.4 SUMMARY

The examination of the circumstances under which Australian sport policy development emerged shows that it was only in the mid-1970s that the Federal Government saw sport policy as a legitimate area for involvement. Since then, this connection has intensified with the Federal Government involvement in developing, formulating and implementing sport policy through the ASC and its NSOs, by funding, resourcing and supporting sport. More importantly, an examination of Federal Government sport policy to date has demonstrated an imbalance, leaning towards the promotion of elitism in sport and paying less attention to mass participation.

McKay et al. (1993) maintained that the government is not a "neutral umpire that safeguards the interests of all Australians" (p. 22). Armstrong (1988) reached the conclusion that the formulation and implementation of public policy is a dependent variable of traditional political power, conflict and ideology. He expressed the belief that "the distribution of public resources will always remain a source of dispute. Policy is the end result of economic, social and political interaction, influenced by the method of formulation, and the nature of political institutions – who gets what, when, and how" (p. 363). Therefore, sport policy in Australia, as an integral part of public policy, has experienced an unpredictable path reflecting the changes in government and their respective ideologies.

While the legitimations for Federal Government involvement with sport and policy formulation have been established and elaborated upon, Chalip (1995) argued that legitimations are insufficient to generate policy action. Therefore, it takes an event of national significance such as national and international elite athlete performances "to symbolize a policy issue and focus policymakers' attention on proposals professing to redress the issue" (Chalip, 1995, p. 5). Hence, focusing events, as described by Chalip (1995), are symbolic representations of policy concern "which give momentum to policymaking" (p. 5) in areas such as sport development. This is the focus of the next section.

2.2 SPORT DEVELOPMENT

Chalip (1995) viewed sport related incidents, such as Australia's failure to win gold medals at the Montreal Olympic Games or to substantially increase mass participation numbers after the Sydney Olympic Games, as symbolic representations of policy concern which give momentum to policy making and use of public resources. Dubnick and Bardes' (1983) contribution to policy making stressed the problematic nature of policies in that to understand policies one "should recognize them as responses to and sources of problems" (p. 5). They argued that a problem "becomes public when it calls for the use of government resources" (Dubnick & Bardes, 1983, p. 6). Where there is some debate over alternative solutions to an agenda item, then Dubnick and Bardes (1983) recognised this as a *policy issue*. Policy issues such as sport development modelling, sport development approaches in Australia, the debate on elite versus mass participation development and the basis for justifying policy formulation in relation to sport development processes are considered as the main impetus for sport policy formulation. Nonetheless, Chalip et al. (1996) argued that it is the national pride associated with successful international sport performances by national athletes and teams that has been "one of the most potent driving forces for sports policy development" (p. x).

Bramham et al. (2001) claimed that the term *sport development* is contested. To define sport development "is inevitably difficult and it does mean different things to different people" (Watt, 1998, p. 64). For instance, Bramham et al. (2001) suggested that the term is "used to describe processes, policies and practices that form an integral feature of the work involved in providing sporting opportunities" (p. 1). Watt (1998) added that the concept of sport development is about "driving forward new initiatives and getting different emphases to various considerations within the sporting fraternity" (p. 66).

Eady (1993) offered another dimension to sport development, the notion of organisational and personal change within the sport development process: "Sport development is the promotion and implementation of a positive change in organisational and personal behaviour, which is planned, structured and achievement oriented" (p. 5). Watt (1998) agreed that sport development is not just about the act of developing a sport but also about developing (a) the individual within the sport, and (b) the sport organisations to better provide for the sport. He suggested that sport development is about "providing and improving opportunities for people to participate in sport at whatever level to the best of their ability and in fulfilment of their interest" (Watt, 1998, p. 64). It is also the process which enhances opportunities for people of all ages, degrees of interest and levels of ability to take part, improve their skills and excel in their chosen sporting activities (Eady, 1993). Watt (1998) argued that Eady's (1993) definition on sport development hits on the very essence of sports management, which is about catering for all levels of interest, ability and desire.

The initial effort to illustrate the sport development process resulted in the *Traditional Sport Development Continuum/Pyramid* (see Figure 2.1), which locates development on a hierarchical basis from foundation to participation, performance and excellence (Bramham et al., 2001). Eady (1993) explained that the term *continuum* is in diagrammatic form an attempt to illustrate "the way in which [the] sports development continuum provides pathways for individuals to progress to the level of performance, which is appropriate/available to them" (p. 14).

The four levels in the continuum are as follows:

(a) *Foundation* is the base of the continuum, and involves the vital first steps of learning basic movement skills.

(b) *Participation* is one level up from the foundation, and involves exercising one's leisure option, taking part in sport for health, fitness, friends and fun.

(c) *Performance* is one level higher than participation, and involves the challenge of increasing proficiency by striving to improve personal standards of participation.

(d) *Excellence* is reaching the top of the continuum and involves accomplishing nationally and publicly recognised standards of performance (Bramham et al., 2001; Eady, 1993; Houlihan, 2000).

Figure 2.1: Model I, The Traditional Sport Development Continuum/Pyramid

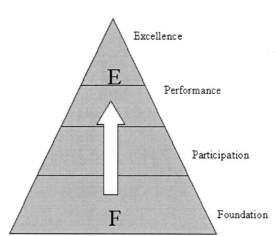

Source: Bramham et al., 2001, p. 3

Farmer and Arnaudon (1996), in their study on Australian sport policy, discussed a minor variation of the Traditional Sport Development Continuum/Pyramid: the *Model of Pyramid-Based Sport*. Instead of four they presented the model with three levels, (i.e.

44

mass participation, intermediate level and high performance sport). They argued that this model "is typical throughout the world" (p. 5). However, there is evidence to suggest otherwise (e.g. Sport England, 2000). Shilbury and Deane (2001) argued that sport development has traditionally been aligned with the *Participation Pyramid Model* which incorporates six levels: (a) School sport, casual, recreational and social participation, (b) Local club sport, (c) Regional, (d) State or Territory, (e) National and (f) International, from the bottom to the top of the pyramid.

Most significantly, the Traditional Sport Development Continuum/Pyramid Model, the Model of Pyramid-Based Sport and the Participation Pyramid Model all take the shape of a pyramid. Shilbury and Deane (2001) claimed that the sports pyramid form assumes that people logically progress to the next level of sport participation without any movement between recreational competitions and semi-elite or elite competitions. Hence, the sporting pyramid has become static and "does not accurately represent the dynamic nature of flows that might exist in sports participation" (p. 198).

A model to illustrate the above mobility resulted in a variation of the sport development pyramid (see Figure 2.2) and shows the different directions participants could take within the continuum (Eady, 1993). As Figure 2.2 illustrates, the pyramid shape of the sports continuum model is abandoned and the four levels from the foundation to excellence are represented as multidirectional.

Figure 2.2: Model 2, The Sport Development Continuum

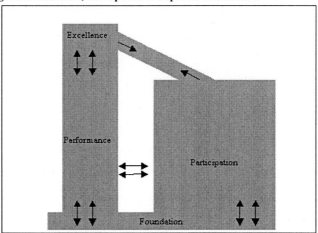

Another effort to better encapsulate this mobility resulted in a more dynamic model, which incorporated the concept of a *performance decision* point where "a conscious decision is made to remain at a particular level of performance for the time being" (Eady, 1993, p. 15). This model keeps the levels of participation mentioned in the previous model, it graphically separates them, adds the introduction and re-introduction stage, returns to the initial graphical representation of a pyramid and allows for the possibility of the individual leaving and re-entering the sport and altering the level at which they aspire to take part over time (see Figure 2.3).

Figure 2.3: Model 3, The Sport Development Continuum/Pyramid

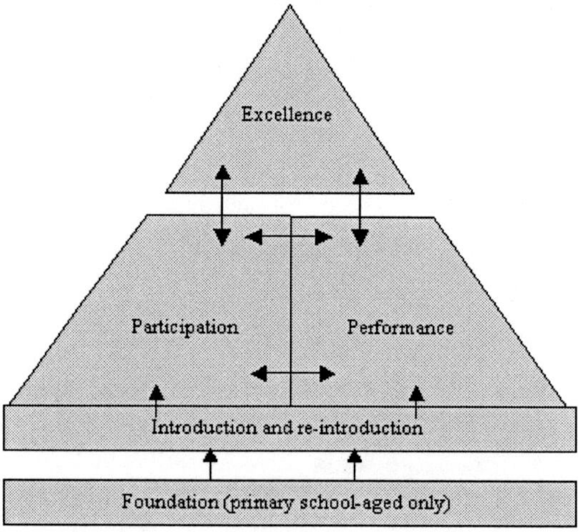

Source: Eady, 1993, p. 15

Even though sport development frameworks, in the best circumstance, may illustrate people's mobility from one level of participation to another, Bramham et al. (2001) argued that the sports development continuum/pyramid has been used by diverse organisations to "provide a logical coherence to their plans, policies and strategies for sport ... This simple and powerful model of sport development has been further modified and refined by sport agencies as a response to and articulation of new policy agendas and initiatives" (p. 3). As such, sport development models are a reflection of policy agendas rather than an actual depiction of the sport policy processes involved.

To test the argument one simply needs to look at Sport England (2000) and its re-developed sport development model, which pictures Sport England's policy programs by means of a new sport development model, the *Active Framework*. This model incorporates and graphically represents all programs involved (i.e. Active Communities, Active Sports, Active Schools and World Class programs) and implemented by the English government in a strategic effort to enhance sport development processes (see Figure 2.4).

Figure 2.4: The Active Framework

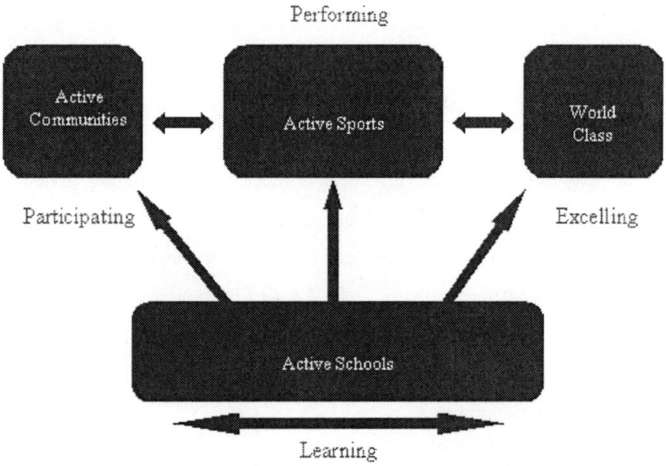

Source: Sport England, 2000, p. 5

While other countries, like England, have developed sport development models to reflect their policy agenda needs, Australia has been historically aligned with the traditional sport pyramid/continuum model (Bloomfield, 1974; Farmer & Arnaudon,

1996). Even though there have been claims that Australia "has abandoned the traditional pyramid structure" (Farmer & Arnaudon, 1996, p. 16) in favour of an approach that recognises more groups and their needs within the Australian society, there is strong evidence, as the discussion that follows suggests, that Australian sport policy is very much a reflection of the sport pyramid/continuum model.

Critics of the sport development models, such as Eady (1993), indicated that the term *sport development continuum* is slightly misleading when used to describe the route that an individual might take when progressing through the different levels of participation in sport. Eady (1993) argued that while "both the term continuum - which implies an imperceptible transition - and the 'levels' of participation are over simplifications" they do "allow practitioners and academics to rationalise and describe in simple terms the process to which the SDO [Sport Development Officer] and others involved in sport and recreation are contributing" (p. iv). Additionally, McDonald and Tungatt (1992) stated that the relationship between mass participation and elite performance is a far more complex interaction than the simple pyramid model would suggest. Nevertheless, Houlihan (2000) asserted that the sport development framework proved to be durable and an effective representation of "disparate policies and interests" (p. 174).

More important, and in relation to this study, the existing models of sport development either are oversimplified attempts to show people's mobility from one level of participation to the others (e.g. the Sport Development Continuum/Pyramid) or simply reflect sport programs (e.g. the Active Framework). People's mobility illustrated in the sport development framework does not explicate sport development processes, the way sport policy influences this mobility or the way one level of the continuum can influence another.

Elite versus Mass Participation Development
McKay (1986) argued that elite sport in Australia comprises a tiny segment of mass participation sport. However, this level receives the largest proportion of funds. This situation has remained since the mid-1980s unchanged if not reinforced. Even though the central feature of sport development has always been providing for all levels of

sporting participants, from elite to mass participation, disagreements as to where the focus should be and differences of opinion about the importance of each level have tormented the area (Bramham et al., 2001). Bramham et al. (2001) noted that the need to work at both grassroots levels and with elite sport is important and contentious.

Farmer and Arnaudon (1996) acknowledged the tension between elite and mass participation. They argued that the balance between elite success and mass participation is always unstable in that "there is always a tension between funding for international competitors to produce world champions, and funding participation in programs to derive national health and socioeconomic benefits" (p. 20). Furthermore, they claimed that there is no longer a debate in Australian sporting circles as to whether funding sport is a government priority. The sports policy debate has shifted to the key issues such as distribution of funding, namely selective versus broad-based, centralised versus decentralised, and elite versus participation. Since the mid-1980s, when Federal Government involvement with sport increased, questions of elite versus mass participation became one of the central themes in Australian sport policy (Farmer & Arnaudon, 1996). Shilbury and Deane (2001) raised the Federal Government concerns about the elite versus mass participation debate. They argued that the sports excellence versus mass participation debate had forced the Federal Government to constantly question its philosophy about "funding and the direction in which it is channelled" (p. 188).

Trickle-up and Trickle-down Effects

Douglas (1978) argued that support of improved performances in international competitions incorporated the argument that "a broader base of participants will yield larger numbers" (p. 139) of elite athletes. In relation to the existing sport development pyramid, theoretically, the wider the base the greater the number of participants at each level above (Donnelly, 1991; Eady, 1993). Hence, governments inject resources at the bottom of the sport development continuum, expecting that a broad base will produce many champions (Veal, 1994). According to Hogan and Norton (2000) this process is referred to as the *bottom-up* or *trickle-up* effect, and was the basis of the Whitlam (Labor) government's sports budget in the early 1970s.

Nevertheless, the pyramid can be examined from another perspective, when government resources are allocated directly at the top of the pyramid and consequently a *top-down* or *trickle-down* effect is expected (ASC, 1994). The top-down (trickle-down) process implies that successful performances by elite athletes encourage people to take part in physical activity and result in an increase in mass participation. The Confederation of Australian Sport (CAS) (1999) argued that the trickle-down effect was the logic inherent in the establishment of the AIS.

Sweany (2000) considered trickle-down effects as the official reason for the Federal Government's commitment to elite development programs. McKay (1990) claimed that the rationale given by the government "for expending so much money on less than 1 per cent of the population is that athletic accomplishments of this elite will inspire young athletes to emulate their performances" (p. 415). He claimed that politicians and state functionaries justify expenditure in high performance sport "on the basis of elite performers' successes having 'trickle-down', 'spillover' or 'inspiration-emulation-perspiration' effects on grass roots participants" (p. 144). Nevertheless, he continued that the evidence on sport participation numbers does not reflect the above argument. Hence, the logic of this 'spillover' is questionable (McKay, 1986), and there is no evidence to suggest that this 'emulation' exists (McKay, 1991).

CAS (1999) believed that "while there is anecdotal evidence of the 'trickle-down' effect there is no objective research data to support it" (p. 25). Sweany (2000) agreed that the argument that international success of Australian athletes would inspire the general population "to get up out of their arm chair and be more physically active" (p. 43) is an assumption. She continued that despite the increasingly successful performances of elite Australians since 1976, this has not been translated into an equivalent increase in participation (if any) by the public.

Hogan and Norton (2000) argued that through the establishment of the AIS, the Australian Government has clearly adopted the trickle-down philosophy as its basis for sports funding. That is, "a large amount of the ASC's budget is directed towards high-performance athletes in a decreasing number of sports" (Hogan & Norton, 2000, p. 205). This trend intensified in the lead-up to the Sydney 2000 Olympic Games.

Nonetheless, after the Sydney Olympic Games, the Howard government in its new plan for sport policy indicated that while focusing on elite excellence, it would promote increased grassroots expansion in the hope of a larger pool of athletes to choose from (DISR, 2001). Evidently, such aspirations match intentions for trickle-down instead of trickle-up effects.

Hidson, Gidlow and Peebles (1994) studied trickle-down effects in New Zealand similar to those of the Australian sport system. Their study, conducted in 1993, examined the possible effects of elite success on mass participation. It raised doubts about one of the assumptions, the trickle-down effect, which is "used to justify considerable expenditure on top-level sport, particularly in the context of Olympic and Commonwealth Games preparation" (p. 18).

In relation to the trickle-down effect, they argued two propositions. The first proposition, which supports the trickle-down assumption and hence legitimates expenditure by the Federal Government and by the NSOs to further develop top-level sport, claims that "successful top-level athletes gain media attention and attendant publicity and become role models. As role models, these athletes attract new people into the sports and into clubs, and encourage existing club members to become more competitive in their approach to sport" (Hidson et al., 1994, p. 23).

The second proposition argues that the demonstrations of sporting excellence can act as a deterrent to grassroots participation. According to this model, "the greater the perceived 'gap' between the level of excellence achieved by top-level athletes and the competence level of new or would-be participants, the greater the likelihood that those participants will resist further involvement in the sport" (Hidson et al., 1994, pp. 23-24). Hidson et al. (1994) argued that the data collected from New Zealand sport clubs and NSOs were indicative only and recognised the need for further research to substantiate their interpretations.

An interpretation of the relationship of *cause and effect* (i.e. allocating resources to one or the other end of the continuum expecting outcomes) has been offered by Hogwood and Gunn (1984) in their study pertaining to policy analysis. They proclaimed that all policies involve assumptions about what governments can do and what the consequences of their actions will be. These assumptions are rarely spelled out, but policies nevertheless imply a theory (or model) of cause and effect. At its simplest, this theory takes the form of "if X, then Y will follow" (p. 18).

However, Hidson et al. (1994) reached the conclusion that cause and effect is an oversimplification of sport policy, since the promotion of the elite "may not be the way to involve more people in the sport, to promote sports club membership or increase the competitive orientation of existing club members" (p. 24). Armstrong (1987) argued that "fostering participation must be deliberate: governments cannot expect trickle-down effects to get the nation on the move" (p. 170).

As Hogwood and Gunn (1984) explained, if one thinks of policy in terms of the simple *if X then Y* theory, one "can see that failure of a policy can arise either from the Government's failure to do X in full or because X fails to have the consequences excepted according to the theory" (p. 18). The sport development model, which Australian sport policy utilises, not only is inadequate to reflect policy deliberations, it also overlooks (at least graphically) the notions of trickle-down and trickle-up effects, which in turn are assumptions by governments justifying policy action or inaction. This allows governments, depending on their political uses, to claim any relationship and to substantiate their funding distributions accordingly (Hogan & Norton, 2000).

The existing conflict of assumptions identified in the sport development continuum implies the acceptance of two opposing strategies: (a) top-down (trickle-down), and (b) bottom-up (trickle-up) process. These two concepts reflect diverse sport policy approaches. Chalip (1996a) explained that this is possible because government policies are formulated based on different legitimations, which may generate subtle yet telling differences in policy implementation.

2.2.1 SUMMARY

Hogwood and Gunn (1984) argued that: "One of the tasks of the policy analyst is to try to tease out the theories underlying policies and examine the internal consistency of the resulting model and the apparent validity of its assumptions" (p. 18). As demonstrated in this section, existing sport development pyramids/continuum lack validity and consistency. Additionally, they fail to answer the question under investigation. McKay et al. (1993) noted that the "inspiration-emulation-perspiration" model of sporting excellence "is defined by the extremely narrow indicator of how efficient and effective Australia is at producing gold medals" (p. 22) and assumes that this success will inspire others to take up physical activity.

With the Australian Federal Government's positioning on sport development modelling, the stressing of the importance of sport development and the exemplification of the questions deriving from the elite versus mass participation debate, this section serves as the symbolic representation of the policy concern that this book examines. More specifically, the policy concern relates to the Federal Government's involvement with sport policies in terms of structure, policies, goals and implications for elite and mass participation levels of sport development.

2.3 THE AUSTRALIAN SPORT POLICY DELIVERY STRUCTURE

According to Webb et al. (1990) there are two distinct levels of policy. At the first level there are two types of policy. These are the policies *for show* and the ones *for real*. Both are designed to "implement change, either to solve a problem, improve a situation or respond to a challenge" (p. 7). At the second level there are two ways of looking at and examining policies. These are *policy content* as opposed to *policy process*, with the latter incorporating two segments (i.e. formulating and implementing policy).

Real-life policy processes do not take place in a vacuum but rather in what Hogwood and Gunn (1984) called *policy space*. This space, as it applies in the Australian context, occurs within national, state and local levels and marks the area of activity for which government takes responsibility, regulates and provides support. The hierarchy of sporting organisations, the relationship between them and the way Federal and state government assistance links with the sporting organisations define the Australian sport policy space (Webb et al., 1990).

Policy space can be used to illustrate the way in which space can become more crowded over time "with more and more governmental interventions and increasingly complex interactions among them" (Hogwood & Gunn, 1984, p. 13). While these theoretical observations have been examined in section 2.1, the remainder of this section illustrates how policy space is organised in Australian sport (i.e. the Australian sport system, the key sport policy players, their relationship, their role in sport development and what the fundamental sports policy goals are set to do).

Bramham (2001) maintained that "political traditions provide general direction to public policy as well as the domain ideological assumptions which map out key institutions and define and empower stake holders in the policy process" (p. 15). Furthermore, Thoma and Chalip (1996) argued that it is imperative before we study sport policy (as well as different systems of sport policy) to consider the different levels at which sport development takes place. While the levels of governance of sport development include local/club, state, national and private, the levels of development include youth, schools, clubs, college/university and professional leagues. However, not all sports are represented at all levels of the structure. For example, while in countries such as the USA the sport structure relies on school or university sport, other countries including Australia rely on club systems of sport almost exclusively.

With the expansion of the Australian Federal Government's involvement with sport, first financially in the 1970s and very soon after in sport policy formulation and implementation, sport government space and its structure have continuously evolved. The sporting organisation structure in Australia is a reflection of the Australian Federated model. This includes the national, state and local levels. Sport organisations are structured accordingly into the same levels and are represented by the NSOs, the State Sporting Organisations (SSOs) and the local clubs.

The Sport 2000 Task Force (DISR, 1999) report provides a simplified yet insightful overview of the components of the Australian sport and recreation system at the national, state and local level, including sporting organisations that are involved with sport at both government and non-government levels. The ASC is at the top of the hierarchy representing Federal Government sports policy. The ASC communicates with the NSOs as the organisations responsible for the delivery of sport through the SSOs.

National Sporting Organisations (NSOs)

As explained, governments and sporting organisations may operate at a local, state, national or international level (Woodman, 1988). The Sport 2000 Task Force (DISR, 1999) report confirmed that at the Australian national level the sporting organisational structure has remained the same since Woodman's (1988) study: the NSOs deliver sport (through SSOs) to the community and the ASC represents the agency responsible for policy.

Sports in Australia are managed and co-ordinated by NSOs. Westerbeek et al. (1995) describe NSOs as the national representatives of their sport. The ASC (2003b) argued that these organisations manage the participation and development of their sports in Australia. Nevertheless, Farmer and Arnaudon (1996) noted that NSOs are involved in

> organizing and conducting national championships, liaising with the international parent body, marketing and promoting national events, fund-raising for national teams, selecting and developing talent, selecting national teams for international events, and liaising with the Federal Government. (pp. 4-5)

For a NSO to be recognised by the ASC, its programs and services must satisfy all the components of the ASC's definition of *sport*, which is "a human activity capable of achieving a result requiring physical exertion and/or physical skill which, by its nature and organisation, is competitive and is generally accepted as being a sport" (ASC, 1997, p. 4).

According to the ASC's 2001 annual report (ASC, 2001), of more than 100 NSOs operating in Australia (ASC, 2002c), around 60 were recognised, hence funded by the ASC. Apart from funding, another major activity of the ASC is the evaluation of NSOs (ASC, 2003b). According to the Sport 2000 Task Force (DISR, 1999) report, there are a number of NSOs that are well managed and strategically focused with development plans that address all aspects of their sports from elite to mass participation. Much of this has resulted from policies and programs of the ASC, such as the OAP and the Active Australia programs that cater for elite and mass participation development needs respectively. As Farmer and Arnaudon (1996) claimed, the actual organisational structure of the ASC and its programs is designed "to facilitate the implementation of these policy goals in cooperation with national sporting organizations and state and territory sports authorities" (p. 16).

NSOs are the primary linkage of sports to the ASC and vice versa. Therefore, the ASC formulates the sport policy that the NSOs implement. The Sport 2000 Task Force (DISR, 1999) report recognises that NSOs are agencies which do not operate in a vacuum. Formal and informal linkages with the ASC have developed over time in an effort to improve outcomes. These have been developed in order to "coordinate activities of agencies that have been established separately but whose activities impact on each other" (p. 65). These two parties at the national level (ASC and NSOs) shape the key sport policy players and receive particular attention within the boundaries of this study in illustrating their involvement in sport policy.

Australian Sports Commission (ASC)

The ASC was established in 1984 as a statutory authority to deliver services to sport in Australia. The ASC is part of the Arts and Sport Program of the Communications, Information Technology and Arts Portfolio. It reports to the Federal Minister for Arts and Sport. The Minister has portfolio responsibility for policy matters relating to sport (ASC, 2003c). A board of 11 Commissioners appointed by the Minister for Arts and Sport governs the ASC, which in turn liaises closely with the Department of Industry, Science and Resources for funding support to channel to sport.

The ASC nationally administers and funds sport on behalf of the Federal Government (ASC, 2003c). Since its establishment the ASC has continued to pursue its mission in order to enrich the lives of all Australians through sport (ASC, 2003c). According to the Sport 2000 Task Force (DISR, 1999) report, from the great number of people and organisations involved in delivering sport in Australia, the Federal Government and the ASC play the most important role in sport policy and provision of finance.

On 1 May 1989, the ASC was reorganised to include the AIS, which had been operating independently since 1981. The ASC Act 1989 formalised this amalgamation, designed to continue the process of improving the efficiency and coordination of the Australian sports system (Shilbury & Deane, 2001). After this amalgamation, there was a need to restructure the ASC to fully integrate the AIS as well as reduce the duplication of services apparent in some areas. As a result, the ASC was streamlined into five divisions, with an addition of another two divisions after a further restructuring occurred in 1993/94 (Shilbury & Deane, 2001). In 1995 the ASC was streamlined in order to ensure the best preparation for the Sydney 2000 Olympic Games (ASC, 2000a).

By the end of 1999, in addition to the AIS division which was responsible for the training and development programs of elite athletes and teams, the ASC had two other main branches: *Sport and Business Services*, for commercial operations, marketing and communications; and the *Sports Development and Policy* division, to coordinate participation programs, conduct research and develop the sporting industry (Sport Business, 2000). In May 2000, the ASC announced that the Commission was to be reshaped to enable Australian sport to maintain its competitive edge in the period after the Sydney Olympic Games. According to the announcement, two separate units would deliver programs in the areas of elite sport and sports development (ASC, 2000b).

The ASC's 2000-2001 annual report (ASC, 2001) depicts its organisational chart having three core units: (a) the *AIS*, (b) *Business Operations Group* (BOG), and (c) *Sport Development Group* (SDG) (see Figure 2.5). While the BOG is responsible for corporate integration of the ASC's complex operations as well as providing general services to sports, the two delivery arms of the ASC, the AIS and SDG, promote the basic sports philosophy of the Australian Federal Government (i.e. performance/excellence and participation).

In relation to ASC's sports philosophy and according to the ASC Act 1989, the three core objectives of the ASC are:

(a) to provide leadership in the development of sport in Australia;
(b) to encourage increased participation and improved performance by Australians in sport;

(c) to provide resources, services and facilities to enable Australians to pursue and achieve excellence in sport while also furthering their educational and vocational skills and other aspects of their personal development (ASC, 1989).

The ASC performs these goals through two of its delivery units, the AIS and the SDG.

Australian Institute of Sport (AIS)

Since its establishment in 1981, the AIS has been responsible for training and developing elite athletes and teams in order to enhance performance and promote success at competitions such as the Commonwealth Games, the World Championships and the Olympic Games. For the purposes of elite sports development, the AIS integrates sport science, medical services and funding as well as the scholarship programs covering 26 sports throughout Australia. The AIS works closely not only with the State and Territory Institutes of Sport, but also in cooperation with the NSOs to provide a coordinated approach to promote elite sport (ASC, 2003a).

Figure 2.5: Australian Sport Commission Organisational Structure 2002

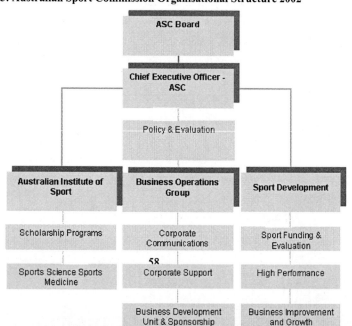

Source: ASC, 2003a

A major aim of the Federal Government was to achieve a continued improvement in the performances of Australians in international sport (via the AIS). The ASC's focus was the strengthening of Australia's international sporting success and reputation. This has largely been achieved through assistance to the NSOs and by providing world-class training facilities, support services and programs (ASC, 2001).

As the ASC (2001) indicated, the Key Performance Indicators (KPIs) for excellence in sports performances by Australian athletes for the financial year ending 2001 were:

1. team and individual world rankings, and
2. representation of AIS scholarship holders within those team and individual world rankings.

The 2000 Sydney Olympics saw Australia finishing fourth on the medal tally, winning 58 medals, 16 of which were gold. This was significantly better (38%) than Australia's previous best performance at the Atlanta 1996 Olympics, winning 42 medals. These were the outcomes of the OAP which was launched by the Federal Government in 1994 and ended after the 2000 Olympic Games. The ASC (1999b) maintained that the principal objective of the OAP was to develop athletes who would win medals at the 2000 Olympic Games. Goward (2000) further stated that the OAP was designed to target exceptional performances and allow athletes to represent their country at the Olympics on home soil. Accordingly, the OAP focused on developing, implementing and refining elite high performance training, and instituting competition programs and sports science support for each of the sports on the Sydney 2000 Olympic program.

In the ASC's 2000-2001 annual report, assessment against the above two KPIs demonstrated a list of successful performances by Australian sports outside of the Sydney 2000 Olympic Games. This included international successes and world rankings (ASC, 2001). Australian athletes have won and been placed at international championships across a wide range of sports, "achieving a remarkable degree of success" (DISR, 2001, p. 1).

In relation to the second performance indicator, 215 AIS athletes and 105 former AIS scholarship holders in 20 sports were selected to represent Australia at the Sydney 2000 Olympic Games. The ASC's programs have met the targets agreed with the government for this outcome (ASC, 2001).

Sport Development Group (SDG)

The SDG sought to develop the base of Australian sport through the Active Australia program. The aim of this program was to increase the number of Australians involved in sport and physical activity in the long term (ASC, 2003a). The SDG provided a full range of advisory and support services to assist NSOs and their affiliated organisations and clubs to conduct their business in an effective, efficient and inclusive way. In addition, the SDG administered the ASC's Sports Excellence and Sport Development grant programs. These programs provided essential funding to NSOs to support the operation of their organisation, high performance activities and sport development programs. In particular, the SDG was responsible for developing a national approach to community sporting activity under the Active Australia banner (ASC, 2003a).

Under the Active Australia banner, the ASC developed and implemented programs that promoted mass participation and added value to the experience of participants in a sporting activity. The ASC's programs are designed to ensure that participation levels increase (ASC, 2001).

The KPIs for improved participation in sports activities by Australians for the financial year 2000/01 were:

1. the total number of Australians participating in sport;
2. the level of participation in organised sport;
3. the demographic trends in participation;
4. the level of community awareness of the benefits of playing sport ; and
5. the number of organisations providing programs to support participation.

When comparing against the above KPIs, the ASC (2001) stated that while the 1999–2000 data indicated a small decline in participation in organised sport and a larger decrease in participation in unorganised physical activity, a true indication of participation rates would require analysis of trend data over a three- to five-year period. As these data have been collected for only three years, since 1998–99, it is difficult to confirm whether this is a national trend towards decreased participation.

Specifically, in relation to the total number of people participating in organised sport the ASC (2001) provides indicative figures. In 1999–2000, 28.9% of adults (4 million people) participated in organised sport and physical activities. This is a decrease of 1.4% on the 1998–99 rate of 30.3%, and similar to the 1997–98 rate of 28.3%.

Australian Sport System Asymmetry
Even though the Federal Government represents sport development processes as a continuum in a pyramid, the nature of the ASC's organisation segregates elite from mass participation development. Accordingly, its structure illustrates its bipolar goals, from excellence in sport performances to improving mass participation in sport. Moreover, all functions of the ASC as they relate to elite and mass participation development, funding allocations, KPIs, outcome measures and variances are independent.

61

Indicatively, the ASC's resources and funding to NSOs are directed to develop sport in different packages, one for the elite and one for mass participation development. Total financial cost to support the national elite athlete development reached $88.077 million[1] in the financial year 2000-2001. In the same year, the total cost of supporting national participation development was $12.798 million[2] (ASC, 2001). It can be seen that there is a difference of $75.279 million worth of dedicated funding between elite performance and mass participation. This difference conveys a message that elite development is in receipt of financial resources from the Federal Government over six times those provided for mass participation development.

2.3.1 BACKING AUSTRALIA'S SPORTING ABILITY: 'A *MORE* ACTIVE AUSTRALIA'

The objective of the ASC's new 10-year sport policy plan Backing Australia's Sporting Ability: A *More* Active Australia (announced by the Federal Government on 24 April 2001) is twofold: (a) to support elite athletes to continue with their national and international successful performances, and (b) to increase the pool of talents at grassroots level from which new elite athletes will emerge.

Sports Excellence

The *Sports Excellence* program provided funding for high performance sport and support services to assist NSOs "to achieve targets in both high performance sport and significantly increased participation" (DISR, 2001, p. 5). It also allowed NSOs greater flexibility "to tailor high performance athlete development programs to meet the needs of their sport" (DISR, 2001, p. 5). Total Federal Government funding for Sports

---

[1] Total ASC costs of outputs is 2.7 percent greater because of greater than budgeted external revenue. The variances between outputs are due to reclassifications because of the ASC's internal restructure and adjustments made after the Olympics. These were internal reallocations only and had no effect on overall achievement of ASC outputs.

[2] Total ASC costs of outputs is 22.4 percent greater because of greater than budgeted external revenue. The variances between outputs are due to reclassifications because of the ASC's internal restructure and adjustments made after the Olympics. These were internal reallocations only and had no effect on overall achievement of ASC outputs.

Excellence to support Australian athletes reached $408 million over the four-year period beginning 2001-2002 (DISR, 2001). The Backing Australia's Sporting Ability package meant an additional allocation of $122.2 million over four years for Australian athletes.

A *More* Active Australia

The Federal Government in its new plan recognised the benefits to be gained from greater participation in grassroots sports including improved fitness and contributions to the development of world-class athletes. More importantly, it was deemed vital that more people take an active part since "more players mean more winners" (DISR, 2001, p. 6).

To this end, the Federal Government has increased funding to encourage participation. It also introduced a new program directed at young Australians. This program provided "effective pathways from participation in sport into high performance development" (DISR, 2001, p. 6) for talented individuals. It also required NSOs to "achieve greater rates of active participation and increase registered membership as a condition of funding" (DISR, 2001, p. 6). Finally, it built on the legacy of the 2000 Olympics by implementing an Olympic Youth Program to provide an enduring message of sport participation and healthy lifestyle (DISR, 2001).

The total Federal Government funding for A *More* Active Australia will reach $82 million over the four-year period beginning 2001-2002 (DISR, 2001, p. 7). This plan includes an additional allocation of $32 million committed to mass participation.

Trickle-up Aspirations

As explained previously, since the establishment of the AIS in 1981 and up until the 2000 Olympic Games, Federal sport policy emphasised Australian elite athletes and their successful performances. This was justified due to the perceived returns such as the inspiration for youngsters to participate (DISR, 1999). The new 10-year policy plan in 2001 pointed the way to increase the pool of talented youngsters at the base of the pyramid to generate elite athletes. The approach fits with the trickle-up aspirations. This clearly indicates a turning point in the history of the Australian Federal

63

Government sport policy approach and its resource allocation justifications. Yet, while a funding increase is apparent in the SDG, which is justified under the assumptions of trickle-up effects, the largest allocation of Federal Government financial support to NSOs according to the new figures is still at the elite level.

2.3.2 SUMMARY

The importance of studying sport development and establishing a model that clearly elaborates the sport development processes assumed by the Australian Federal Government (trickle-down and trickle-up effects) was illustrated in section 2.2. The current section (Section 2.3) established that the key policy players in Australian sport are at the national level and consist of the ASC (with its two delivery arms, AIS and SDG) and the NSOs acting as the national agents of their sports. This section also outlined the roles of the key policy players and their relationship, their structure, policies and goals, and their implications in relation to the focusing event.

As indicated, one of the characteristics of the Australian sports system is the separation of sport development processes into two segments, elite and mass participation development. Consequently, policy goals, policies, KPIs and impacts on sports are bipolar. This also reflects the Federal Government's funding allocation asymmetries, which clearly lean towards elite sport. More important, recent Federal Government policy signifies a change in sport development approaches, which articulates principles in relation to sport development attitudes different from those previously espoused.

With regard to the above policy issue, there is a plethora of foreign literature expounding the approaches of governments with different or similar ideological justifications and sport systems. According to Chalip (1995), to fully prepare for and cover all aspects of sport policy analysis, comparisons of the policy problem under examination with other practices are required to indicate and provide information on opinions available in relation to the issue under investigation.

2.4 SPORT DEVELOPMENT COMPARATIVE STUDY

Chalip (1995) explained that comparisons of the same policy problem under different settings are the parts of the analysis that determine the information and the opinions available with regard to the focusing event that may or may not be pertinent to the policy problem. Chalip's (1995) recommendation of appreciating further information on the same issue, hence possibly different approaches, leads to the need to examine alternative sports policies in a comparative study. The aim of this section is to illustrate the different approaches that have been adopted by different countries and their governments concerning the sport policy issue under examination.

From the number of scholars worldwide (e.g. Armstrong, 1987; Booth, 1995; Bramham, 2001; Chalip, 1996b; DaCosta, 1996; Farmer & Arnaudon, 1996; Girginou, 2001; Gittins, 2000; Haynes, 1998; Henry & Nassis, 1999; Hogan & Norton, 2000; Houlihan, 1997a; Johnson, 1978; Johnson & Frey, 1985; Macintosh, 1996; Macintosh, et al. 1987; Mishra, 1990; Oakley & Green, 2001; Ogle, 1997; Olafson & Brown-John, 1986; Olin, 1981; Pettavino & Pye, 1996; Puig, 1996; Riordan, 1993, 1995; Semotiuk, 1987; Shilbury, 2000; Stewart-Weeks, 1997; Thoma & Chalip, 1996; Webb et al., 1990; Woodman, 1988; Zilberman, 1996) who have built a body of literature on sport policies, there are relatively few sport policy comparative studies (e.g. Chalip et al., 1996; Landry et al., 1991).

Riordan (1993) argued that this is mainly due to the problematic nature of comparative sport policy analyses that limits the validity of any study. He explained that any comparative analysis of sport runs the risk of comparing like with unlike. There is "no single model of capitalist or socialist sport, however similar many of the structural features may be" (p. 245). He continued that it would be a mistake to posit the British and Soviet models as representative of capitalist and socialist sport respectively "as it would be to export them unadapted" (p. 245). While in liberal capitalist development sport came to be regarded typically as the concern primarily of the individual, in state socialist development it came to be regarded as the concern primarily of the state (Riordan, 1993).

65

However, previously Woodman (1988) argued that it is worth examining how sport systems developed under different regimes to see if there are facets that could be successfully applied to the Australian system. Thoma and Chalip (1996) claimed that "the nature of funding for programs and facilities, as well as the specifics of program and facility administration, is determined, at least in part, by national sport policies" (p. 63). Just as forms of government differ (e.g. democracy, dictatorship, monarchy), so do national systems for administering sport.

Chalip (1995) suggested that legitimations and ideological traditions provide useful bases for cross-national comparison of sport policies. The purpose of this section is not solely to present different government and policy agendas as such, but to illustrate the differing approaches to the same policy issue of a number of ideologically and politically different countries and their policy approaches to sport development. The following cases have been chosen because they represent the diverse range of sport system and policies:

(a)   United States of America (USA) as representatives of an arms-length approach to sport policy, showing minimal intervention in sport development processes;

(b)   Canada to show the Federal Government involvement with the elite level of sport development and organisational dependence;

(c)   Chinese sport policies to demonstrate the communist emphasis on mass participation sport development; and

(d)   United Kingdom to illustrate conservative approaches to sport policy. The latter includes a *Sports for All* initiative to sport development as well as a trend towards increasing support for the elite level.

In an effort to see different responses to the same sport policy issues (sport development), the following section shows how different countries, their governments and political systems have espoused various methods.

USA's minimal influence

An enduring principle of American politics is that government should be minimal. According to Douglas (1978) and Clumpner (1986), this *laissez faire* approach is reflected in the sport policy domain. Chalip and Johnson (1996) remarked that "despite the importance of sports to Americans, there has never been a demand for institutionalized, direct government participation in the world of sport" (p. 426). It was therefore the nation's values and beliefs that dictated the Federal policy towards sport. In this case Federal Government sport policy is fragmented and limited (since there is no Federal agency responsible for professional or amateur sports nor any specific subsidy to the industry) and the governance of sport is in the hands of managers and entrepreneurs (Chalip & Johnson, 1996).

It was only after the defeats of USA athletes by communist nations (e.g. the former Soviet Union) that the USA government was prompted to pass the Amateur Sports Act in 1978. This act designated the United States Olympic Committee (USOC) as the sole non-government authority to develop sport at the international level. USOC sources of funding are derived largely from private fund raising, licensing and sponsorship arrangements. They obtain minimal funding from government. Thus, Federal money does not provide a means for indirect control of USA sport with overall responsibility for sports lying in the hands of USOC and the national governing bodies of each individual sport (Chalip & Johnson, 1996).

The Amateur Sports Act requires USOC to promote participation in sports. However, USOC focuses mainly on the development and support of elite competitors (Chalip & Johnson, 1996). Sport development has been concerned with the training and control of elite athletes, while mass participation in sport has been left to the schools, local government and non-profit organisations. It is a system based on the schools, universities and private clubs and not community clubs. Chalip and Johnson (1996) and Woodman (1988) argued that, as in the Eastern bloc countries it is the universities rather than the state that support elite athletes. Hence, while at the national level sport is supported by private investment, at the local level it is assisted through public investment.

Canadian governance and control

While sport governance in the USA is explicitly non-government, Thoma and Chalip (1996) supported the argument that a distinct contrast is provided by Canadian sport policy and development which have been substantially influenced by the government agency, Sport Canada. During the late 1950s and early 1960s Canadian sport experienced declining international success such as poor performances at the Olympic Games (Baka, 1976). At the same time as concerns about international performances emerged there was growing pressure from physical educators and physical fitness advocates for the Federal Government to take action regarding the low level of physical fitness amongst Canadians.

As a response, the Federal Government turned its attention to the promotion of high-performance sport. It was judged that better international performances were essential if sport was to be effective in the promotion of national unity. To this end the Federal Government took greater control of high performance sport from the NSOs (Macintosh, et al., 1987). Sport Canada's 2003 mission statement spells out a clear and almost sole priority, which is support be given to high performance sport to boost Canada's nationalism. It supports the achievement of high performance excellence and development of the Canadian sport system to strengthen the unique contribution that sport makes to Canadian identity, culture and society (Sport Canada, 2003).

Thoma and Chalip (1996) commented that since 1961, the Canadian Federal Government has exerted considerable influence over sports primarily through the distribution of funds to the NSOs. Following the passage of the Fitness and Amateur Sport Act in 1961 the government's investment in sport rose sharply and the growth of such investment was accompanied by greater external Federal control. Olafson and Brown-John (1986) and Macintosh, Franks and Bedecki (1986) argued that these changes result in a very complex and increasingly bureaucratic system and involvement from a government which sought to distance itself from American and Chinese practices. Macintosh et al. (1986) recognised that this bureaucracy was not without problems. According to Thoma and Chalip (1996), NSOs developed substantial dependence on government funding and this dependence permitted increased government control. This control is implemented through Sport Canada, which is an arm of the Federal Government.

A core result of the Canadian sport system was the creation of a well-articulated support system for Canada's high performance athletes and sophisticated sport science and support system for athletes and coaches, and training centres. Macintosh (1996) argued that "this system has been the envy of many other countries and has been a model for the development of sports in Australia" (p. 61). In its vision for sport in the year 2012, Sport Canada is moving towards a "dynamic and leading-edge sport environment that enables all Canadians to experience and enjoy involvement in sport to the extent of their abilities and interests" (Sport Canada, 2002, p. 13) rather than a sole focus on elite athletes. In addition, it shows a move away from its autocratic approach to sport governance aiming to coordinate sport as a "result of the committed collaboration and communication amongst the stakeholders" (Sport Canada, 2002, p. 20) rather than a centralised and bureaucratic governance of sport.

China, Communism and sport development
Chinese communist practices realise an alternative way of perceiving sport development and its governance. Xiangjun and Brownell (1996) suggested that communist regimes, as in China, view sport as a means to promote national integration, health and production, and use it as for national defence and military purposes.

After the end of the Cold War in December 1991, when the Soviet Union ceased to exist, some Western commentators looked to the demise of the communist regimes in the Soviet Union and Eastern Europe to predict the collapse of the communist regime in China. However, instead of collapsing, China has experienced astonishing economic growth (Suisheng, 1999). The All-China Sports Federation created in 1949 is the organisation responsible for coordinating, organising and promoting sports in China (Yin & Roberts, 1995; Xiangjun & Brownell, 1996).

The State Physical Culture and Sports Commission which was formed in 1952 is the state organisation most actively involved in sports policy making, and took over many of the functions of the All-China Sports Federation (Xiangjun & Brownel, 1996). Chinese sports policy is issued and administered by these two organisations, and is ideologically guided by the Communist Party. Ying and Roberts (1995) pointed out that a noteworthy feature of the above system is that it is highly centralised, with the central government in China making most decisions regarding funding, sporting events and the management of teams.

Ever since the founding of the People's Republic of China in 1949, the Chinese government has focused on developing mass physical culture and sports programs. Their motto has been to promote national physical culture, whilst at the same time speeding up their development of mass participation. By the mid 1950s Chinese elite performances quickly improved and China began to mount the stage of international sports. According to Ying and Roberts (1995), elite athlete excellence has been built upon a base of mass participation.

In addition, China adopted its policy from the Soviet sports development and training model and many Soviet Union and Hungarian professionals have taught and trained Chinese athletes. The sport school systems were instituted in 1955 again replicating the Soviet model (Xiangjun & Brownell, 1996). As physical culture became more and more an integral part of China's daily life, at the elite level China's top athletes saw their status rise in the international sports arena. In the past 50 years China has demonstrated remarkable sporting achievements with many medals and world records broken.

Henry (2001) argued that even though socialist/communist countries view competitive sport critically as it reinforces capitalist structures, they are keen to promote sport for military, political and social reasons. Riordan (1986) summarised the major reasons for concern by communist nations for sporting excellence as: a) inspiration and patriotism, b) the parity of mental and physical culture, c) gaining world recognition and prestige, d) maintaining and reinforcing unity of the communist countries, and e) demonstrating the advantages of the communist way of life.

In comparison to state socialist/communist countries, conservative governments cast the state in an enabling role that avoids the directive approach associated with state socialism (Henry, 2001). However, unlike the minimalist liberal practices, this enabling role is consistent with the sort of indirect funding that is operated in the *arm's length* approach to support sport (Henry, 2001). Hong (1997) argued that the national sport management system has changed direction and promotes the commercial benefits of elite sport. Sport is expected to be financially viable and not rely on state support.

United Kingdom, Conservative regime and New Labour approaches

In Britain the role of sport and leisure has been seen as a means of *soft* policing by Labour and Conservative governments from the early 1970s until the mid 1980s (Henry, 2001, Wilson, 1988). The emphasis in sport and leisure provision was directed towards groups of people that were perceived troublesome, such as young inner-city male residents. The justification for government provision was based on the rationale of the *externalities* that accrue from leisure provision (Veal, 2002), such as the reduction of hooliganism and delinquency among young people and social control (Henry, 2001; Veal, 2002). Houlihan (1997a) argued that the concern of the Sport for All philosophy was to employ sports and recreation as a form of social control to reduce anti-social behaviour. As a response to such policy orientations the prime responsibility for implementation rested with local government and the Sports Council that was established in 1972 to provide sport and recreation for disaffected British youth (Bramham et al., 2001; Houlihan, 1997a).

Throughout the late 1980s and early 1990s, the liberal-oriented conservative governments of Thatcher and Major saw sports more as a source of problems than a source of policy opportunities (Houlihan, 1997a). A large reduction in government funding was justified under the conviction that social regeneration was largely dependent on economic regeneration (Henry, 2001). A shift in ways to attract private sector investment in sport, competitive tendering for the management of the sport centres, the restructuring of the Sports Council spending with emphasis placed on incentive funding and the abandonment of the policy of Sport for All were the core characteristics of the sports policy in the early 1990s. However, the advent of the National Lottery in 1994 enabled intervention in the policy domain of leisure and sport and allowed decisions about sport to be taken by advisory groups (Henry, 2001).

The Major government showed an inclination towards the promotion of elite sport as a means of boosting national identity as the main tenet of its liberalistic ideology (Henry, 2001, McDonald, 1995). Houlihan (1997a) pointed out that the Major government also put a greater emphasis on traditional team sport in schools. McDonald (1995) argued that during the mid-1990s there was a shift of government focus to services supporting excellence and a withdrawal from the promotion of mass participation. Nevertheless, an emphasis on junior and school sports was an initial step on the road to excellence.

Henry (2001) asserted that as with the establishment of a core curriculum in physical education, the emphasis within schools was placed on competitive sport. According to McDonald (1995), the expansion of the provision of sport services by local authorities during the same era justified the government's shift away from mass participation and Sport for All. The Major government's principal policy goal to aid elite athletes resulted in the establishment of the British Academy of Sport to foster British sporting success as well as the promotion of sponsorships and schemes funded in essence by the National Lottery (Henry, 2001).

In power since 1997, the Blair government, inspired by the social democratic (Third Way) regime, "is driven by a hybrid ideology, which draws selectively from the roots of liberalism and social reformist" (Bramham et al., 2001, p. 14-15). Henry (2001) argued that the "avowed commitment to tackling social exclusion in and through sport" (p. 96) and the promotion of access to sport were probably the most significant policy differences between the Blair government and its predecessors. While the Conservatives abandoned the Sport for All policy in 1994, Labour reasserted its commitments to Sport for All. Henry (2001) claimed that policy changes were also felt at the school level where promotion of sport was not solely talent-oriented but a means of fostering community.

The English sport policy aim appears to be more people involved in sport, more places to play sport, and more medals through higher standards of performance in sport (Sport England, 1999). Along with mass participation development, the Blair government recognised the ability of sport to project a positive image of a nation and provide significant diplomatic and economic spin-offs as well as a sense of pride for the people (Sport England, 2003). Oakley and Green (2001) argued that one of the main characteristics of government sport policy post-1995 has been the increasing importance placed on Olympic sports and elite athlete performances. Additionally,

Houlihan (1997a) maintained that with the restructuring of the Sports Council to Sports England, a narrower policy focus on grassroots enhancement and elite athlete performance was apparent.

The financial priority given to elite support in the UK is undoubtedly lower in absolute and relative terms than, for example, in Australia. Additionally, neither the government's nor Sports England's (nor the Sports Council's before that) involvement with sport policy matched the situation in Canada where, for reasons of national unity and prestige, sports dependence on finance from the Canadian government and the government's influence on sport policy resulted in the monopolising of elite sport (Collins, 1991).

2.4.1 SUMMARY

Chalip et al. (1996) maintained that governments establish their policies with different legitimations, which in turn may create slight yet telling differences in policy implementation. For example, Canada's concerns for nation building resulted in a focus on the development of elite athletes and Olympic sports. Unlike Canada, several European governments, including the UK, have sought to promote health through the physical activity that sports generate. Therefore, traditionally, they have promoted Sport for All programs rather than the development of programs to select and train a few elite athletes.

Thoma and Chalip (1996) argued that there is a relationship between the form of government and the structure of sport administration. For example, in countries like China where the government controls the economy, it also exercises control over sport. Sport is regarded to be too important to be left to the whims of private clubs with restricted entrance and commercial promoters. It is developed for health, hygiene and defence and is state-controlled (Riordan, 1993).

However, sport governance features in countries with similar forms of government do not necessarily mean they administer sport similarly. Thoma and Chalip (1996) indicated that "policies that specify the structure of sport governance have emerged over time in response to each country's particular social, economic, and political

73

history" (p. 63). The USA and Canadian sport policies reflect individual responses to circumstances and therefore differ substantially.

Levine (1974) argued that the examination of differences between nations to isolate characteristics in relation to a policy issue is a macro-perspective approach, whereas examining specific processes of sport development is a micro-perspective. This research examines specific sport development processes as they emerge in Australia and espouses the micro-perspective approach of policy examination.

2.5 CONCLUSION

Chapter 2 reviewed the germane literature that relates to Australian Federal Government sport policy with respect to sport development modelling. It demonstrated the explicit needs for research into sport development policies and argued for an extensive empirical study of sport development practices as manifestations of sport policies. The tenet of this book is that research into the sport development processes and the trickle effects needs to be undertaken due to the tension between (a) elite and mass participation development and (b) mass participation as an end and mass participation as a means (larger pool of talented athletes) in Australia.

1. The questions that need to be answered in relation to sport development policies in Australia are:
   (a) What are the sport development processes in Australia?
   (b) What has been the impact of Federal Government involvement with sport policy on the sport development processes at a national level?
   (c) Who is engaged with the sport development processes in Australia and in what ways?
2. The theoretical importance of this book lies in its contribution to the sport management literature, since:
   (a) sport policy studies in Australia are limited to a small number of scholars;
   (b) there has been no literature in Australia that addresses sport policy and sport development issues since the early 1990s;

(c) sport development processes in Australia lack legitimate theoretical justification: hence, there is no work to provide firm evidence to support the contention that trickle effects do accrue;

(d) studies that examine sport development modelling are limited and, based on existing studies, associations between sport development process and policy deliberations have not been taken into consideration; and

(e) existing sport development frameworks explain only people's mobility rather than policy deliberation and impact on the sport development spectrum.

3. The practical usefulness of this book to sport management, sport policy and sport development is multiple, since:

(a) it offers policy makers, sport managers and development officers a greater understanding of the sport development processes in Australia;

(b) it aims for explicit policy formulation and implementation processes;

(c) Australia could experience an improved sport development system with sports flourishing at all sporting levels;

(d) it may provide a potential benchmark for international sport development practices; and

(e) it will offer a model of sport development with the potential for further quantitative studies on testing the theory generated from this study.

In conclusion, this chapter illustrated that the theoretical setting for this book is located within the realm of public policy analysis. Australian sport policies, as components of public policy, are shaped and reshaped by the existing governments and their ideological tenets. Section 2.2 explains the focusing event that prompted this study, that is, sport development and, in particular, the *elite versus mass participation* issue. The trickle-up and trickle-down aspirations of governments and the desire for elite excellence act as an event of national significance and the core sport development policy issue in Australia. As this section showed, this focusing event generates the attention of policy-makers in Australia and becomes the focus of policy agenda.

Section 2.3 provided a discussion on the *Australian sport policy delivery structure and policy goals*. Hence, this section was a reflection of what sport policies within the given government space 'must do' (i.e. to continue to produce champions and encourage participation). It specified Federal Government policy goals in relation to the focusing event and the aspects of the policy (i.e. the trickle-up and -down effects of theoretical inefficiency to justify policy deliberations) that require redress. Similar or opposing approaches adopted by governments outside Australia in relation to the aspects of the focusing event that require redressing were illustrated in section 2.4 in a *sport policy comparative study*. This analysis offered additional information and other countries'/governments' approaches to the same policy issue. The remainder of this book examines the phenomena under investigation that is sport development processes in Australia by way of an *empirical study*.

CHAPTER 3: METHOD

3 INTRODUCTION

This research sought to investigate the sport development processes underpinning the Australian sport system. In doing so, a qualitative approach using the principles of grounded theory research was employed. This chapter explicates and justifies the methodological considerations and procedures that were adopted in this study.

3.1 NATURE OF THE STUDY AND STRATEGY OF INQUIRY

The aim of this study was to explore sport development processes in Australia and the ways in which Federal Government sport policy impacts on these processes. Drawing from organisations involved in the sport development processes in Australia, the questions for which the research was designed to provide answers were:

1. What are the sport development processes in Australia?
2. How do the Federal Government sport policy and other stakeholders' involvement impact on these processes?

Chapter 2 demonstrated that existing sport development frameworks do not adequately answer the research questions. The lack of theory or models to explain the questions under examination directed this study. The limited theory available in this area was explored in Chapter 2 and consequently this study suggests that there is a theoretical vacuum with regard to sport development processes in Australia. However, in order to incorporate the 'what is already known' so that it can be challenged in the course of inquiry, this study utilised a *scaffold*. According to Morse (2002), a scaffold is used when "information is known about a phenomenon, or concept, but not enough for a researcher to work deductively" (p. 296) and the scaffold "enables the researcher to focus but leaves intact the freedom to explore inductively the internal structures of the concept" (p. 296).

Denzin and Lincoln (2000) argued that the positivist and post-positivist traditions, which hold specific positions concerning reality and its perception, shape both quantitative and qualitative perspectives. While positivists see reality as being out there to be captured using quantitative methods, post-positivists argue that reality can only be approximately comprehended. Denzin and Lincoln (2000) noted that post-positivists rely on multiple methods of capturing reality, largely through qualitative techniques, and emphasise the discovery of theory as it is found in its natural setting. They capture the differences in research designs between quantitative and qualitative research as follows:

> Positivist research designs place a premium on the early identification and development of a research question, a set of hypotheses, a research site, and a statement concerning sampling strategies as well as a specification of the research strategies and methods of analysis that will be employed. (Denzin & Lincoln, 2000, p. 368)

Moreover, they continued:

> [i]n interpretive research, a priori design commitments may block the introduction of new understandings. Consequently, although qualitative researchers may design procedures beforehand, design should always have built-in flexibility to allow for discoveries of new and unexpected empirical materials and growing sophistication. (Denzin & Lincoln, 2000, p. 368)

Perry (2000) indicated that the most striking difference between the two approaches is that while quantitative research problems ask who and what, how many and how much, qualitative research stresses how and why social experiences are created and given meaning. Denzin and Lincoln (2000) added to the differences arising from the methodological stances, observing that while quantitative research explores causal relationships between variables, qualitative inquiry is concerned with the inductive analysis of processes. Patton (1990) explained that inductive analysis means that the patterns, themes and categories of analysis "emerge out of the data rather than being imposed on them prior to data collection and analysis" (p. 390).

Hassard (1990) argued that a research problem involving constructions of meanings that have not previously been explored requires a qualitative methodology. Therefore, the nature of the present research problem indicated a qualitative approach as the most appropriate. Additionally, if a research question concerns a process, the method of choice for addressing the question is grounded theory (Strauss & Corbin, 1994). Glaser (1992) suggested that grounded theory is a general technique that can be used successfully by researchers in many disciplines. Haig (1996) maintained that although grounded theory "has been developed and principally used within the field of sociology" (p. 1), it has been successfully employed by researchers in a variety of disciplines including political science. In terms of research carried out with the aim to either expand theory or generate new theory, Strauss and Corbin (1998) noted that grounded theory has come to rank among the most influential and widely used modes of qualitative research.

3.2 GROUNDED THEORY: SUITABILITY AND DIVERSITY

Grounded theory is a qualitative research approach formulated by Glaser and Strauss in 1967 as a means of generating theory which is embedded in systematically gathered and analysed data (Bryman, 1988; Glaser & Strauss, 1967). Wells (1995) suggested that the aim of grounded theory is to explain social phenomena and processes, the structural conditions that support the processes, the consequences of the processes and the conditions that support changes in those processes. Hence, the objectives of this study were to explain sport development processes, the circumstances and setting within which sport development processes occur, the impacts of these processes on sport and the conditions that support changes in sport development.

Strauss and Corbin (1990) argued that grounded theory is inductively derived from the study of the phenomenon it represents. That is, "it is discovered, developed and provisionally verified through systematic data collection and analysis of data pertaining to that phenomenon. Therefore, data collection, analysis, and theory stand in reciprocal relationship with each other" (Strauss & Corbin, 1990, p. 23). In contrast to *abstract theory* that develops from hypotheses that are deduced in accordance with logical rules and then tested, observations of data through a process of coding, description, conceptual ordering and theorising lead to *inductively* derived theory (Strauss & Corbin, 1998). Therefore, grounded theories "are likely to offer insight, enhance understanding, and provide a useful guide to action" (Strauss & Corbin, 1998, p. 12).

The inquiry for this study directed the choice of grounded theory for a number of reasons.

1. There is minimal conceptual work in the area of sport development and a lack of cohesive theory in the field. Consequently, there is little theory to postulate hypotheses. Therefore, this study was exploratory and designed to better understand the area of sport policy and sport development.
2. The understanding of social processes by using grounded theory meets the requirements and nature of this study to investigate and explain *sport development processes*, their context and implications for sport.
3. The study aimed to construct a theory on sport development processes which would be available for further research and hypotheses testing. By utilising inductive reasoning, grounded theory allowed a substantive theory that fits the situation that was researched, deals with the specific area of inquiry and explains the processes and interactions under study to emerge. This theory is readily available for further research in order to test its applicability and to develop a formal theory with wider scope in sport development.

It should be acknowledged that since the late 1960s grounded theory has evolved, reformed and been repudiated by critics as well as by its own pioneers (Charmaz, 2000). Consequently, there appear to be conflicting opinions, misconceptions and unresolved issues regarding the application of grounded theory. The controversies related to grounded theory gave rise to two versions: the traditional, espoused by its originator Glaser, and that which was adapted by Strauss, co-originator of the traditional grounded theory, and Corbin. Even though similarities between the two approaches exist, significant deviations in coding data result in considerable practical implications for researchers utilising grounded theory.

Babchuk (1997) argued that the central difference between the Glaser and Strauss versions of grounded theory derived from ontological, epistemological and methodological chasms. Annells' (1996) interpretation of the above is that analyses of the ontological, epistemological and methodological perspectives suggest that grounded theory has traditionally been sited in a post-positivist inquiry paradigm but has evolved and moved toward the constructivist[3] inquiry paradigm. As a result, Strauss is perceived to have taken the path towards constructivism. The main practical implication of grounded theory variations is that Glaser's approach is more deeply committed to the principles and practices of the qualitative research paradigm while Strauss seems to be more concerned with producing a detailed description and is more closely aligned with the traditional quantitative doctrines. Therefore, depending on the approach espoused by the researcher, the research process and analysis, as well as the results of the study, may vary (Babchuk, 1997).

The debate emerging from Strauss and Corbin's (1990) work centred on the methods of *coding* and the role of *emergence* in grounded theory. Cutcliffe (2000) recommended that researchers proposing to utilise this method should consider these conflicting opinions. Therefore, a critical evaluation of the existing literature on grounded theory method and an overview of the most controversial areas of grounded theory are provided in Appendix 1. Kendall (1999) asserted that even though "one grounded theory approach is not necessarily superior to another", the decision to use a particular approach "depends on the goal of the research study, description, or theory generation" (p. 756). In addition, Wilson and Hutchinson (1996) argued that researchers are "obliged" (p. 122) to specify the grounded theory approach they employ.

The aim of this study was to generate theory on sport development processes. Additionally, since the nature of the research led to the conclusion that the use of grounded theory would allow sport development processes to emerge, ontological, epistemological and methodological considerations indicated the choice of the most appropriate variation of grounded theory. Because post-positivism was the main paradigm guiding this study, the research problem was more clearly aligned with the classic tenets of grounded theory.

Once it was established that the research was to be influenced and guided by classic grounded theory practices, the implications of this choice and the ultimate aim of this

---

[3] The constructivist paradigm of inquiry perceives the nature of reality as a "local and specific mental construction formed by a person and multiple mental constructions collectively exist regarding reality (relativism)" (Annells, 1996, p. 385).

research were the implementation of theoretical coding in conjunction with constant comparisons[4] of data to produce conceptually rich theory on sport development processes. The intent was to generate theory that related to a particular situation or, according to Creswell (1998), "closely related to the context of the phenomenon being studied" (p. 56). It is important to recognise that some components from both versions of grounded theory, such as open coding, overlap. Therefore, both Glaser's (1978; 1992) and Strauss and Corbin's (1990) literature is used in this chapter where applicable.

3.3 NATURE OF THE DATA

From the variety of surveying options available, this study used public documents as its primary source of data generation. More specifically, it involved the collection of NSOs' annual reports. The justification for examining NSO annual reports lies in the nature of these documents and the fact that they constitute the main formal written source of information that reflects both NSOs' operations with regard to sport development policy and practice and interactions with the Federal Government and other key players. Additionally, these reports constitute the annual contributions of all SSOs, staff and members of the boards of directors collectively in a reliable form available to the public.

Silverman (2000) maintained that documents offer information on social facts but not necessarily transparent representations of organisational day-to-day routines and processes. The implication of this is that we cannot learn how organisations operate. However, the scope of this book is not to attain an understanding of the NSOs day-to-day operations. Instead, the aim of this research is to examine the sport development processes as they are reflected at a national level. Therefore, annual reports were approached for what they were and for what they were used to accomplish. Silverman (2000) suggested that the embedded elements of social facts depicted in document necessitates that they are treated in a serious manner. Hence, researchers using documents are more concerned with the "processes through which text depict 'reality' than with whether such texts contain true or false statements" (p. 826).

---

[4] The process of taking information from data collection and comparing it to emerging categories.

The Confederation of Australian Motor Sport Limited (CAMS) in its 2000 annual report (CAMS, 2000) argued that the purposes of NSOs in producing annual reports are to create a transparent relationship with members and organisations with which they interact and to communicate their operations and activities for the year in review more comprehensively. Therefore, annual reports reflect a commitment to accountability by the organisation to its members and offer a greater degree of transparency regarding its activities. Finally, this type of data offers stable sources of evidence with a broad coverage of events and settings (Yin, 1994[5]).

Dick (2000) argued that in grounded theory any data collection method could be used. The research endeavour takes place in natural settings and the data are drawn from sources that vary from questionnaires to participant observations, interviews and documents (Benoliel, 1996). Glaser (1992) argued that grounded theory is "not bound by either discipline or data collection" (p. 18) and that a variety of material is "all data for the analysis" (p. 11). Furthermore, Glaser and Strauss (1967) stated that "no one kind of data on a category nor technique for data collection is necessarily appropriate. Different kinds of data give the analyst different views or vantage points from which to understand a category and to develop its properties" (p. 65).

Documents are considered as "atypical" (Creswell, 1998, p. 56) data forms that can help develop theory. Strauss and Corbin (1990) argued that investigation of archival material has been reported in qualitative studies and considered that a cache of archival material is equivalent to a collection of interviews and field notes. A number of authors, such as Bryman (1988), Glaser and Strauss (1967) and Grbich (1998), discussed the advantages of gathering document data in terms of effort, cost and speed compared to interviewing. Bryman (1988) argued that document material is non-reactive which means that it is not the product of investigations in which individuals are aware of being studied. Ultimately, "the possible biases which are often recognized to derive from interviews and questionnaires are removed" (p. 197). Grbich (1998) claimed that collecting documents is also a means of establishing comparable information from

---

[5] Yin (1994) explored the use of document data in case studies. Regardless of the methodological choice of data analysis, organisations such as NSOs may be viewed as cases.

organisations, since it can provide sources of comparison for field data. Also, documentary material "can provide access to information about individuals who are normally fairly inaccessible to conventional approaches" (Bryman, 1992, p. 197).

3.4 POPULATION AND THEORETICAL SAMPLING

The purpose of the research was to examine the impact of Federal Government involvement in and policy on NSOs' sport development processes. According to the 2001 official directory of sporting organisations published annually in Australia by the ASC, there were approximately 100 sports represented by NSOs. Subject to producing annual reports, the ASC's 2001 annual report records 60 sports funded by the Federal Government.

This research excluded sports that were not funded by the ASC during the financial year of reference as being out of the research focus. Therefore, the population under investigation was comprised of the 60 NSOs funded by the ASC during the financial year 2001. According to information derived from ASC annual reports (1996 to 2002), even though Federal Government grants allocations to NSOs varied throughout the time, the number and type of NSOs receiving ASC grants were largely consistent through those years. This trend increased the population's reliability.

In order to maximise participation in the study and thus variety among respondents, a letter was sent to the population. The letter was forwarded to the highest person in the organisation's hierarchy who was a member of the senior management (usually the General Manager or the CEO, depending on the organisational structure of each NSO) at the postal address appearing on the ASC's official directory listing NSOs. The letter (see Appendix 2) introduced the study, explained its benefits and invited all NSOs to participate by dispatching annual reports from 1999 to 2002. This timeframe covers a four-year period consistent with the Federal Government four-year funding cycle. Additionally, the arraying of events into a chronology "permits the investigator to determine causal effects over time, because the basic sequence of a cause and its effect cannot [be] temporally inverted" (Yin, 1989, p. 119).

To this extent, the initial sampling process was *convenience* in terms of gathering a large pool of data. This data was then analysed using *theoretical sampling* procedures. Theoretical sampling is used to develop emerging categories and to make them more definitive and useful. This is achieved by using the findings on the first set of data analysed to direct further selection of data. As the grounded theorist refines the categories, it is likely to find gaps in the data. As the researcher goes back to the field or pool of data and collects delimited data, they conduct theoretical sampling. Thus, the aim of this sampling is to refine ideas, not to increase the size of the original sample (Charmaz, 2000).

Theoretical sampling was undertaken in this study following the collection of annual reports from NSOs as they responded to the initial letter of introduction. The specific sampling decisions evolve during the research process itself (Strauss & Corbin, 1990). To facilitate the selection and theoretical sampling of annual reports for analysis, Minichiello, Aroni, Timewell and Alexander's (1995) *"analytical induction method"* (p. 249) was used.

Figure 3.1 displays the analytic induction method as a spiral process whereby the researcher collects the first set of data (i.e. first document) and, after analysing it, develops propositions about the area of inquiry. Then, "on the basis of the material and analysis" (Minichiello et al., 1995, p. 251) from the first set of data, the researcher "locate[s] a negative case that will extend" (Minichiello et al., 1995, p. 251) their understanding of the social process under investigation. This zigzag process (Creswell, 1998) allows for theoretical sampling, that is, the process of data collection where "the analyst jointly collects, codes, and analyses" (Glaser, 1978, p. 36) data and decides what data to analyse next in order to develop a theory. As concepts emerge, further sampling is guided by the need to test assumptions about emerging analytic concepts and their properties.

The scope of theoretical sampling was to reach *theoretical saturation*, that is, the point at which new categories or variations on existing categories cease to emerge from new data (Soulliere, Britt & Maines, 2001) and no new information is discovered (Smith & Stewart, 2001). Glaser (1978) argued that sampling ceases only when categories and their properties and dimensions are saturated, elaborated and subsequently integrated into a theory. Similarly, Minichiello et al. (1995) asserted that the analytic induction process continues until an adequate level of explanation of the social process under investigation is provided. Specifically, after analysing 50 per cent of the annual reports (37 annual reports), 90 per cent of the concepts and categories had evolved. However, saturation was not reached until 94.6 per cent of the annual reports had been analysed. The remaining 5.4 per cent represents four annual reports that yielded no new information concerning any category (Turner, 1981) and offered no additional information to this study.

Figure 3.1: The Analytical Induction Model

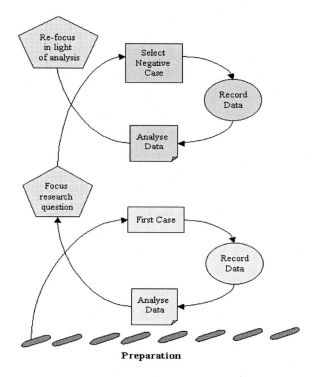

Adapted from Minichiello et al., 1995, p. 250

3.5 NSOs AND ANNUAL REPORTS COLLECTED

Table 3.1 shows the 35 NSOs that responded to the research letter. In total, 74 annual reports were dispatched (a reference list of all the annual reports collected is provided in Appendix 3). According to the tenets of theoretical sampling, there was no specific order or minimum/maximum number of annual reports sought to be collected from each NSO. Rather, the choice of each annual report was guided by the emerging concepts.

Additionally, the choice of each annual report was made in order to a) fill theoretical categories to extend the emergent theory, b) replicate previous case(s) to test the emergent theory, or c) select a case that was dissimilar/negative to extend the emergent theory (Yin, 1989). Therefore, the fact that some NSOs' annual reports covered a range of years while others reported on one year did not present a limitation to the study. The collection of annual reports from the same source through different years facilitated data comparisons within sports when necessary. Hence, 'time' triangulation of data sources enhanced the validity and reliability of the study.

Table 3.1: NSO Annual Reports [6]

No.	NSO	Year of annual report collected			
		1999	2000	2001	2002
1	Athletics Australia		☑	☑	
2	Australian Football League	☑	☑	☑	
3	Australian Baseball Federation		☑	☑	☑
4	Basketball Australia	☑	☑	☑	
5	Bocce Federation of Australia		☑	☑	☑
6	Bowls Australia			☑	
7	Australian Canoeing			☑	
8	Australian Cricket Board		☑	☑	

---

[6] NSOs' annual reports based on the financial year are represented by the last year of reference (e.g. the financial year of 1999-2000 is ticked in the table for the year 2000). Additionally, at the time of data collection only a small number of NSOs had produced their 2001/02 annual reports. Due to theoretical sampling procedures, none of these issues presented a limitation to the study.

9	Croquet Australia	☑	☑	☑	
10	Diving Australia		☑		
11	Equestrian Federation of Australia			☑	
12	Australian Golf Union		☑		
13	Australian Gymnastic Federation	☑	☑	☑	
14	Women's Hockey Australia	☑	☑		
15	Judo Federation of Australia			☑	
16	Australian Lacrosse	☑	☑	☑	
17	Confederation of Australian Motor Sport		☑	☑	
18	Netball Australia	☑	☑	☑	
19	Orienteering Australia	☑	☑	☑	
20	Roller Sports Australia			☑	
21	Australian Rugby League		☑	☑	
22	Australian Rugby Union	☑	☑	☑	
23	Australian Yachting Federation		☑		
24	Skiing Australia		☑		
25	Soccer Australia		☑	☑	
26	Softball Australia		☑	☑	
27	Squash Australia	☑	☑	☑	
28	Surf Life Saving Australia		☑	☑	
29	Australian Swimming		☑	☑	
30	Synchro Australia		☑	☑	☑
31	Taekwondo Australia			☑	☑
32	Tennis Australia		☑	☑	
33	Australian Water Polo	☑	☑	☑	
34	Australian Weightlifting Federation		☑	☑	
35	Australian Wrestling Union				☑

The annual reports provided an extensive range of NSOs' responses covering sports that varied considerably in their participation size, geographic location, purpose, goals, resources, government funding and popularity. Annual reports were collected from organisations of professionally played and governed sports, such as the Australian Football League (AFL), as well as amateur sports, such as croquet. Data from annual reports covered both Olympic and non-Olympic NSOs (see Table 3.2) and ranged from high profile sports (Olympic or non-Olympic NSOs), such as athletics and cricket, to low profile and awareness sports, such as orienteering.

Table 3.2: ASC Grants Above/Below $1 million in 2001

| ASC Grants Above $1 million in 2001 | | ASC Grants Below $1 million in 2001 | |
Olympic	Non-Olympic	Olympic	Non-Olympic
Athletics	Cricket	Synchro	Australian Football League
Baseball	Netball	Taekwondo	Bocce
Basketball		Tennis	Bowls
Canoeing		Weightlifting	Croquet
Gymnastics		Wrestling	Golf
Women's Hockey		Diving	Lacrosse
Yachting		Equestrian	Motor Sport
Soccer		Judo	Orienteering
Softball		Skiing	Roller Sports (Skating)
Swimming			Australian Rugby League
Water Polo			Australian Rugby Union
			Squash
			Surf Life Saving

Another feature was the variance in the level of ASC grants they received. As Table 3.2 illustrates, from the 35 NSOs only 13 sports (two of which were non-Olympic) received more than $1 million from the ASC during the financial year 2001, while 22 sports received less than $1 million in total grants.

The characteristics of sports such as popularity, funding and operations that have been taken into consideration suggest that the NSOs participating in this study varied extensively in size and scope. Consequently, the information offered in these documents varied in volume from sport to sport and to a lesser extent within the same sport in different years in terms of its depth and variance of information. Nevertheless, it is only reasonable that sets of data collected by any technique, including interview transcripts, may differ in data volume and quality.

Yet these documents were produced by NSOs for the same purpose (i.e. to report to and inform the public regarding their developments and objectives and to comply with funding criteria) and their content comprised patterns of thematic similarity relevant to the study. They provided information on the mission, vision and objectives of sports and their organisational structure, and profiled their boards and other members. Board members, individuals like coaches and referees, corporate sponsors and affiliated organisations such as SSOs all reported and reflected on the year as well as on key challenges and future issues.

For example, the NSO presidents' messages provided overviews of milestones and activities as well as future issues or problems. The NSO CEOs' messages offered overviews of achievements and key challenges ahead. Other types of sport development information included more in-depth reports from the referee board, the coaching board report and reports on commercial operations, public affairs and communication, data and publications, marketing and promotions. Most notably, reports were available on elite and mass participation programs, membership, events and results. Finally, the annual reports presented financial reports with detailed financial reviews and statements of financial positions. Federal Government and other stakeholder involvement with sport development was represented throughout the reports and the 'voice' of the affiliated state organisations was presented by means of special reports on their developments. This was incorporated in the NSOs' annual reports.

3.6 DATA MANAGEMENT, CODING AND ANALYSIS

Incoming annual reports were photocopied, clustered according to sport and stored for archival purposes. Photocopied documents were accumulated and subsequently transcribed in Nvivo software. Nvivo facilitated the management of the bulk of data. Fielding and Lee (1998) claimed that the sheer volume of information produced in qualitative research makes data vulnerable to disruption. This in turn justifies the use of computers in qualitative studies as the use of software assists in data management. Additionally, the use of software assists with the maintenance of precision and rigor in the analysis of data (Richards & Richards, 1994).

Cases stored in Nvivo as documents were selected as they facilitated understanding and made individual contributions towards the emerging theory. It was this selecting that ensured that the theory is "comprehensive, complete, saturated, and accounts for negative cases" (Morse, 1999, p. 5). Dissimilar cases raised questions regarding how to incorporate them into the overall analysis and provided variation that contributed "to greater complexity of analysis" (Oshansky, 1996, p. 402). This reinforced skepticism and prevented "reification of interpretation" (Oshansky, 1996, p. 402). More importantly, data from different annual reports and sports were sought to provide further clarification of the emerging concepts, in accord with the theoretical sampling tenets of grounded theory.

In addition, Nvivo was utilised for the initial stage of conceptual coding. The coding features that Nvivo encompasses are in accordance with the principles of grounded theory generation. For example, nodes (codes) can be initially free in open coding stages and formed in trees (categories) and sub-trees (subcategories and properties) as the researcher moves to theoretical coding. The researcher in turn can utilise Nvivo's browser to display the coding stripes for a full visual representation of the codes and sub-codes developed. Triangulation by 'researcher' involved the inclusion of more than one investigator to reflect on the formation of codes and categories as well as the emerging theory.

In summary, Nvivo allowed the management of large quantities of textual material and convenient coding and retrieval functions for searching patterns (Tak, Nield & Becker, 1999). These ways of handling information offered by Nvivo permit a more rigorous and detailed exploration of data (Qualitative Solutions & Research, 2003). Nevertheless, Nvivo was only used at the first stage of open coding and the development of concepts because the following stages of coding required the researcher's ability to link substantive codes and their properties, develop hypotheses and connect the categories to develop theory.

In addition to Nvivo software, *memos* and *diagrams* were used for the purposes of data integration around the main categories and the refinement of the emerging theory. Dick (2000) identified memos as notes that the researchers make to themselves about hypotheses they have concerning a category or property and particularly about relationships between categories. Glaser (1992) defined memos as "the theorizing write-up of ideas as they emerge, while coding for categories, their properties and their theoretical codes" (p. 108). Dick (2000) suggested that while coding makes visible some of the theory's components, formulating memos adds to the relationships, which link the categories to each other. The following Table 3.3 shows how concepts identified from one particular case, the 2000 Rugby Union annual report, lead to further exploration of relationships and concept development.

Table 3.3: Example of a Memo

> The 2000 Rugby Union annual report states that *'Participation, income, attendances, media profile: all these litmus tests for the health of the game are good. We can build on this with a continuing commitment from all levels of the ARU's operations and the continued harmony between the ARU and its member unions'*. There are three issues of importance here: a) the continuation of commitment, b) the recurring emphasis on the teamwork (harmony) between different parties involved as an important ingredient for successful sport development, and c) that the health of the sport is a result of a number of components rather than success at one level. These issues are regularly appearing in annual reports so far. However, it seems that these concepts are not fully elucidated. I need to explore these issues further by selecting more cases and make comparisons between them. It would be interesting to see whether a smaller sport such as squash experiences similar relationships.

Collectively, the use of memos in grounded theory is important since, based on Strauss and Corbin (1998), memos "force the analysts to work with concepts rather than with raw data", "act as reflections of analytic thought" (p. 220), provide "conceptual density and integration" (p. 218) and "help the analyst to gain analytical distance" (p. 218). Essentially, the sorting of all memos in this study put the fractured data and memos back together. The emergent product of this sorting of memos was the outline for writing. Hence, "as memos sort themselves out, the outline for writing emerges and the analyst just follows it" (Glaser, 1992, p. 113) to formulate "the theory presentation to others in words or writings" (Glaser, 1992, p. 109).

Diagrams acted as visual representations of the relationships among concepts or visual memos. Strauss and Corbin (1998) argued that diagrams might vary considerably from the early to the final stages of coding. In this study, at the early stages of coding diagrams were difficult to form since relationships between concepts had not yet emerged. However, a listing for each category, illustrating its properties, operated as a good starting point and led to diagrams during later coding stages. Diagrams have been comprehensively used throughout Chapters 4, 5 and 6 and illustrate the theory on sport development as it emerged.

In an attempt to simplify grounded theory data analysis, Turner (1981) suggested the activities involved in each of the nine stages that follow. Consequently, selected cases were read and re-read comprehensively and passages of relevance to the study were highlighted and were analysed in order to:

1. develop categories that closely fit the data;
2. saturate categories until new data yields little new information concerning a category;
3. formulate abstract definitions of categories to articulate the criteria for particular categories;
4. use the definitions to guide further analysis towards emerging features of importance;
5. exploit categories fully, which requires the researcher to be aware of additional categories and particular variations of existing categories;
6. note, develop and follow up links between categories and hence formulate hypotheses about the links between the categories;
7. consider the conditions under which the hypotheses hold;
8. make relevant connections to existing theory; and
9. examine whether the relationships hold in comparisons of extremes to test emerging relationships.

Soulliere et al. (2001) argued that the process of *constant comparison* enables emerging concepts to be informed, shaped and reshaped by the variety of conditions encountered, resulting in dense, complex theory which corresponds closely to data. Eisenhardt

(1989) proposed as the central idea that the analyst constantly compares theory and data, moving toward a theory that closely fits the data. Therefore, constant comparison is one way to ensure validity of findings (Brink 1989; Glaser 1978). Eisenhardt (1989) continued that a "close fit is important to building good theory because it takes advantage of the new insights possible from the data and yields an empirically valid theory" (p. 541).

Constant comparison has been applied through every step of data analysis and coding, from the initial identification of concepts to the very end of theory generation and its integration with the extant literature. In particular, the constant comparison of incident to incident, a concept to more incidents, and concept to concept with the purpose of finding the best fit of concepts to a hypothesis as suggested by Glaser (1978) was employed in this study. Ultimately, similarities and differences indicated patterns that were utilised as part of the theory development.

More specifically, constant comparison facilitated the coding processes used in this study:

1. Substantive (Open) Coding (i.e. unravelling substantive codes, their properties and the core category);
2. Theoretical Coding (i.e. linking substantive codes and their properties, and developing hypotheses – or building a 'story' that connects the categories); and
3. Writing and Theory Advancement (i.e. formulating an analytic story and integrating extant literature).

These activities encapsulate Turner's (1981) previously stated analytical steps. The coding methods are sequential and interrelated, and each is built upon the previous step (Smith & Stewart, 2001). Nevertheless, having specified coding techniques does not necessarily mean that the researcher moves from open through theoretical to selective coding in a strictly consecutive manner, since some categories are easier to move on to saturation levels than others (Pandit, 1996). The remainder of this chapter describes in detail these stages and the way each stage was realised within the current research by providing coding examples at each stage.

3.6.1 SUBSTANTIVE (OPEN) CODING

Pandit (1996) argued that the first stage of grounded theory analysis, open coding, aims to develop concepts[7], categories[8] and properties[9]. Glaser (1992) argued that open coding is "the initial stage of constant comparative analysis, before delimiting the coding to a core category and its properties - or selective coding" (p. 38). He continued:

> This initial categorizing of incidents through the constant comparative method is the first basic analytical step into the data. During open coding the data are broken into incidents, to be closely examined and compared for similarities and differences, while constantly asking of the data the neutral question what category or property of a category does this incident indicate? (p. 39)

By using this method, data were read line by line, examined and approached by asking questions such as what, where, how and when, and comparisons made of incidents so that similar incidents were grouped together and given the same conceptual label. For example, when reading data and asking 'who', the concepts that arose related to the parties involved with sports such as athletes, participants, members, volunteers, coaches, referees and so forth. When examining the data while constantly asking 'what', the concepts revealed a number of issues and strategies such as events and competitions, finances, teamwork and marketing.

Subsequently, data were re-examined and concepts were organised by reoccurring themes and grouped under a more abstract, higher order concept, a *category*. Categories or *substantive codes* constitute the cornerstones of developing theory (Corbin & Strauss, 1990) and link a number of associated concepts. This stage revealed three categories: a) *Stakeholders*, b) *Strategies*, and c) *Processes*. These three categories were labelled as closely to the data as possible to ensure that they remain and reflect the meaning of the category, "preferably by using *in vivo* labels" (Morse, 2000, p. 715), that is, the very words found in data that describe what is happening (Hutchinson, 1986). A small section of the Australian Swimming 1999/2000 Annual Report is

---

[7] According to Pandit (1996), concepts are the building blocks of theory.

[8] A category is "a type of concept. Usually used for a higher level of abstraction" (Glaser, 1992, p. 38).

[9] A property is "a type of concept that is a conceptual characteristic of a category, thus at a lesser level of abstraction than a category" (Glaser, 1992, p. 38).

provided as an example of an annual report that reflects the three categories: A (Stakeholders), B (Strategies) and C (Processes) in Table 3.4.

Table 3.4: Example of an Extract from the Australian Swimming 1999/2000 Annual Report

The high performance and talented coaches programs were supported with funding from the ASC. Whilst Australian Swimming will review and refine our programs to meet the challenge of a drastic reduction in government support beyond 2000, it is obvious that this will impact on our ability to support our swimmers and coaches as they prepare for 2004.	A. Stakeholders
This report reveals that our elite program has provided our swimmers and coaches with the support to succeed; the presentation of our major events is now of world standard and the public profile of Australian swimming is at an all time high. However, our elite swimmers need a strong grass-roots program from which to emerge. The transition from learn-to-swim to club competition is an area of concern, which is being investigated.	B. Strategies C. Processes
Sponsors and government support allowed us to put in place a high performance support program to assist our swimmers reach the performance levels they have.	A. Stakeholders C. Processes
Australian Swimming in conjunction with State Swimming Associations continues to support the grassroots levels of the sport.	A. Stakeholders
In recent years, the Federal government, through the ASC, have urged National Sporting Bodies to implement specific Sport Harassment policies in the areas of administration, coaching, athlete participation and officiating.	A. Stakeholders B. Strategies

The main characteristics of the categories are that they reoccur frequently and link various data, allow for maximum variation in data sources (Byrne, 2001) and "sum up the patterns found in the substantive incidents in the field" (Glaser, 1992, p. 27). Furthermore, these categories have explanatory utility and analytic power because they have the "potential to explain and predict" (Strauss & Corbin, 1998, p. 113). Their properties/concepts represent multiple perspectives on them (Creswell, 1998) and define the how, when, where, why and so on of a category (Strauss & Corbin, 1998), in an effort to give a category "specificity through definition of its particular characteristics" (Strauss & Corbin, 1998, p. 116).

Following the reordering of data into categories, the analysis continued by constant comparison within categories and the grouping of passages where comments on each category were evidenced. An example from a small number of annual reports from different NSOs where comments about category A (Stakeholders) were evidenced is illustrated in Table 3.5.

Table 3.5: Example of Various Annual Report Passages on Code A (Stakeholders)

Sponsors and government support allowed us to put in place a high performance support program to assist our swimmers reach the performance levels they have (Swimming Australia, 1999/2000).
The ACB is responsible for international and interstate cricket, national development programs, coaching and umpiring programs ... The state associations are responsible for cricket within their respective states and for the delivery of national programs developed and funded by the ACB (Australian Cricket Board, 1999/2000).
The association [sic] [received] substantial funding from [the state] government, including special funding for projects associated with the International Year of the Older Person and ensuing Y2K compliance. Without this support for programs and personnel, the sport would not be able to function at the current level (Women's Hockey Australia, 1999).
The NSW Department of Sport and Recreation continues to be a major sponsor and supporter of squash in the state. Michelle's achievements as a player are well documented with her many successes gaining much-needed media coverage for the sport. However, in her role as a person she has no peer. Her frequent nights mingling with local pennant players, attending coaching clinics, visiting country squash centres for promotion, local school visits and generally making herself available as required within a hectic international playing schedule, separates Michelle from all others (Squash Australia, 1999).

Glaser (1992) argued that open coding ends "when it yields a core category" (p. 39), which is the central phenomenon setting out how participants or cases "process their main concern or problem" (p. 64). Judging the appropriateness of a category as the central phenomenon should be automatic. The core category for this study was the *stakeholder's involvement* with sport development as it is central in relation to all other categories, frequently occurring in the data, inclusive and easily related to other categories, clear in its implications for a more general theory, theoretically powerful and allowing maximum variation (Creswell, 1998).

The regular involvement of the key sport-related stakeholders with Australian sport addresses the problems encountered in developing sport successfully. Indeed, sports interact with a number of stakeholders that provide the resources, policy and framework for sport development processes to occur. The basic social process of stakeholders' involvement with sport development is the core category in this study. It accounts for most of the variation in the question under investigation and is pivotal to the theory presented on sport development in Australia.

3.6.2 THEORETICAL CODING

Glaser (1992) argued that, once identified, the core category must be saturated by theoretical coding to ensure, from its relationship to its properties and other categories, that it is core. Only then can the researcher be "confident that it was not a premature choice brought on by the instant grab of such a catchy category" (p. 80). He further asserted that besides substantive codes, examined in open coding, there is another type of code (i.e. theoretical) that represents the relationships that are discovered "to relate the substantive codes to each theoretically" (p. 27).

Subsequent coding of code A (Stakeholders) for identification of its properties revealed that stakeholders were involved with the following strategies/properties: (a) facilities, (b) coaching and officiating, (c) administration/management, (d) player development, (e) media/marketing, and (f) competitions/events. Using player development as an example of theoretical coding, the following Table 3.6 shows the extracts of open coding with the sentences that refer to player development strategies.

Theoretical codes enabled the analyst "to see the research, the data and the concepts in new ways to be used for generating theory" (Glaser, 1992, p. 29). Therefore, theoretical coding was a "property of coding and constant comparative analysis" (p. 38) that generated the conceptual relationship between categories and their properties as they emerged. Figure 3.2 represents the relationships between substantive and theoretical categories for this study. As illustrated, the three substantive codes identified in open coding were comprised of nine sub-codes that were identified by using theoretical coding and were related to each other.

Table 3.6: Example of Extracts from the Theoretical Code 'Player Development'

- Performance support program
- International and interstate cricket, national development programs
- Delivery of national programs
- Projects associated with the International Year of the Older Person
- Mingling with local pennant players
- Local school visits

Figure 3.2: Substantive and Theoretical Codes

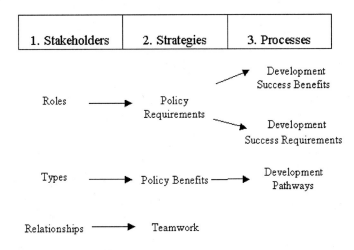

Glaser (1978) argued that it is the theoretical coding and the conceptualisation of how substantive codes may relate to each other as hypotheses which enable the substantive codes to be integrated into a theory. It is this theoretical coding that can provide the full and rich understanding of the social processes and human interactions which are being studied. Hence, while substantive coding facilitates the researcher's asking the questions 'What is this?' and 'What are the components of this social process?', introducing theoretical coding enables the researcher to ask questions such as 'What is happening here?' and 'How do the substantive codes relate to each other as hypotheses?'.

Another crucial requirement at this stage of coding was *theoretical sensitivity*. Theoretical sensitivity refers to the researcher's "manipulation of the data to yield explanations that best reflect the reality that is being apprehended" (Hall & Callery, 2001, p. 263). Strauss and Corbin (1990) explained that theoretical sensitivity reflects the investigator's ability to use personal and professional experiences to see the research situation and data in new ways and exploit the potential of data for developing theory. They further explained that theoretical sensitivity is used to maximise analytic procedures so that potential biases are countered and hypotheses that do not fit the reality of the situation are revisited. The researcher's awareness of the subtleties of meanings of data that was achieved though familiarity with the literature, professional and personal experiences and the analytic processes undertaken in this study, as suggested by Talbot (1995), enhanced its theoretical sensitivity.

Following the coding processes, the analyst began an attempt to establish a *storyline*, which is a brief descriptive account that "encapsulates the essence of what the research is about" (Fielding & Lee, 1998, p. 37). The aim of this step was "to elaborate the core category around which the other developed categories can be grouped and by which they are integrated" (Flick, 1998, pp. 184-185). In this way, the story of the study was elaborated by descriptive overviews. However, the analysis went beyond this descriptive level when the storyline was elaborated through an *analytical story* (Creswell, 1998; Fielding & Lee, 1998). According to Strauss and Corbin (1990), the production of a grounded theory depends on the transformation of the descriptive account of the codes and sub-codes using storylines into an analytical story.

This stage of analysis transformed the nine sub-codes (theoretical codes) into precise themes that formed the section headings for the results and discussion Chapters 4, 5 and 6. 'Equivalence', a test of reliability for qualitative research projects suggested by Brink (1989), was tested using more than one expert to observe the same event and compare the collected data (i.e. triangulation by research). The equivalence test of reliability has been fulfilled in two ways. Firstly, equivalence was achieved through the involvement of two research experts with the book. In particular, these experts were involved with the coding and categorising process of the book. Secondly, a grounded theorists and Nvivo (a qualitative analysis software) expert was involved with the initial coding and grouping of categories. These three experts, collectively, were aware of what the research was about and were asked to discuss the key factors that were reoccurred in the data and assisted in revealing concepts that were more salient (e.g., they recommended the use of information provided in the annual reports on NSOs financial statements).

Goulding (2002) and Hodder (2000) maintain that peer reviewed feedback and guidance in relation to the concepts/categories identified and their relationships, as well as their relevance and their fit in a study, result in a successful interpretation of the results. The iteration between data and concepts culminated when enough categories and associated concepts had been defined to explain the phenomena under investigation, any additional data collected added no information to the set of concepts and categories developed, and theoretical saturation was achieved.

3.6.3 WRITING AND THEORY ADVANCEMENT

Creswell (1998) suggested that for the purposes of building a thorough analytic story, the literature is used for *supplemental validation*; that is, the analyst references the literature to validate the accuracy of the findings or to point out how the findings differ from published literature. For the purposes of theory validation, constant comparison, suggested by Dick (2000), remained the researcher's core process. The aim was to compare existing literature to the emerging theory in the same way that data were compared to the emerging theory. According to Eisenhardt (1989), this involves asking "what is this similar to, what does it contradict, and why" (p. 544).

As Turner's (1981) steps of analysis indicated and Eisenhardt (1989) recommended, grounded theory involves building bridges from the emergent theory to the existing literature by comparing the two in terms of *similarities* and *differences*. In this way the relevant literature became integrated into the evolving theory. The key to this process was to consider a broad range of literature (Eisenhardt, 1989). This included the examination of a) literature that conflicted with the emergent theory, and b) literature that discussed similar findings. Theories and studies from diverse disciplines such as sport marketing, sport management, event management, sport sociology, organisational theory, strategic management, project management, stakeholder and policy analysis and human resource management were compared for similarities and differences.

Pandit (1996) argued that comparisons with *conflicting* frameworks improve construct definitions and therefore internal validity. Eisenhardt (1989) added that if the researcher ignores conflict findings, then "confidence in the findings is reduced" (p. 544), which in turn causes a challenge to internal validity and generalisability.

The importance of integrating literature that discusses *similar* findings is that "it ties together underlying similarities in phenomena normally not associated with each other. The result is often a theory with stronger internal validity, wider generalizability, and higher conceptual level" (Eisenhardt, 1989, p. 544). Pandit (1996) added that the comparison with similar frameworks improves external validity by establishing the domain to which the study's findings can be generalised.

The researcher confronted the challenges concerning a) the timing when the theory validation should occur, and b) how to go about integrating the relevant literature. Cutcliffe (2000) stated that the stage at which the researcher begins to weave in the literature for theory validation purposes appears to depend upon which version of grounded theory is being used. While Strauss and Corbin (1994) argued that it should be woven into the emerging theory, Glaser (1978) claimed that the researcher should refrain from theory validation until the theory has emerged from the data. The researcher may ask when is it appropriate to stop iterating between theory and data. Eisenhardt (1989) claimed that the key for closure is once again saturation.

3.7 LIMITATIONS

This study presents a number of potential limitations. First, the study investigated sport development processes from a particular perspective. It explored the phenomena as they were represented at the national level because that level was closest to the Federal Government involvement with sport policy. Even though NSOs reported on how sport development processes occur at all levels, the fact that this study did not explore sporting organisations at state, local level or the contribution of the private sector in sport development represents a limited perspective on sport development processes. For instance, the data in annual reports did not report on the increased private sector involvement with sport development which was one of the key recommendations from the Shaping Up report (DISR, 1999), as sponsorship and corporate funding offers subsidies for sport development programs and events at all levels of participation. This limited perspective arguably raises two further limitations to this study in relation to the validity of the data collected and the reliability of the method used.

Even though annual reports are public documents, it is impractical to verify that their content depicts the reality in all its possible forms. Additionally, a single source of data can be seen as weak representations of organisational reality. However, the book examined the global sport development processes in Australia, and not those of individual organisations. In light of this, annual reports presented an invaluable source of collective information with volume and depth for the analysis of the phenomena under investigation and contained insights into policy rather than reporting on sports' best outcomes. As such, national sport development trends became apparent. The latter contributed to the decision to utilise annual reports as the sole source for data collection.

Regarding the generalisability of the findings, the selection of each annual report for its contribution towards the emerging theory ensured that the theory was "comprehensive, complete, saturated, and accounts for negative cases" (Morse, 1999, p. 5). Nonetheless, Smith and Stewart (2001) argued that qualitative research is not strictly generalisable but offers a depth of insight that cannot be achieved by statistical procedures. The limited generalisability, therefore, may be considered a legitimate price to pay for the equally important enhancement in depth and quality (Krueger, 1994).

Dick (2000) maintained that grounded theory has its own sources of rigour. It is responsive to the situation in which the research is done and it *works* (i.e. it helps the people in the situation to make sense of their experience and to manage the situation better). Hutchinson (1986) argued that a quality theory will "inevitably identify a basic social process relevant to people in similar situations" (p. 59). In a quality theory, knowledge is generalised, the process is applied to new conditions and the findings can be applicable to any setting in which the problem of governments' involvement in sport development processes is of concern. According to Glaser and Strauss's (1967) definition it is a theory that will

> ...fit the situation being researched, and work when put into use. By "fit" we mean that the categories must be readily (not forcibly) applicable to and indicated by the data under study; by "work" we mean that they must be meaningfully relevant and be able to explain the behavior under study. (p. 3)

Morse (1999) argued that the knowledge achieved from the theory "should fit all scenarios that may be identified in the larger population" (p. 5). She added that the theory is also applicable beyond its immediate set of cases "to all similar situations, questions, and problems, regardless of the comparability of the demographic composition of the groups" (Morse, 1999, p 5).

The second potential limitation of this study lies in its use of grounded theory According to Strauss and Corbin (1994) the major distinguishing factor between grounded theory and other qualitative research methods is its emphasis on theory development, either *substantive* or *formal*. Glaser and Strauss (1967) distinguished between substantive theory or localised knowledge and formal theory or abstract knowledge produced through qualitative inquiry. Benoliel (1996) maintained that the analytic process of grounded theory "results in codes, categories, hypothesized relationships among categories, and a basic social process interpreted to explain the phenomenon being studied and to provide the core of a substantive theory" (p. 407).

According to Strauss and Corbin (1994), a substantive theory is grounded in research on one specific content area and evolves from the study of a phenomenon situated in one particular context. In contrast, formal theory pertains to a conceptual area and therefore emerges from the study of a phenomenon examined under several different types of situations. The present study offers a substantive theory on the sport development processes as it pertains to a specific rather than general context and situation and deals with a specific area of inquiry. Subsequently, it presents the potential for a formal theory with a wider scope to emerge from subsequent studies.

Third, Tak et al. (1999) argued that employing computers might reinforce the mechanistic aspect of qualitative data management such as indexing, sorting and filing at the expense of analysing data more theoretically. It is important to recognise that the use of software has the potential to undermine the emergence of data. Hence, becoming aware of the disadvantage of using software is a crucial step in preventing the analyst from using the software for the wrong purposes. In this study, Nvivo software was restricted to data management purposes and the initial open coding process.

Pandit (1996) argued that the principal advantage of using a software program in qualitative research is that it simplifies and speeds the mechanical aspects of data analysis without sacrificing flexibility, thereby freeing the researcher to concentrate largely on the more methodological and analytical aspects of theory building. Accordingly, despite the great number of services that qualitative software can offer, it is important to acknowledge the tasks which software is not capable of performing. Tesch (1991) argued:

> The thinking, judging, deciding, interpreting, etc., are still done by the researcher. The computer does not make conceptual decisions, such as which words or themes are important to focus on, or which analytical step to take next. These intellectual tasks are still left entirely to the researcher. (pp. 25-26)

3.8 SUMMARY

Chapter 3 commenced with arguments for choosing a qualitative approach to studying the research questions and in particular the adoption of grounded theory. This chapter recognised the critical elements of the debate regarding grounded theory procedures and justified the adoption of a traditional approach to grounded theory as suitable for this study. The chapter detailed the research processes implemented by the researcher supported by coding examples. It indicated that the selection of data from the annual reports was guided by theoretical sampling and that constant comparison was the core element pertaining to the analysis. Chapters 4, 5 and 6 are the product of the practices described above and provide details concerning the results and the discussion of the findings of this study. They show that the data gathered for the study provided sufficient for this book insight into sport development practices in Australia to construct a theory.

CHAPTER 4: THE SPORT DEVELOPMENT STAKEHOLDERS

4 KEY TO DATA INTERPRETATION AND INTRODUCTION

The following conventions have been adopted within the results and discussion Chapters 4, 5 and 6 to indicate categories, codes, in-vivo codes, sub-codes, and properties. In addition, appendix 3 provides a full annual reports reference list.

- Word(s) in **CAPITAL & BOLD** = Category
- Word(s) in **bold** = Code
- Word(s) in 'quote' = In-vivo code
- Word(s) in *italics* = Sub-code
- Word(s) underlined = Code/sub-code property

The following shapes and colours have been adopted within the results and discussion chapter's figures to indicate categories, codes, in-vivo codes, sub-codes and properties.

Represents
Stakeholders

Represents
Practices

Represents Sport
Development Segments

Represents
Practices' Benefits

Represents any
Sub-groups

The purpose of this study was to explore the nature of sport development processes in Australia and to assess the Federal Government's role in these processes as it affects the attitudes and behaviours of NSOs. In addressing the research questions, annual reports from 35 NSOs were examined and the ensuing data provided information that fell into three categories. They were: (a) the **SPORT DEVELOPMENT STAKEHOLDERS**, (b) the **SPORT DEVELOPMENT PRACTICES**, and (c) the **SPORT DEVELOPMENT PATHWAYS**. This chapter presents and discusses the results on the Sport Development Stakeholders. Chapters 5 and 6 present and discuss the results on the Sport Development Practices and the Sport Development Pathways accordingly.

This chapter, on sport development stakeholders, provides a stakeholder analysis that examines the parties involved with sport development and their dynamics by introducing them and studying their relationships. In addition, this chapter identifies relevant Federal Government sport policies and explores the impact of ASC sport policies in setting the agenda for NSOs. The importance of the sport development stakeholder relationships in delivering sport development (through sport development practices) in Australia and its implications for sport in general terms are also presented. Therefore, this chapter makes the connection between sport policies and the sport development practices that follow in Chapter 5.

The fundamental significance of this category (i.e. sport development stakeholders) and its function in this study is reflected in the fact that it forms the core category and by implication, according to grounded theory method, is central to all other categories, concepts and themes. It is essentially the platform for the other categories, codes and properties of this study. More specifically, the sport development stakeholders' relationships and their involvement in sport lead to the availability, implementation and evaluation of sport development practices, and the provision of appropriate sport development pathways for sport development processes.

Chapter 5, sport development practices, details the ways in which the sport development stakeholders put sport policies into practice or the ways they are involved in sport development. This chapter explores the essential strategies for the delivery of sport development and demonstrates how the sport development practices benefit sport development.

Finally, Chapter 6, on sport development pathways, explores three different yet associated processes of developing sport and the appropriate combination of stakeholders and practices involved with each individual process in order for sport development to be successful. These processes are the **attraction**, the **retention/transition**, and the **nurturing processes**. These three processes collectively provide the necessary pathways from mass participation to elite sport and vice versa.

The three main categories interrelate as the sport development stakeholders formulate and implement sport development practices that in turn generate the sport development pathways. These three categories exemplify the way sport development processes occur in Australia. In essence, the three results and discussion Chapters 4, 5 and 6 that follow offer a *macro*, *meso* and *micro* policy analysis respectively. Houlihan (2000) indicated that at a macro level, policies may reflect broad government sport ideologies (e.g. sports excellence and performance) which become clear at a meso level (e.g. the prioritisation of the Olympic Games) and specific at a micro level (e.g. the selection of particular sports for elite funding).

4.1 SPORT DEVELOPMENT STAKEHOLDERS

This chapter identifies the sport development stakeholders (i.e. all the parties involved in the delivery of sport development processes), discusses their roles, importance and relationships where applicable and offers a macro-analysis of sport development. The results show a number of agencies involved in sport development, from governments and organisations at all levels to corporate companies and individuals functioning inside or outside these governments and organisations. However, after extensive coding and analysis of the documents, three central groups of stakeholders were evident. These were: (a) the **governments** at the federal, state and local level including the statutory authority of the Australian Sports Commission (ASC) and the Federal Government policies; (b) the **sporting organisations** at the national, state and local level; and (c) **significant other stakeholders**, such as volunteers, paid staff, various participants and sponsors, that operate within or for the sporting organisations.

Figure 4.1 illustrates the sport development stakeholders. As this chapter will show, these stakeholders have either an interest in and the power to affect sport development (through sport policy formulation and implementation) or a stake in the achievement of sport development objectives (through sport development practices). This is in accord with Freeman's (1984) definition of a stakeholder: "any group or individual who can affect or is affected by the achievement of the organization's objectives" (p. 46).

Figure 4.1: Sport Development Stakeholders

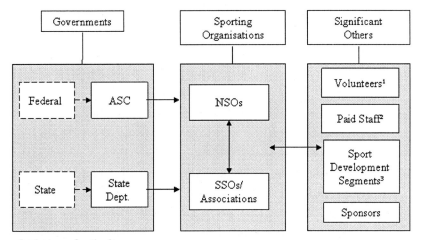

------ Instigators of authority
[1]   Volunteer administrators, coaches, umpires and board members
[2]   Sport development officers, coaches and administration/management personnel
[3]   Elite, talent, junior, membership/participation, and supporter/spectator segments

The sport development stakeholders establish various relationships at multiple levels. Initially, the relationships between governments and sporting organisations through the ASC illustrate the government's active role in and importance to sport development. This is followed by the relationships formed internally within national and state/local sporting organisations, which show how these sporting organisations establish an **intra-organisational cooperation** for a balanced approach to sport development. Finally, the relationships and contributions of significant other stakeholders that operate within these sporting organisations are reported. The first two types of stakeholders, namely the governments and the sporting organisations, are combined and discussed together in the first part of this chapter. This is followed by a discussion of the roles of other significant stakeholders that operate within the sporting organisations. These include (a) volunteers such as non-paid administrators, members of boards, coaches and umpires; (b) paid staff such as sport development officers, paid coaches and administration/management personnel; (c) the sport development segments such as the elite athletes, talented juniors, mass participants and sport spectators/supporters; and (d) sponsors.

4.1.1 GOVERNMENTS AND SPORTING ORGANISATIONS

This section links the two types of stakeholders, the governments and sporting organisations that operate at different levels. More specifically, it includes a discussion of: (a) the relationships between the ASC and the NSOs, (b) the relationships within sporting organisations (NSOs, SSOs and clubs/associations), and (c) the relationships between the state departments and the SSOs. Initially, the areas of Federal Government involvement with the NSOs and the relationships between the ASC and the NSOs are illustrated followed by the nature and ramifications of Federal Government funding for sport development. Next, the discussion shifts from the national to state and local sporting organisational levels and illustrates the NSOs' and SSOs/clubs' responsibilities and interaction. Moreover, this section illustrates that the support of governments and the intra-organisational cooperation of national and state organisations facilitate a balanced approach to sport development across the development spectrum from mass participation to elite in Australia.

The Relationship between the ASC and NSOs

The ASC, the Federal Government statutory authority, is responsible for the delivery of the Federal Government's sport policy and the funding of NSOs for the development of sport in Australia. NSOs indicate that interaction between the ASC and NSOs often takes place through consultation or sports consultants. This is best illustrated by the following quotation from the Australian Baseball Federation (2000/01):

> The relationship between the ABF [Australian Baseball Federation] and ASC was facilitated primarily through Sports Consultant Tony Wynd. Tony's supportive style and clear communication skills assisted [the] ABF significantly in ensuring

funded programs were properly designed and delivered to achieve performance targets. (p. 19)

Over time, the ASC and the NSOs have developed a close working relationship, a partnership, to achieve sport development goals. The Australian Weightlifting Federation (2001) provides support for this point by arguing that "this partnership between the AWF [Australian Weightlifting Federation] and ASC will work harmoniously in an effort to meet recognised outcomes that once realised will benefit communities throughout Australia" (p. 14). Two-thirds of NSOs express similar views on the benefits realised from their partnership with the ASC. As an example, in 1997 the Australian Yachting Federation's interaction with the ASC was limited. Yet, in 2001 it had "a positive open relationship with the ASC", which resulted in its being "recognised as a leading National Sports Organistion [sic]" and "specifically invited to participate in targeted programs" (Australian Yachting Federation, 2001, p. 2).

(a) ASC Areas of Provision and Requirements

NSOs recognise that the ASC provides for both the <u>elite athlete</u> and <u>membership/ participation</u> ends of the sport development continuum. According to the Australian Gymnastic Federation (2001), the ASC's contributions allow NSOs to provide the necessary resources, both financial and human, to achieve the objectives in their strategic plan which covers "both the High Performance and Participation elements" (p. 3). As a further illustration, the Bocce Federation of Australia (2002) acknowledges that without the financial contribution of the ASC, "the BFA [Bocce Federation of Australia] could not carry out its development program or be in a position to field teams to international competition" (p. 6). Pfeffer and Salancik (1987), who studied the external control of organisations, recognise the importance of resources as a critical factor in determining the dependence of one organisation on another.

Athletics Australia (1999/2000) also recognises the support and financial commitments of the ASC to the development of its "national teams' up and coming talent and Australian representatives" (p. 2). The Australian Rugby Union's (ARU) (1999) description of the twofold ASC involvement in relation to sport development is that "the ASC provides a grant to support the Union's participation initiatives and coaching program, while the AIS supports the development of elite players" (p. 50).

There is a common belief that Federal Government funding to NSOs allows the ASC to implement performance benchmarks in return for allocating grants. In this regard, Squash Australia (2000) states that the ASC "regards itself as a purchaser of sporting results. Put simply, if the sport expects ASC financial support, it will need to produce results" (p. 5) both in terms of elite international success (Sports Excellence Program) and participation numbers (Sports Development Program). The Australian Yachting Federation (2000) is another case in point. It maintains that "the success of our sailors overseas and of programs such as the National Membership Scheme, together with the positive contribution that the AYF [Australian Yachting Federation] has made to the ASC, has seen their commitment to sailing increase significantly" (p. 9). Pfeffer and Salancik (1987), in their interpretations of organisations' environmental dependence, maintain that for an organisation to continuing provide what another organisation needs, "the external groups or organizations may demand certain actions from the organization in return" (p. 43).

One-third of NSOs agree with the above suggesting that success goes hand in hand with increased expectations and demands from all types of stakeholders. Australian Swimming (2000/01) believes that as a result of their success it is faced with "ever increasing demands from all interest groups holding a stake in this sport. Coaches, sponsors, media, administrators, managers, the paying public and the swimmers themselves have all experienced this rather swift intensification" (p. 33).

Overall, NSOs believe that the ASC provides direction and guidance for both elite and mass participation elements. This involvement allows the ASC to establish success criteria at all levels. In order for the ASC to allocate grants to NSOs, the latter reveal **participation/membership** and **elite athlete requirements**. The participation/ membership requirements relate directly to the popularity (*public profile*) of the sport and its membership numbers (*growth*). The elite athlete requirements relate to athlete performances (*elite success*). These two areas of funding requirements are reported in NSOs' *strategic plans*. Therefore, **management/administration requirements** relate to the submission of plans where NSOs' objectives for mass participation and elite development programs are stated.

Management/Administration Requirements

The ASC is formally advised of the NSOs' sport development objectives through their strategic plans. NSOs have to formulate and revise long-term strategic plans, as it is a "condition of Federal funding" (Squash Australia, 2001, p. 7). Furthermore, Squash Australia (2001) continues, formulating and revisiting strategic plans give them "the opportunity to reassess our priorities and re-focus on a realistic number of primary objectives" (p. 7). According to Australian Lacrosse (2001), business/strategic plans form the "basis" (p. 2) of funding applications to government and their future operations. Overall, NSOs describe strategic or business plans as the glue between ASC funding allocation and sport development at all levels.

Whether NSOs submit a request or a business/strategic plan, the point is that a request or plan has to be endorsed and approved by the ASC before any funding allocations are approved. For instance, the ASC informed the Judo Federation of Australia (2002) that they were "to have a Strategic Plan in place if we were going to attract any more funding" (p. 43). The Australian Gymnastic Federation provides another example, having secured strong financial support from the ASC following its endorsement of its 2001-2004 business plan. Similarly, Orienteering Australia (2000) argues: "Another success was the level of funding achieved from the Australian Sports Commission as a result of our new Strategic Plan" (p. 2).

Membership/Participation Requirements

In relation to the ASC requirements for funding mass participation, NSOs suggest that the public profile of the sport and its membership/participation growth are crucial factors. Membership/participation growth represents the frequency and volume of participation, or what Houlihan and White (2002) describe as "getting more people to play more sport" (p. 3). Public profile is anything that causes the consumer to experience or be exposed to a brand (be it a sport, club, team, facility, event, or athlete) and has the potential to increase awareness (Irwin, Lachowetz, Cornwell & Clark, 2003).

With regard to ASC financial support, NSO opinion is divided into two groups. The first group stresses the importance of increased profile to obtain grants. In response to enhanced public profile and participation numbers, NSOs call for increased Federal

Government funding. The Confederation of Australian Motor Sport (CAMS) (2000), for example, claims that "the popularity of Motor Sport in Australia is immense" (p. 3) and thus "we are calling on both Federal and State governments to support our sport to a greater degree" (p. 3). Australian Lacrosse (2001) faces the task of increasing the public profile of its sport as well as its participation numbers before it is eligible for any increased funding. It suggests that "the sport of Men's Lacrosse was simply too small and had too low a public profile, and therefore did not fit with the political imperatives of 'those that the ASC answered to'" (p. 1).

The second group, in their efforts to obtain, increase or retain funding, aims to achieve growth in membership/participation by complying with ASC's requirements to employ Sport Development Officers (SDOs) or become/remain Active Australia Providers. Indicatively, the employment of a SDO was a condition for Roller Sports Australia (2000/01) to retain its funding. Their Executive Officer declared that he was pleased "to announce that the Australian Sports Commission has increased funding to RSA [Roller Sports Australia] on the condition that we employ either a part or full time Sports Development Officer" (p. 4). To be eligible for funding, being or becoming an Active Australia Provider was a condition in other cases. For example, in 1999 Squash Tasmania became an Active Australia Provider "as required for further Government support" (Squash Australia, 1999, p. 21).

Elite Athlete Requirements

The ASC assesses NSOs' funding applications based on a number of factors. At the elite athlete level, the ASC looks closely at elite success and the performances of athletes at world and international championships. As a consequence of regaining the world champion title in 2000, Surf Life Saving Australia (SLSA) attracted Australian Institute of Sport (AIS) funding, and softball's overall success in Sydney in 2000 "resulted in the Federal Government increasing Sport funding" (Australia Softball Federation, 2000/01, p. 9). The signals were also apparent for the Australian Yachting Federation (2000):

> Throughout the OAP [Olympic Athlete Program], it was made very clear that we were being continuously assessed on the results of our sailors at international events. These results were good and generated additional funding for the OAP.

They directly resulted in sailing becoming an Australian Institute of Sport program sport for the first time from 2001. (p. 5)

Similarly, Orienteering Australia's High Performance allocations are closely tied to and dependent on elite performances in world competition and in achieving benchmark performances in world events. As Diving Australia (1999/2000) states, with generous support from the Federal Government there is "a requirement to produce results and maintain standards" (p. 7). The Australian Softball Federation (1999/2000) argues that when considering future funding allocation the ASC assesses Key Performance Indicators (KPIs): "the ASC/AIS will measure our success in achieving these KPI's" (p. 9). In addition, the Australian Softball Federation admits that government funding allocations are heavily weighted according to performances. Therefore, the success of the team determines future funding levels. Along the same lines, the Australian Water Polo's (2000) major aim is to professionally prepare and do everything possible for Olympic success, because "this success, was and is, vital for the survival of our elite programs, to deserve the continuous support of the Australian Olympic Committee and the Australian Sports Commission" (p. 11).

Indeed, success is "vital for the survival" of the Australian Water Polo elite programs if it is "to deserve the continuous support" (Australian Water Polo, 2000, p. 11) of the ASC. The Australian Softball Federation's women's division funding allocation is "heavily weighted according to the performances of the Australian Women's Team, and therefore the success of the team was to [sic] determine future funding levels" (Australian Softball Federation, 1999/2000, p. 11). As a further illustration of the importance placed on elite success, the Australian Baseball Federation (1999/2000) argues that future government funding from the ASC and various state institutes and academies of sport is dependent on the success of its national senior and junior teams and suggests that "simply put, our future Government funding will be dependent on the ability of our national league to develop elite baseballers" (p. 6).

To identify a full range of possibilities and in order to test the proposition that successful elite athlete performances are followed by Federal Government funding, a comparison of organisations was made. Paradoxically, Australian Lacrosse presents the case where successful athlete performances at the world and international stage were not necessarily followed by Federal Government recognition and funding. However strong the evidence that elite success is crucial for ASC recognition and the continuation of support, the case of Australian Lacrosse suggests that world success is not the only factor taken into consideration. Australian Lacrosse (2001), though ranked third in the world in 2001, raised concerns over the continuation of its ASC funding. It states: "Currently ranking third in the world it is to be hoped that the Australian Governments decision to remove all elite funding from the sport of Lacrosse does not in any way temper the results of this enthusiastic group of elite athletes" (p. 3).

This case represents a strong contradiction of the data presented so far in that Australian Lacrosse have had its grants revoked despite being ranked third internationally. Australian Lacrosse argues that funding from the ASC and the complete absence of High Performance funding would not change until its sport was able to clearly demonstrate significant and measurable growth in participation numbers and a corresponding elevation in public profile. Australian Lacrosse is counting on growth in the membership/participation numbers to obtain grants for its high performance program. This argument reflects the importance of increasing the public profile of the sport and its membership/participation numbers in order to attract Federal Government funding. Hence, it appears that international elite success will not deliver Federal Government grants to Australian Lacrosse until the sport is also popular and has a high public profile.

Figure 4.2: ASC-NSOs Areas of Provision and Requirements

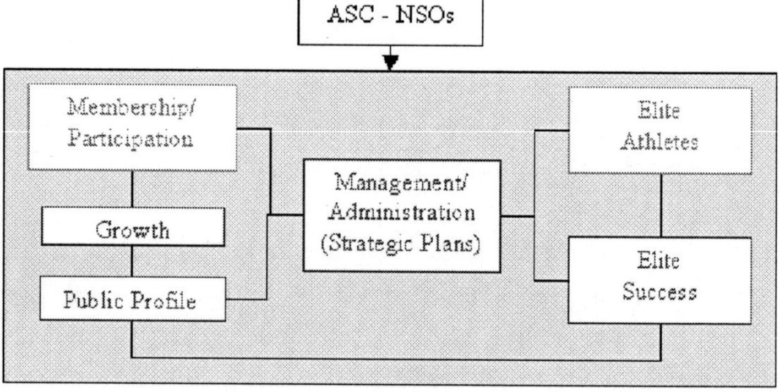

116

Figure 4.2 summarises the areas of ASC contribution (*provision*) to the NSOs and the areas of NSO accountability (*requirements*) to the ASC. It illustrates that management/administration, membership/participation and elite athletes form the three areas of both ASC involvement and NSOs' accountability.

(b) The Nature of ASC Funding and Implications

As the discussion on the nature of the ASC funding that follows shows, NSOs indicate that not only have ASC grant allocations fluctuated over the years but also the nature of funding is somehow provisional and uncertain. This is best demonstrated by the examples of the Australian Yachting Federation (2000) admitting to a "lack of certainty over the levels of Government funding that will be available on an on-going basis" (p. 5), and the Australian Water Polo (1999) disclosing that it has been "overshadowed by possible cuts from the Federal Government and uncertainty" (p. 2). Pfeffer and Salancik (1987) recognise that organisational interdependence, such as the relationship between the ASC and the NSOs, can create problems of uncertainly or unpredictability for the organisation. They suggest that "when the supply of resources is stable and ample, there is no problem for the organization. Organizational vulnerability derives from the possibility of an environments' changing so that the resource is no longer assured" (p. 47). The uncertain nature of ASC funds results in NSOs *lobbying* the government or searching for alternative funding. The most common sources of income for NSOs' financial viability derive from the membership/participation *fees* and *sponsorships*.

Lobby

ASC grant fluctuations and NSOs' uncertainty over future grants and long-term financial contributions cause NSOs to actively lobby the ASC. Di Gioacchino, Ginebri and Sabani (2004) make a useful distinction between lobbying used to influence electoral competition and result, and lobbying that is enacted post-election in an influence-driven approach. The influence-driven approach to lobbying represents the lobbying efforts of the NSOs through Sport Industry Australia (SIA) and is used to exert pressure over the ASC. Lobbying appears to be an important mechanism available and the response to defending and securing additional funding to support programs and operations. For example, the Australian Gymnastic Federation (1999) is actively involved in "lobbying the ASC Board in order to defend the AIS MAG and WAG programs from adverse post 2000 recommendations made to the ASC" (p. 1).

Numerous NSOs provide evidence of lobbying efforts. Indicatively, CAMS (2000) explains: "We have lobbied strongly for 2001 funding and the result has been positive" (p. 3). The Judo Federation of Australia's (2001) lobbying endeavours were also successful: "Fortunately, through some very good negotiating by personnel within the Federation, Judo was given some reprieve with the announcement of a small increase in funding" (p. 41). Squash Australia (1999) argues that the indications were that after 2000 funding levels could have been inadequate and that it was "up to Sport to lobby the Government (and the Opposition) to ensure that funding is maintained at a satisfactory level" (p. 5). In his examination of organisational environments and interorganisational relationships under various political conditions, Hall (2002) reinforces the argument that "lobbying can be very successful" (p. 207).

Insecurity over future grants from the Federal Government led NSOs on one hand to lobby for continuity or increased ASC grants and on the other hand to seek financial independence, self-sufficiency and the identification of alternative sources of income. For example, the Australian Gymnastic Federation (2000) realises "that the Federation's future can no longer be dependent on Government funding" (p. 1) and is "determined to take all possible steps to secure alternative revenue opportunities" (p. 1). Australian Swimming (2000/01) aims to "ensure that the organisation becomes more self-reliant and less dependent on government funding" (p. 51). Squash Australia (1999) presents another example of a NSO seeking alternatives sources of income:

> Squash Australia will continue to find it difficult to operate effectively as long as we are heavily reliant on Government funding and affiliation fees from State Associations that have their own financial difficulties and finding alternative funding sources will be one of our top priorities in 2000. (p. 6)

Alternative sources of income and resources to overcome Federal Government funding reliance which have been identified can be divided into two groups: (a) support from membership/participation fees, and (b) financial assistance from sponsors. Identification and employment of these sources of financial security confirm Mewett's (2000)

118

suggestion that sport in contemporary Australian society must be financially viable if it is to survive and prosper. Shilbury's (2000) cluster model emphasised and drew attention to the need to be less reliant on government funds. Additionally, a large spectator base and corporate sponsorship lend support to Shilbury's (1990) characteristics of corporate sport, especially its ability to generate substantial income.

Membership/Participation Fees

The NSOs' response to the volatile nature of the ASC's financial support is often the adjustment of membership fees or intensified efforts to increase membership/ participation numbers. Pfeffer and Salancik (1987) suggest that organisations can take a number of actions to avoid or minimise dependency. A common and direct solution is to develop an organization which is dependent on a variety of exchanges and less dependent on any single exchange" (p. 109). Bowls Australia (2000/01) supports this argument. After having a successful year (2000/01) as a result of the continued growth of its National Merchandising Program (which shows its potential and demonstrates that NSOs can generate revenue streams outside of corporate sponsorship and government funding), it argues that "serious consideration should now be given to investigating other avenues of revenue generation from the membership base" (p. 7).

The Australian Gymnastic Federation (1999) also seeks "business opportunities to generate new income streams" (p. 2). These include club development and delivery of services to increase membership and enhance benefits. In addition, the Australian Yachting Federation Board (2000) considered a membership fee increase in order to achieve its future coaching and development strategies and ensure it capitalises on the success of its elite athletes.

More important, the NSOs that present membership as an alternative source of income argue that this income is significant in financing their operations and assisting sport development. For instance, the Australian Yachting Federation's (2000) membership scheme is an important revenue stream to the NSO. Its annual report encapsulates the above argument:

> We are anticipating a reduction in Government funding after the Olympics, however with increased income from our new membership program and continuing

endeavours [to] expand other recurring sources of income, our aim is to place the AYF [Australian Yachting Federation] in a position to ensure the future viability and success of our sport. (p. 18)

Further analysis drew on additional data from NSOs' financial reports. Selection of annual reports based on membership fees reinforces the importance that NSOs place on this income source. The Australian Yachting Federation (2000) in their profit and loss statement for the year ended 30 June 2000 shows that its income from membership subscriptions reached more than $491,164, a figure twice as large as the $228,000 grant allocation from the ASC. Taekwondo Australia's (2002) statement of financial performance for the year ended 30 June 2002 shows an income of $31,205 deriving from membership fees compared to a $21,785 grant received from the ASC. Roller Sports Australia (2000/01) also agrees on the role of membership fees: "membership fees paid to RSA have been a large slice of the sports funding over the recent years" (p. 8). Moreover, in its profit and loss statement for the year ended 31 December 2001 the Australian Gymnastics Federation (2001) received nearly $286,000 from membership fees compared to $158,510 general sponsorship revenue and a nearly $250,000 government grant income.

The Australian Gymnastic Federation (1999) acknowledges the importance of membership fees to their state associations' financial performance, noting: "The continued decline in gymnast registrations has had an impact on the Association's [Gymnastics Western Australia] annual financial performance" (p. 35). Similarly, the Australian Softball Federation (1999/2000) indicates that "the diminishing membership is bringing its own financial woes" (p. 44). It recognises that it needs to grow "to ensure that total operating costs are divided between more members and therefore maintain, or possibly reduce, costs per head" (p. 44).

Sponsorship

The NSOs aim to ensure that their organisations become more self-reliant and less dependent on government funding. Unless they do so, and as long as they remain heavily reliant on Federal Government funding and affiliation fees from state associations that have their own financial difficulties, the majority of them will continue to find it difficult to operate effectively. Therefore, finding alternative funding sources appears as one of their top priorities along with the need to deliver competitions which are attractive to corporate partners. In support of this, previous research (e.g. Shilbury 2000) recognised the growing trend for NSOs to "identify organisations relying on the success of a sport to leverage support" (p. 217).

Women's Hockey Australia (2000) provides an example that illustrates best the view expressed by many NSOs on the importance placed on the injection of sponsorship to the survival and growth of the sport:

> In the last twelve years we have been fortunate in securing sponsorship from a number of sources; this has made the financial burden lighter and enabled the development of a number of programs that provided for a sound basis on which to build our future successes. (p. 1)

The constant comparison of cases showed that although all NSOs recognise sponsorship as an important source of revenue, not all of them manage to attract corporate funds. Australian Canoeing (2000/01), for example, argues that "in the post Olympic climate, the sponsorship market has been difficult, and unfortunately we remain reliant on Federal government funding for a majority of our programs" (p. 4). In evidence of this, a comparison between their profit and loss statement for the year ended 30 June 2000 and that of the year ended 30 June 2001 shows a decrease in sponsorship funds from $115,741 in 2000 to almost half, $67,709, a year later. In the same year, its government grant was nearly 15 times higher than its sponsorship income which shows its marked reliance on government funds. Another NSO suggests that without a national database and data, or enough resources to pay for a national survey, its "chances of major sponsorship, particularly national sponsorship are slim" (Bocce Federation of Australia, 2001, p. 5).

In light of the evidence of the ASC's funding instability, in a more focused analysis and in conjunction with theoretical coding and the making of constant comparisons, a funding typology emerged. The typology is comprised of cases where *continuous*, *increased*, *withheld* or *decreased* funding was evidenced. Further analysis of these types of ASC funding based on similarity patterns indicated a further grouping of results into *Continuous/Increased* and *Reduction/Withdrawal* of ASC funding.

Continuous/Increased ASC Funding

Even though the ASC commits its support and policy direction covering all aspects of sport development from elite to mass participation, NSOs associate *continuous or increased funding* from the ASC with *elite success*. Additionally, they claim that continued or increased funding from the government results in funding *reliance* and increases their *accountability* to the ASC.

The NSOs perceive successful elite performances as a requirement not only for Federal Government grants, but also for their consistency. The Australian Baseball Federation (1999/2000) illustrates this point by arguing that "the performance of our junior and senior national teams on the world stage since 1995 has been quite extraordinary and can be significantly linked to the support through the Australian Sports Commission" (p. 5). Women's Hockey Australia (2000) was also pleased with the continued support of the ASC deriving from the national squad's successful performances. Moreover, Basketball Australia argued that the continued support of the ASC through the OAP was essential to its programs. The Australian Gymnastic Federation (2000) noted that its "Olympic results would not have been possible without the continued financial support of the ASC and our High Performance Network" (p. 2). The Australian Baseball Federation (2000/01) also experienced a "fair degree of funding consistency from the Australian Sports Commission throughout the 1997 to 2001 period" (p. 19). The Federation argues that this is indicative of a stable relationship and "a successful run of winning programs" (p. 19).

There is a fundamental view that NSO finances rely greatly on these grants. Therefore, the continuation and consistency of this funding are crucial to Elite Success. Australian Canoeing is one of many bodies expressing the belief that NSOs are not alone in acknowledging the importance of regular and consistent ASC grants to elite success. The Federal Government also admits that continuous funding is important if sports are to keep the momentum of success. Australian Canoeing (2000/01) explains:

> Whilst there has been a distinct shift in policy towards funding broad-based participation in sport from the previous focus on high performance, the Government has acknowledged that to maintain the Sydney [Olympic] performances, there must be a long-term commitment to sport funding, and they have addressed this in their funding programs. (p. 4)

The great importance of continuous financial support is illustrated on many occasions. Athletics Australia (1999/2000), for example, maintains that "the importance of ongoing Government support, particularly for athletics' high performance program, is evidenced by the fact that the Commission's grant represented 49.7% of Athletics Australia total revenue for the year" (p. 17). Similarly, Roller Sports Australia (2000/01) suggests that the "principal source of funding ... has been the grants funds that RSA receives from the Australian Sports Commission" (p. 7).

Given that Roller Sports Australia is only one of the many sports to argue that ASC grants form its principal source of funding and that even high profile and well-funded sports such as Athletics Australia confirm the great proportion of their overall funding consists of the ASC grants, it is understandable that the ASC plays an active role in sport development. Larson and Wikstroem (2001) argued that the relative power of a stakeholder is based on the degree of authority and resources available to them. Consequently, issues of increased funding reliance and accountability emerge for NSOs in their relations with the ASC. Thus, according to Mitchell, Agle and Wood (1997), ASC power gains authority through legitimacy, which gains exercise through urgency on the part of NSOs.

The extent to which the ASC supports and finances NSOs justifies the belief that the ASC is the most important sport development stakeholder and is at the hub of the sport development processes. Although some NSOs, such as Squash Australia (2000), directly admit that "the Australian Sports Commission is our most significant stakeholder" (p. 3), others provide examples of the importance of the ASC's role in their sport. To illustrate this, between the financial years 1996/97 and 2001/02, the Australian Yachting Federation received grants from the ASC that represented an increase of around 360 percent. This funding turnaround has resulted in tremendous developments for the sport of sailing. In 1997, the Yachting Youth Program was limited to the selection of a team to represent Australia overseas. In 2001, the Australian Yachting Federation (2001) was in a financial position to hold "a Youth Championship, coordinated with the relevant Class Championship, giving a focus to the program and national training camp opportunities, as well as increasing support for state youth programs from your [sic] High Performance coaches" (p. 1).

Almost half of the NSOs claim to be reliant on the ASC's "outstanding support" (Australian Gymnastic Federation, 2001, p. 1). Such NSOs further argue that they strongly endorse the Federal Government's objectives because of their significant Federal Government funding reliance. For example, Squash Australia (2000) and its members recognise that the ASC is their most significant stakeholder and that the AIS and High Performance Programs are critical to the future of their sport. Consequently, they suggest that it is important that Squash Australia continue to "actively support the objectives of the Federal Government" (p. 3).

For that reason, however positive the ASC's relationship with the NSOs is for sport development practices, their partnership presents an impediment, namely the NSOs' partial dependence and reliance on Federal Government grants. By implication, continuity of finances means increased levels of accountability. The Judo Federation of Australia (2001), amongst other NSOs, supports this view by noting that "following the great success at the Olympics" (p. 47) the increase of grants was associated with greater accountability requirements. It faced a position where it was required to support the ASC's strategic plan "or risk the loss of ASC funding" (p. 47).

Nevertheless, it appears that both the Federal Government and the NSOs agree on the need to identify measures to attain certain levels of self-sufficiency and autonomy. The ASC in collaboration with the NSOs makes some efforts to overcome this financial dependency by providing greater distribution flexibility. Hence, the NSOs expected the ASC to give them a greater degree of flexibility with their funding allocation "to distribute resources according to program priorities, and as such the ability to manage their affairs with less involvement and direction from the ASC" (Australian Canoeing, 2000/01, p. 14). Moreover, the Australian Softball Federation (1999/2000) notes that "the major change to the funding program is in the area of High Performance Program funding, as we will now be given a greater flexibility to distribute resources according to our priorities, with less involvement by the ASC" (p. 11). The Australian Weightlifting Federation (2000) reinforces this view.

It is envisaged that NSO's will have greater flexibility to use government funds after their high performance program has been signed off by the Commission and that associated reporting obligations will be further reduced and simplified – which is welcome news for sports administrators around the country. (p. 17)

The Australian Weightlifting Federation was looking forward to more success in the next quadrennium due to the flexible funding policy adopted by the ASC.

Reduction/Withdrawal of ASC Funding

Since continuation or increase in ASC funding relates directly to the elite athlete successful performances, it is understandable that the NSOs express the view that Federal Government funding fluctuations and in particular *reduction or withdrawal* of ASC grants, rather than membership/participation, affects the elite athletes (*elite success*). The following examples illustrate the NSOs' opinions on this point. Australian Swimming (1999/2000) reviewed and refined its programs to "meet the challenge of a drastic reduction in Government support beyond 2000" (p. 15). It was obvious to them that actual or expected funding reductions would impact on their "ability to support our swimmers and coaches as they prepare for 2004" (p. 15). Finances and future costs also became a hot issue for Croquet Australia (2001) when it was no longer eligible for High Performance grants. "While the Australian Sports Commission has been supportive with grants over the past year, croquet will no longer be eligible for High Performance grants which will make the control of our future costs, an important issue" (p. 11).

One-third of NSOs raise concerns regarding reductions or withdrawal of ASC grants in relation to their overall *operations/services*. The Australian Gymnastic Federation (1999), for example, recognises its substantial dependence "upon Government funding to maintain its level of operations" (p. 1). NSOs believe that this is due to their difficulties in attaining the number of staff necessary to meet operational needs. Shilbury (2000) argued that immaturity on the part of some sporting organisations in Australia limits their ability to be financially autonomous. He claimed that "the readiness to manage increasingly complex structures, and their willingness to consider alternative forms of organisation, structure and management procedures to ensure best practice...[have] not yet fully reconciled" (p. 200).

In addition, NSOs express the problematic nature of their funding dependency in terms of staffing their organisations. Basketball Australia (1999) is one NSO to experience financial pressures and argue that the "resulting decisions that we had to make led to a substantial down-sizing in BS's [Basketball Australia's] staff" (p. 4). Although NSOs believe that continued support results in an increase in or retention of existing staff members and the recruitment of highly qualified and experienced coaches (e.g. increases in Federal grants for Squash Australia meant the recruitment of a national coaching director), the following example best illustrates the converse, that reductions in Federal Government funding may result in termination of employment contracts. "The employment of a part-time position [of a National Development Officer] in Queensland was terminated due to withdrawal of ASC funding" (Australian Lacrosse, 2001, p. 3).

As further illustrations, the Australian Weightlifting Federation (2000) claims that "due to [a] major reduction in funding, this position [National Coaching Coordinator] is not a paid one" (p. 21), and the Judo Federation of Australia (2001) states that "during the time of our funding uncertainty and the Sports Commission ruling on [the fact that] only 10% of the funding could be used for administration, the FJA (Inc) [Federation of Judo Australia] National Executive Director resigned" (p. 41).

The NSOs which experienced a reduction or withdrawal of funding subscribed to the notion that termination of employment contracts or staff resignations result in an increasing workload for the remaining employees or volunteers. Therefore, while low funding or withdrawal of grants may lead to the conclusion of staff employment contracts, this in turn increases the workload on remaining staff. Basketball Australia's downsizing, for example, placed greater pressure on those who remained. The workload increased within other NSOs, such as the Australian Gymnastic Federation and Squash Australia, when financial restrictions precluded the recruitment of replacement staff, which led to duties and responsibilities being reallocated. Consequently, operations and services become a challenge to manage.

On a more positive note, in one-third of the cases where reduction in funding from the Federal Government was experienced, NSOs suggested that they developed higher levels of *teamwork* and realised the potential that joint efforts have to offer to their future survival. Teamwork as the result of reduced ASC grants may be illustrated by Squash Australia (1999) where reductions "resulted in a great team effort that by the end of the year appeared to have ensured the survival of the Unit" (p. 5).

Figure 4.3 illustrates the ASC grants to NSOs discussed above as continuous, increased, decreased or removed and their implications. The nature of ASC funding demonstrates an instability which stimulates NSOs' efforts to lobby the government and/or search for alternative sources, mainly from membership/participation fees and/or sponsorship deals.

Figure 4.3: The Nature and Implications of ASC Funding to NSOs

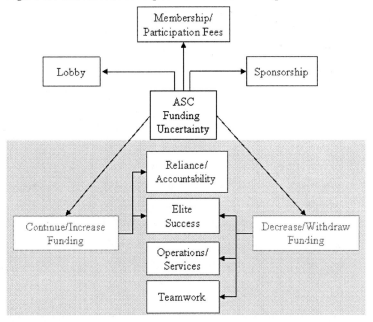

Overall, the ASC's financial support to the NSOs largely relates to elite athletes and their success rather than a balance between elite athlete success and growth in the membership/participation area. This is probably because according to the ASC annual reports since 1999 the NSOs receive significantly more money for elite athlete successful performances and less for membership/participation (ASC, 1999; ASC,

2000c; ASC, 2001; ASC, 2002b). Although continuity of ASC finances is important for maintaining successful performances at the elite level, some NSOs believe that continuing relationships with the ASC are beneficial for membership/participation and management/administration aspects of their organisation. For example, Women's Hockey Australia's continuous working relationship with the ASC helps it to encourage maximum ongoing participation and Australian Swimming (2000/01) states that its close links with the ASC results in "continuing its focus on Management Improvement, Sport Development and community based programs" (p. 37).

Hence, although sports believe that they gain benefits from their partnership with the ASC in membership/participation, ASC funding fluctuation and their implications impact more on elite athletes and their success. At this stage of data analysis, a question arose whether the proposition that elite success leads to increases in participation is the basis on which grants to elite programs are made. In order to answer the above query, further analysis led to the examination of the relationships sporting organisations form within a sport as well as the relationships available between state governments and state sporting associations. As the discussion that follows shows, NSOs delegate membership/participation policy implementation to state associations, and support and funding are devolved and filtered down from NSOs to their state associations. This in turn shows how NSOs have an indirect involvement with mass participation rather than a sole focus on elite success. Through growing intra-organisational cooperation between these sporting organisations, a balanced approach to sport development catering for all participation levels is achieved.

The Relationships Within Sporting Organisations and Between State Governments and SSOs

The ASC recognises NSOs as what Australian Canoeing (2000/01) describes as "the responsible bodies for development at all levels" (p. 10) or, according to the AFL (2000), as the "keeper of the code" (p. 51). In support of this, Australian Swimming (2000/01) claims that history has proven that "athlete representative bodies are extraordinarily beneficial to the growth and development of not only the athletes they represent, but equally important the much broader scope of the sport" (p. 34). As the sports' national governing bodies, all NSOs agree with Athletics Australia (1999/2000)

128

when it suggests that it is "responsible for the governance, management, promotion and development" of the sport "at all levels and across all disciplines throughout the country" (p. 4). This responsibility operates internationally, nationally, at the senior and junior elite and mass participation levels. The following quotation from Squash Australia (2001) illustrates the magnitude of importance of the very existence of the national bodies to sport.

> It is through our national body that our sport has national teams, funds development programs for juniors, supports high performing and elite players, coaches, referees, and so on...without our national body, and by its very existence, the support of the Federal Government in funding the Australian Institute of Sport and various other ASC programs, most of which are delivered through Squash Australia, our sport would be in desperate trouble. (p. 5)

Within this context, strategies and programs are shaped in order to develop sport for more Australians without compromising sports' international competitiveness. This injects enthusiasm for the game and all it represents among young and future players whilst at the same time fostering participation and enjoyment by "older" players.

Even though NSOs are the bodies responsible for both participation and elite development, it appears that NSOs are more directly concerned with the latter rather than being involved with both elements of sport development equally. The previous section showed that the ASC's financial involvement at the NSO level is closely related to the development and success of elite athletes rather than membership/participation growth. As will be illustrated here, even though NSOs are responsible for all levels of sport development, they manage by means of different strategies and collaborative patterns at the organisational and governance level to share responsibilities for mass participation and junior and talent identification programs with their SSOs. NSOs suggest that sporting organisations form alliances and nurture teamwork at two levels: (a) internally, and (b) at governance level.

(a) Internal level

Internally, benefits are realised by flexible *organisational structures*. Internal restructuring (with the flexibility to restructure as required) is a common practice within sporting organisations to ensure they are well placed to meet the challenges and demands of moving forward. Athletics Australia provides a good example of this. Ryan

(2002) claimed that Athletics Australia's organisational restructuring since 1998 has boosted its performance and helped it realise its full potential. He suggested that small NSOs seeking to run their sport like a business "could do well to follow the governance overhaul example set by Athletics Australia" (p. 1). NSOs express the view that organisational structuring and flexibility of restructuring present powerful tools to ensure sporting organisations are right for the environment in which they have to operate. For example, South Australian Swimming reviewed its organisational structure "creating the role of Participation Development Officer to more clearly define the role and more closely align the key objectives of the Strategic Plan" (Australian Swimming, 2000/01, p. 45).

It is commonly accepted by the ASC (2003d) that governance structures promote appropriate financial controls, unity of purpose and successful risk management practices, and hence have a "significant impact on the performance of a sporting organisation" (p. 1). NSOs express the opinion that flexible structures facilitate their efforts to develop networks with each other and to work in collaboration. As an example of this, Netball Australia's Board recognises the need to continually review and adapt its structure when necessary and to "ensure that all levels of the structure were aware, and understood, their appropriate roles and responsibilities" (Netball Australia, 2000, p. 3).

(b) Governance level

At the governance level, collaborative patterns involve partnerships of sporting organisations within a sport. NSOs' views on collaborative patterns within governance are divided into two approaches. Amalgamation relates to the merging of sporting organisations or the takeover of one of them by another at the national level while intra-organisational cooperation involves no merging but rather focusing on sporting organisations of all levels working together for the health and future development of sport. Henry and Chao Lee (2004) described these approaches to governance as *systematic governance*, which is "concerned with the competition, cooperation and mutual adjustment between organisations" (p. 26). These characteristics of systematic governance are explored next.

Amalgamation

Amalgamation is the unification process that brings selected sporting organisations under one national umbrella. Brown (2003) argued that in the recreation and sport industry amalgamation generally takes two forms: a merger that brings two or more organisations forming a new entity altogether; and a takeover "when one or more organisations cease to exist in their own right and their resources, assets and roles are consolidated into an existing entity" (p. 1). Mahony and Howard (2001) referred to the synergy between sporting organisations and the merging of teams, leagues and organisations in the same industry as horizontal integration. Soccer Australia (2000) provides a case in point, where the amalgamation of the sport was achieved under a national body in order to "capitalise on the vast family of football for everyone's benefits and the good of the game" (p. 4). In its effort to unify the game, the code of soccer came together under one umbrella through the unification of "the NSW [New South Wales] Soccer Federation and NSW Amateurs, together with the Womens [sic] Soccer Association and Futsal [10]Australia" (p. 3).

Brown (2003) stated that even though Soccer Australia reaped the benefits of less duplication of activity and resources and gained sponsorship, "it has taken time to build trust amongst the group" (p. 6), share information and put aside many past difficulties. However, other examples of sport amalgamations such as the Women's Hockey Australia and the Australian Hockey Association's unification have also led to disadvantages such as loss of volunteers and members, loss of jobs and clashes of cultures, and may be complex and intricate. Phillips (2002) explained that "amalgamating sporting associations often faces financial barriers and inequalities, clashes over facilities and debates over board representation - all flavoured by egos both strong and fragile" (p. 1). For example, following hockey's international body's recommendation in 1998 for Women's Hockey Australia and the Australian Hockey Association to unify, gender issues made the process more complex. Specifically, women's hockey felt their independence was in jeopardy while the men representing Australian Hockey were more open to the change because their role was unchallenged.

---

[10] Futsal is a modified version of indoor soccer run by the International Federation of Football Association

However, quite the opposite was true. The men saw an opportunity to capitalise on the strong profile of the women's hockey team.

Schraeder and Self (2003) demonstrated that mergers and acquisitions are becoming a strategy of choice for organisations attempting to maintain a competitive advantage. As such, whilst in the past "these two organisations have worked well together" (Women's Hockey Australia, 2000, p. 1), with their strengths merged they have the potential to "complement each other in the future" (Women's Hockey Australia, 2000, p. 1). The amalgamation of the two national bodies of hockey provides "a window of opportunity for hockey to be seen as a sport that is producing world class athletes, coaches, administrators, and facilities. There must be positive long-term goals to provide a legacy for the sport" (Women's Hockey Australia, 2000, p. 1).

Intra-organisational Cooperation

There is an underpinning belief that organisations at the national, state and local level must work closely with each other for the successful development of sport in Australia. In their study examining tourism development and stakeholders, Sautter and Leisen (1999) produced similar results and support the argument that collaboration "among key players is a fundamental ingredient in sustainable development efforts" (p. 312).

The various sporting associations across Australia look ideally to unify and cooperate in order to, as Athletics Australia (1999/2000) illustrates, "work together on a range of long-overdue initiatives for the strengthening and expanding of the sport into the future" (p. 2) and to develop "coordinated national programs for high performance, marketing, sponsorship and event scheduling, together with development programs for schools, coaches and the ever-expanding fun-run market" (p. 2). Another example of cooperation in the governance of sport is "One Basketball"[11]. Basketball Australia (2000) developed a vision and set an agenda for the future of the sport which is "the result of the cumulative efforts of those in the basketball community" (p. 10). "One

---

[11] "One Basketball" is a strategy of Basketball Australia (2000) vital for the growth and prosperity of the sport as it highlights the need for 'consistency in branding and program delivery' (p. 10). This strategy was the result of an ongoing dialogue involving all stakeholders and the cumulative efforts of those in the basketball community.

Basketball" highlighted the "need for integration and unification in all that we do, and the need for consistency in branding and program delivery" (p. 10).

Nevertheless, literature on the characteristics of sport, for example Mullin (1985), shows that sporting organisations may simultaneously compete and cooperate. Economic theorists such as Leeds and von Allmen (2004) argue that *industrial organisation* is "the study of firms and markets as they relate to employees, consumers, government, and perhaps most importantly, each other" (p. 6). They offer the example of National Basketball Teams and illustrate how sporting organisations may compete fiercely on the court and cooperate as a single entity off it. The way sport is organised in Australia is based on organisations representing the national, state and local club levels. While there needs to be communication between and within all levels, still and especially in professional organisations, there is a lot of competition between, for example, leagues. In his effort to understand sporting organisations and in particular in terms of managing conflict, Slack (1997) explained that the more sporting organisations differentiate themselves, that is, breaking down work and allocating it to different sub-units (in this case NSOs allocate sport development responsibilities to SSOs), "the greater the likelihood of conflict, because the greater the differences" (p. 200) created between organisations.

Regardless of levels of differentiation within organisations, there is a strong call from sports for cooperation. The element of intra-organisational cooperation is of special importance to this study because it illustrates the way sporting organisations approach sport development, and the filtering of responsibilities between them. This combined with the proactive role of the ASC previously described achieves a balanced approach to sport development. Therefore, the intra-organisational cooperation processes are elaborated in detail.

The Australian Gymnastic Federation (1999) is one of many NSOs to state that its official "mission" is to work together with state members "to promote, develop and continuously improve the image and quality of, and participation in, Gymsports in Australia" (p. 41). State associations often report that their relationship with their national body is excellent and that "[a]ssistance is as near as the phone along with support and understanding between the State and Federation" (Australian Gymnastic Federation, 2001, p. 32).

Arguably, this example is one of many that illustrate the desire of sporting organisations at different levels to work together. The NSOs explain that they support SSOs and work together on a variety of issues and the SSOs in turn recognise that "[a] nationally united sport is a strong force, much stronger and much more effective than a sport with divisions and internal wrangling" (Australian Gymnastic Federation, 2000, p. 34). Overall, the NSOs recognise that they have to continue to work together with their state associations 'for the good of the game' and to 'remain strong'.

One belief that is common among NSOs is that intra-organisational cooperation and transparent policies increase *communication* across affiliates which in turn improves relationships and levels of teamwork. Indeed, Slack (1997) explained that clear and adequate communication as well as clear policies, procedures and rules within and between sporting organisations reduces ambiguity and contributes to decreased levels of conflict. This is illustrated by the Australian Weightlifting Federation (2001):

> A concerted effort, through more open communication and transparent policies, has been made to enhance the feeling of 'ownership' of the sport by stake holders [sic], with the result of improved relationships and cooperation between the AWF and its affiliated State and Territory Associations. (p. 6)

Sport organisations show an appreciation of increased leadership levels and recognise that improved communications also give sport a clear direction towards effectively achieving common goals. The Bocce Federation of Australia (2002) is one of many NSOs to acknowledge the potential that organisational solidarity with its state associations can bring to sport. The Federation states that "it's only by working cooperatively together that bocce will triumph" (p. 6). Squash Australia (2001) reinforces Bocce's view noting that its "potential for success will only ever come from a collaborative and genuine contribution by all of us" (p. 6). It argues that with the cooperation of all the state affiliates, the organisation can "proceed with its designated plans and provide the national direction and focus" (Squash Australia, 2000, p. 12).

Australian Swimming (2000/01) states that "with clear direction, open lines of communication, and cooperation between all stakeholders" (p. 30) it is in a position to achieve its goals. It continues that through improved communication and collaborative, consultative and cooperative efforts the national and state sporting associations can "work more closely together with clear objectives and a vision for the future" (p. 15).

Overall, NSOs argue that intra-organisational cooperation plays a key role in successful sport development. It enhances their ability to effectively communicate within their organisations, assists organisations to focus and achieve their goals and aids them in the implementation of national initiatives. NSOs present numerous initiatives/goals and areas of actively supporting their SSOs. They explain that this support and funding assist the states in important development work and the creation of resources and programs. As a result, many players, coaches and officials (based in every state of Australia) benefit from a range of programs that are funded by the NSOs. For example, assistance with clinics and resources from Women's Hockey Australia (2000) "has increased the communication and responses to Country Victoria" (p. 22). Also, Tennis Australia's (1999/2000) Women in Tennis Coordinators initiative in each state and territory around Australia was set to increase opportunities for females in tennis in areas such as leadership, playing, coaching and officiating.

The unified approach to sport development emphasises the NSOs-SSOs partnership in achieving the promotion, development and continuous improvement of the image, quality and participation in sport in Australia. For these tasks to bear fruit there are two interrelated components: (a) *SSOs sport development plans;* and (b) *NSOs distributions.* That is, SSOs seeking additional funding from NSOs submit *sport development plans* as a requirement for the NSOs' *distributions* of their surplus to SSOs.

Each state association is requested by its NSO to actively pursue its development plans designed to enhance participation growth and advance standards. In such plans, the SSOs are concerned with the promotion and development of their sport within their respective states. This is achieved by the continuous work and contribution of the development staff of all state associations in promoting the sport at the grassroots[12] level by actively pursuing development plans "designed to achieve participation growth and advancing standards" (Australian Lacrosse, 1999, 2000, 2001, p. 4).

NSOs, being not-for-profit sporting organisations, are accountable for financing their state members subject to their fund availability and profitability. As an example, Tennis Australia's (1999/2000) member association grants dropped from almost $562,000 in the financial year ending 30 June 1999 to just $28,000 in the following year. This may be seen as a reflection of their total income changes which show a decrease from $21,719,128 to $17,839,564 within the respective years. Most NSOs view an increase of their surplus as a key financial focus in order to maximise their distributions to SSOs. As the Australian Cricket Board (ACB) (1999/2000) illustrates, NSO distributions can "assist state associations to stimulate development and growth" (p. 29) of the sport at all levels. Moreover, "the significant increase in distributions to the states enhances investment in the development of the game at the local level" (p. 31). Nevertheless, not all NSOs are profitable, let alone able to consider distributing funds to states. For example, the Judo Federation of Australia (2001) reported a loss of $79,557 in the year ending 30 June 2001.

These results are congruent with Shilbury's contention (2000) that NSOs-generated surplus may be directed to state-based programs aimed at developing sport. This "filtration" of money to the states contributes towards funding participation within states and is allocated on the basis of the expected levels of participation. Ongoing support of this nature is perceived to be extremely important for the viability of the state associations and their development programs as it enhances investment in the development of sport at the local level. Examples of financial assistance to SSOs are numerous; however, the most important point suggested by NSOs is that these grants are the "tangible" evidence of how the top end of sports and elite success are helping to fund growth and development at the grassroots level.

---

[12] Grassroots is "anything that is not elite or where people play and are paid for their skills and crowd pulling power" (Terry, 2001, p. 12).

Regardless of NSO financial assistance, all sports recognise building good relationships with state associations and working together with them as a requirement for successful sport development. They express the view that this intra-organisational cooperation allows sports to enhance their ability "to do more things better" (Australian Baseball Federation, 2000/01, p. 6). As a further demonstration, the ARU (1999) argues: "We can achieve great things by working together, on and off the field. If we can capture this spirit for the years ahead, we will succeed in building our game at all levels" (p. 12). Two years later it declares that "if there has been one factor which has contributed more than any other to the success of the past few years it is the unity of purpose among the ARU and its member unions" (ARU, 2001, p. 7). The focus is to ensure that a coordinated approach exists "with a clear delineation of roles and responsibilities between stakeholders of the sport guaranteeing there is minimal duplication of resources" (Australian Swimming, 2000/01, p. 30). In addition, Soccer Australia's (2000) critical success factor is to develop "a corporate structure which integrates elements of the game at all levels throughout Australia and commits all stakeholders to national strategic objectives for the game as a whole" (p. 2).

The AFL Commission recognises that its state members need "continuing support to maintain and build their strength at grassroots level" (AFL, 2000, p. 51). Furthermore, increased income from the national bodies enables associations such as Tennis Australia (1999/2000) "to increase its activities and expenditures for tennis development and promotion. The company specifically targeted junior programs, junior development, participation, marketing and media" (p. 38). Even though the sphere of the NSOs' support to SSOs seems to be extensive, the central areas of provision arising from the intra-organisational cooperative approach to sport development fall into the following groups:

1. Promotions and programs to attract and retain membership/participation numbers. In support of this point, Australian Swimming (2000/01) in partnership with its state associations points out that it is exploring ways "to attract and retain members particularly in the non-elite area" (p. 21). By providing more hands-on and financial assistance to its state members, the Australian Baseball Federation (2000) attempted to reverse the falling participation rate and grow it. With the shift by the government sport agencies (both state and federal) "to base the funding of sporting

organisations on club membership rather than participation numbers, Orienteering Australia urgently needs to assist the states to explore innovative ways to encourage new memberships" (Orienteering Australia, 2001, p. 2). Australian Swimming (1999/2000) argues that before the Sydney 2000 Olympic Games it was imperative for South Australia Swimming "to work together to maximise the benefits that can be derived from this great sporting event, and further develop the sport of swimming at all levels" (p. 41).

2. Promotions and programs to identify and develop talented players. For example, the AFL (2001) in partnership with the state and territory football associations conducted "a comprehensive program of activities that identifies the talented player and then nurtures that talent in specialised training programs" (p. 71). The support for and confidence shown by the Australian Gymnastic Federation (1999) and its national staff in "Men's and Women's programs and our staff has greatly assisted our ability to develop gymnasts capable of National representation" (p. 32). The Australian Gymnastic Federation's Club 10 program provides an example of the success that a coordinated approach throughout all governance levels can bring to sport development. In addition, some NSOs' surplus translates to player payments for both NSOs and state-contracted players.

3. Initiatives to develop coaches/umpires and assistance in the management/ administration. For example, while the Australian Softball Federation provided support to state and territory associations in conducting accreditation courses, the Vic Synchro community looked forward "to further support from the national body through the coming year, with the introduction of a coaching development program" (Synchro Australia, 2001/02, p. 6). An example of administrative support is provided by Queensland Swimming that "recognise[s] the assistance Australian Swimming has provided in the sport administration arena, namely with iMIS database Management" (Australian Swimming, 2000/01, p. 44).

Notably, the NSOs support SSOs in actively pursuing what they fund the least at a national level, namely membership and participation. Therefore, intra-organisational cooperation between NSOs and SSOs, as well as the flexibility for organisational restructuring, assists sporting organisations at the national level in filtering down funding, support and sport development responsibilities to the state level which assists in providing a balanced approach to sport development within Australia. The ARL

(2000) describes this as follows: "It is vitally important that the governing body, whatever name it takes, recognises that the decisions it makes flow through to the grassroots of the game" (p. 7).

In addition to their relationships with the SSOs, NSOs also receive funds from the ASC to assist clubs/associations at the local level. For example, the Australian Croquet Association receives annual funding from the ASC for club development. CAMS (2000) works closely with clubs "to attract more young people and encourage clubs to appoint junior development officers to facilitate this process" (p. 12).

In cricket, the ACB (1999/2000) provides money and help to clubs through the Club Assist Program and administrative/managerial support. It describes this support as "a hands-on initiative providing guidance for the effective management of club cricket" (p. 44). The Australian Gymnastic Federation (2000) states that "with active support from the State Associations, and funding support from the ASC, this project [Club 10] is providing direct support to 30 clubs across Australia" (p. 1). It continues that one of the most important factors that contribute to the success of the Club 10 is "the management structure established from the onset of the project. This saw Gymnastics Australia and State Associations working together to develop, coordinate and manage the entire project through the Club 10 Advisory Committee" (Australian Gymnastic Federation, 2001, p. 25).

Examination of the relationship between the ASC and the NSOs revealed ASC and NSOs' requirements. Similarly, the relationships between sporting organisations reveal a number of areas of NSOs' involvement with SSOs/clubs and their requirements. Figure 4.4 illustrates these areas of provision and requirements.

A comparison between Figure 4.4 showing the provision and requirements deriving from the NSOs-SSOs/clubs relationship and Figure 4.2 showing the type of requirements and areas of provision between the ASC-NSOs highlights the fact that at the national level the ASC's requirements and provision to NSOs cover elite success and membership/participation growth and public profile. Nevertheless, in the relationships between NSOs and SSOs/clubs, importance is placed on the processes within membership/participation, such as increasing participation numbers and identifying and developing athletes and coaches/umpires, rather than on concern with elite performances as such.

Figure 4.4: Intra-organisational Cooperation Provision and Requirements

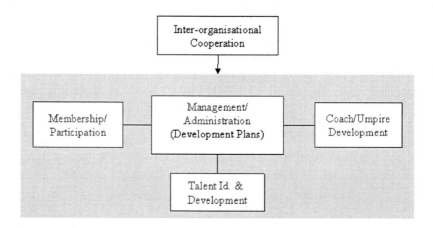

SSOs and clubs/associations are responsible for the delivery of programs developed and funded by the NSOs. Thus, the state associations do all that is possible in partnership with their national body. However, NSOs are not alone in their attempts to support SSOs financially because state governments/departments finance and support SSOs. State governments, through their diverse offices for sport and recreation such as the Office for Recreation, Sport and Racing of South Australia, Sport and Recreation Victoria and the NSW Department of Sport and Recreation, financially support many SSOs' activities. For example, the Western Australia State Office of the CAMS (2001) "secured funding from the State Government Department of Sport and Recreation to fund projects and programs being run by CAMS and its affiliated clubs" (p. 15).

Similar to NSOs with regard to ASC funding reliance if to a lesser extent, SSOs vacillate between the need for continuity and the need for financial independence and self-reliance from state department funds. The following statement from Squash Australia (1999) illustrates this point:

The NSW Department of Sport and Recreation continues to be a major sponsor and supporter of squash in the state…It is hoped this arrangement will remain in place for several years however it is important that steps are put in place to position the sport where it can be self-funded and control its destiny. (p. 24)

In addition, some SSOs, such as the Western Australia Rugby League Association express the opinion that grant applications to state governments appear to be more successful when accompanied by increased membership and participation numbers. In that respect, the common belief among some state associations is that they are 'stuck in a catch 22 scenario' where they are unable to receive funding because they do not have the numbers; however they will not have the numbers without permanent or at least semi-permanent staff.

4.1.2 SIGNIFICANT OTHERS

This section discusses other significant players that are actively involved with sport development in Australia. This group of stakeholders, in comparison to the first group, does not involve sporting organisations or governments and their departments. Rather, it is comprised of various individuals who operate within or for the sporting organisations and sponsors from non-sporting organisations that contribute to sport development in Australia. Even though governments and sporting organisations are the cornerstone institutions for sports development, significant others provide the necessary additional support. They provide multiple benefits to sport and play an increasingly vital role in order for the sport development processes to be realised.

(a) Volunteers

By and large, volunteers are perceived by all NSOs as their most valuable asset. Volunteers, whether active participants or not, may include members of the board, club members, court operators, family and friends. Their involvement with sport development varies from player development, coaching, refereeing and officiating in programs at all levels, to administering sporting organisations and making decisions of strategic importance as members of boards. The variety of involvement areas and roles that volunteers undertake, from website services at the Bocce Federation of Australia, to officiating at the CAMS, promotions and development work for Orienteering

Australia and the smooth running of programs and events in many occasions, shows the important role they play in sport development.

Cuskelly, McIntyre and Boag (1998) claim that despite the trend towards hiring paid staff to follow professional sport management procedures, volunteers remain important to the operation of many sports organisations. Indicatively, when examining their involvement in sporting events, all NSOs claim that volunteers contribute to the success of their events and the peak performance of the athletes in the events. For instance, Squash Australia (2001), despite having paid staff, claims that "to have successful events you require dedicated volunteers" (p. 24). Without them, the Australian Gymnastic Federation (2000) argues it "would not be able to provide the number of events and services" (p. 28) that it offers. Moreover, the Australian Gymnastic Federation (2000) claims that "the Olympic Games could never have happened without the amazing efforts of the volunteers" (p. 8). These statements support Strigas and Jackson's (2003) study of volunteer recruitment programs which stresses the significance of volunteer involvement in the overall success of recreation sport competitions.

The Australian Softball Federation (2000/01) claims that "volunteers contributed to the outstanding success" (p. 9) of championships, while Australian Swimming (2000/01) maintains that "technical officials and other volunteers ensure the competitors are provided with a smoothly conducted competition at which to perform at their peak" (p. 15). Hollway (2002), the former Director General of the Sydney Organising Committee for the Olympic Games in Sydney, used his Olympic experience to explain the vital role of volunteers. He claimed that the value, services and generosity of volunteers in contributing towards the efficient delivery of sporting events cannot be underestimated.

Auskick presents an example of the AFL's junior development program where family and friends are voluntarily involved in the delivery of sport development: Auskick "which has grown by an average of 12 percent per annum since 1995 … sees boys and girls aged five to 12 years play specially modified AFL games and activities for fun and enjoyment in a safe environment" (AFL, 2001, p. 71). While managed through the AFL's Game Development Department, Auskick is "owned and operated" (AFL, 2000, p. 6) by parents and friends of football. This is possible because it is conducted "by parents and friends" (AFL, 2000, p. 6) and it is "managed by the community" (AFL, 2001, p. 71).

Whether by becoming involved in coaching, event management or anything that is requested of them, volunteers give their time and energy freely to sporting organisations. Cuskelly et al. (1998) maintain that the nexus between volunteers and sports organisations is important because the delivery of community-based sport "is reliant upon the willingness of a large number of volunteers to commit their time and energy" (p. 181). Significantly, this time and energy is translated by almost all NSOs into considerable fiscal savings and ultimately the future viability and health of sports. For instance, the Australian Gymnastic Federation (2001) points out that "thousands of hours of volunteer work contribute significantly to the ongoing future viability of the sport, whilst maintaining relatively low fees for membership and competitions" (p. 30).

NSOs including the AFL, Basketball Australia, the Bocce Federation of Australia, ACB, the Australian Gymnastic Federation, CAMS, Netball Australia, Orienteering Australia, the ARU, SLSA, the Australian Softball Federation, Squash Australia and Australian Swimming express similar views on the significance of volunteer contributions to the future viability, survival and health of their sport. Even though it is not easy to put a monetary valuation on volunteer contributions, economic analysis of sport studies (e.g. Gratton & Taylor, 2000) elucidates the immense value of the resources the voluntary sector contributes to sport.

The following acknowledgement sums up NSOs' views on volunteer significance: "The strength of an organization, (in this case a sport) relies so heavily upon its volunteer coaches, judges and parents to grow the sport" (Australian Gymnastic Federation, 2001, p. 28). Without the contribution of such people, "the game simply would not survive" (Netball Australia, 2001, p. 4). For example, "…motor sport simply could not exist without the willingness and dedication of its volunteers" (CAMS, 2001, p. 2). Volunteers are "the lifeblood of the club cricket" (ACB, 1999/2000, p. 44). Without them, Gymnastics Victoria states that "gymnastics in this state would not be in the healthy position it finds itself" (Australian Gymnastic Federation, 1999, p. 34) and the Australian Gymnastic Federation (2000) adds that "this great sport would cease to exist" (p. 22).

(b) Paid Staff

Although volunteers do much of the work within sports organisations, NSOs acknowledge the contributions of paid officers and personnel. Paid staff positions may vary from contracted officers and support staff to coaches, umpires and administrators or members of the board, and provide the human resources infrastructure of sport. Significantly, the roles of coaches, SDOs, members of management and the board are discussed in brief in annual reports.

Coaches and Sport Development Officers (SDOs)

A statement from the Australian Softball Federation (1999/2000) encapsulates the purpose and role of coaches as follows: "Every person who undertakes a coaching position, irrespective of the level at which they coach, should be ensuring that they are assisting each and every player to achieve their goals, whatever those goals may be" (p. 20). Similarly, the general purpose of the Lacrosse National Coaching Body is to develop the sport and promote a core set of values "to advance the sport of lacrosse at all levels of its development" (Australian Lacrosse, 2000, p. 1).

Overall, there is a fundamental belief that the results achieved by athletes would not be possible without the support and hard work of coaches, and an acknowledgement that in today's competitive and professional sporting environment, coaching resources are vital in making sure Australia continues to groom stars of the future. These results are congruent with those of previous enquiries (e.g. Heah, 2003) that describe coaches as co-pilots lending their experiences and enabling and guiding athletes to navigate and reach desired goals.

In addition to coaches, SDOs play a significant role in achieving the objectives of growth of sport by promoting it and increasing its public profile. However, there are instances where, in addition to their role in implementing programs for mass and junior participants, SDOs' responsibilities may cover the development of sport across the spectrum. For example, the National Development Director of Orienteering Australia assisted with elite performances and supported the states in their grassroots promotional activities, ultimately improving the public profile of the sport. In the same example, there is evidence that SDOs are involved with the management/administration of their organisations. The National Development Director of Orienteering Australia took responsibility for their strategic planning and their funding submissions.

Administration/Management and Board of Directors

The professional and effective management of NSOs is considered important for the survival of their operations in an increasingly complex and volatile environment. One-third of NSOs state that environmental conditions place increasing demands on their management/administration staff and the boards of directors. For example, the ACB (1999/2000) argues that its "issues-rich environment requires effective management" (p. 62). Similarly, the boards have a significant role to play in relation to rapid environmental and societal changes, which leads some NSOs to implement a more professional and commercial approach to sport. In relation to sport organisations' changing role in society, CAMS (2000) observed a role that has changed "from providing competition rules and dealing with mainly sporting issues and the administration thereof". Now, "the increasing commercial involvement has seen a shift in focus towards business, governance issues and risk management" (p. 12).

As the professional end of the sporting spectrum becomes more commercial, NSOs are exposed to a range of new pressures. It is becoming increasingly challenging to ensure that sport is "appropriately stewarded, governed and nurtured in an increasingly aggressive, litigious environment" (CAMS, 2000, p. 2). Hence, the professional management of sports (by administration staff and board of directors) and a commercialised approach to sport have the potential to ensure growth. The Australian Gymnastic Federation (2001) recognised this:

> While acknowledging that we are a not for profit sporting organisation, the sport will only prosper from improved management and accountability of the business, that will in turn provide the financial base to ensure growth for the sport... The contribution made by the Board of Directors has been significant in directing the company on a more professional and business like course. (p. 30)

The boards' central role in the future health of sports is perceived by sports including the ARL, the Australian Gymnastic Federation, Squash Australia, and the Australian Water Polo. The health and future of the sport are evidenced in sound participation numbers, development at all levels, income, attendances and media profile. Squash

Australia and the ARL recognise their commitment and efforts to investing in and ensuring their long-term future. The Australian Gymnastic Federation also recognises their contribution to the health of the sport and its healthy position, and the Australian Water Polo (2001) values the commitment and contribution of the members of the board "for endless hours of personal time for the welfare of our sport" (p. 3).

Finally, NSOs' management/administration and members of their boards deliver successful sport development programs. The following examples best illustrate this view. According to Diving Australia (1999/2000), "The success of the program relies heavily on the administrative support of Andrew Heath and management support from Bob Murphy and John Boultbee from the AIS in Canberra" (p. 9). More generally, Soccer Australia (2000) states that its board is comprised of "professional sport administrators, dedicated to delivering a better level of service to all our stakeholders" (p. 4).

Two-thirds of NSOs argue that regardless of their roles, the main attributes of the paid personnel are 'dedication' and 'professionalism'. Netball Australia (2001), for instance, claims that its organisation "would not be held in the same regard without the staff that we have" and that "the staff of Netball Australia have shown their dedication and professionalism" (pp. 4-5). Squash Australia (2001) also argues that its head office staff "deal with the day-to-day challenges and crises of our organisation, and their professionalism and dedication is a credit to them individually and as a team" (p. 5). Additionally, Australian Swimming discusses staff professionalism in relation to the smooth running of events and productivity.

(c) Sport Development Segments

Even though all sport participants are unique individuals with numerous personal characteristics, the roles they play within sports development place them into the following five sport development segments: (a) *membership/participation* segment, (b) *junior* segment, (c) *talent* segment, (d) *elite* segment, and (e) *supporters/spectators* segment (see Figure 4.5).

Figure 4.5: Sport Development Segments

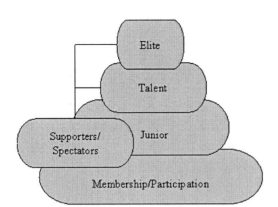

Members, Participants or Volunteers?

The membership/participation segment is comprised of the registered members and participants of sporting organisations, clubs and associations around Australia. This segment includes indigenous people, people with disabilities, the young enthusiasts, senior and elderly persons, women and all those individuals who are members or participants of a sport in a sporting association. However, membership numbers do not equate to participation numbers because members do not have to be active at all times.

Many NSOs use the two terms interchangeably because there is neither clear distinction nor an agreed term. Sporting organisations strive to establish membership databases in order to measure participation. Nevertheless, not all NSOs have a database in place to provide precise registered members. Establishing a member database is an initiative reinforced by the ASC and a promising practice for attracting government funding in this area of membership/participation. In addition, it helps to clarify that volunteers may or may not be members and/or participants.

Junior, Talented, Elite, Supporters/Spectators

The junior segment involves all the young players and represents a part of the membership/participation segment. A proportion of junior participants in the junior segment forms the talented athlete segment, which includes all the talented young players. The talented athletes are likely to reach higher levels of participation and

147

performance and become the elite athletes of the elite athlete segment. Therefore, even though the junior segment is part of the membership/participation segment, it is considered a separate entity and a step closer to the talented athlete segment. Yet again, the talented athlete segment, which is a sub-segment of the juniors, is a separate entity placed even more closely to the elite athlete segment, illustrating the path to elite (see Figure 4.5).

As the analysis that follows will detail, a large number of members and participants make available a greater pool of junior members. Similarly, high junior membership levels increase the chances of drawing talent. These elite juniors provide the source for the top-level athletes who in turn have the potential to stimulate membership/participation and increase the sport supporters/spectators base. Green (2001) identified two types of sport participation, namely direct and indirect. She defines direct participation as the actual physical participation in an activity or competition. Active participants range from general or mass participants to the aspiring elite athletes (Houlihan & White, 2002). Indirect participation includes viewing, reading, discussing with others and purchasing sport products. Green (2001) concluded that the two forms of participation may occur together.

The sport supporters/spectators form the group of people who follow sport through the different types of media, predominantly television broadcasts, and/or attend sporting events and competitions. Studies on spectator types (e.g. Giulianotti, 2002) developed typologies that classify spectators according to the time they invest in following sport, their level of involvement with the team/club or athlete and the amount of sport products consumed as well as the type of media preferred to follow sports. Supporters/spectators can be of any age, be active participants or not, and may acquire any level of participation skills. The importance of this segment to sport development is reflected by its contribution in 'easing' sports fiscal burdens.

The Judo Federation of Australia (2001) defines an elite athlete as "one who is the highest achiever in their respective division in Judo" (p. 8) or the highest achievers in their sport if one is to generalise. Elite athletes are credited not only for their successful performances at national and international championships but also for their special role in promoting and enhancing the public profile and development of sport. Wong and

Trumper (2002) assert similar views and reinforce the argument of the dual role of athletes in occupying and informing both the national and international spaces in terms of spectatorship.

(d) Sponsors

The NSOs which have received corporate money from sponsorship in the past argue that corporate sponsors make their financial problems "lighter". This financial inclusion enables them to achieve sport development and growth goals through the implementation of development programs, competitions across all levels and in due course elite success. SLSA (2001), for example, recognises sponsors' contributions to its sport since due to this support its clubs are able to "implement the new strategies, training programs and enjoy an environment for safe competition" (p. 21). In addition, Soccer Australia's (2000) future success "will be largely dependent upon the support it receives from its television partner, as well as its ability, with the IEC [International Entertainment Corporation], to attract blue chip corporate partners into the code" (p. 27).

Even though corporate money appears to be largely related to supporting high profile leagues/teams, player wages, televising and sponsoring major events, a number of high profile sports report sponsorship grants contributing directly to sport development programs. For example, the AFL states that in late 2001 Simpson (a leading Australian household appliance company) "became the sponsor of the leading junior development program in Australia AFL Auskick" (p. 58). MILO sponsors all Junior Tennis Programs (Tennis Australia, 1999/2000). Nike is the official sponsor of the Junior Tennis Tour and Wilson Sporting Goods also sponsors the Junior Tour as well as other Player Development Programs for Tennis Australia (1999/2000).

Overall, NSOs view sponsors as important sport development stakeholders. The AFL (2001) summarises this importance by admitting that "the AFL's relationship with its corporate partners is vital to the survival and growth of the game. These relationships assist the game from the junior to the elite level" (p. 58). Sports organisations agree that continued support of sponsors is crucial to continuously developing sport. However, they explain that sponsorship is external to the sport source of funding, and sponsors' requirements from NSOs can occasionally be demanding.

As a result, NSOs realise that external stakeholders' funding can be unpredictable in nature. This is best illustrated by Bowls Australia (2000/01).

> Another major hurdle the sport faced was the breakdown of the Premium TV contract. The Board has taken steps to rectify the arrangement for 2002, however it is a testament to the financial management of Bowls Australia that a surplus of more than $37,000 was achieved. These issues, coupled with the recent ABC-TV debate over free-to-air television coverage of bowls and Esandas's decision to discontinue its successful sponsorship arrangement, highlight the unpredictable nature of our external funding sources. (p. 7)

4.1.3 SUMMARY

The first half of this chapter provides ample evidence on the connection between Federal Government sport policies (through the ASC) and the impact they may have on NSOs managerial and sport development practices. More specifically, in working closely with the NSOs the ASC sport policies aim to achieve sport development goals such as:

1) Increase membership/participation through policies and programs for various groups of people including junior, women and people with disability, indigenous people, and the elderly.

2) Achieve international elite athlete success (through Sports Excellence and High Performance programs).

To achieve sport development goals, the ASC is involved with formulating and providing policies to NSOs. This ASC involvement and policy may take the form of resources (financial and human) and programs. However, what is crucial in policy formulation and implementation processes is to establish that the sport development goals are communicated and 'commonly' shared. A critical ASC policy towards this direction requires NSOs to report to the statutory authority on their long term use of these resources and programs through Strategic Plans as well as reporting on the way these resources and programs have been used in the past year through Annual Reports.

Strategic plans and annual reports outline and reflect the ways NSOs intend to or have implemented the ASC policies. Strategic plans need to be approved by the ASC before any grants are approved and before any NSO can implement any of what meant to be a most effective and efficient way of putting ASC policies into practice. Hence, NSOs need to adapt their sport development practices to what is 'commonly' shared with the ASC. Other ASC requirements may pertain to specific levels of participation. For example, at the membership/participation level increased public profile, awareness of programs and participation numbers are some of the ASC policy requirements for funding assistance. In relation to elite athlete policies, the main ASC requirement is to produce elite athletes and maintain their international success. In essence, the ASC sport policy priorities will guide the NSOs practices. Therefore, NSOs sport development practices are shaped and guided by the Federal Government's sport policy deliberations.

In addition, the nature of ASC funding has implications on NSOs and the delivery of sport development practices in that ASC grant fluctuation guide NSOs lobbying practices and search for alternative sources of income. The NSOs lobby to secure Federal Government funding while simultaneously striving for financial independence. These two NSO funding efforts display the controversial reality of their strategies, trying to attract maximum funds from all sources. Stewart-Weeks (1997) speculated that post-2000 Australia's third wave of policy would be a combination of less public funding to sport (in relative terms) at all levels and growing expectations for service and performance. Shilbury (2000) recognised the need for NSOs to reduce their dependence on Federal Government funding in the post-2000 policy agenda and explained that this "is not an argument to reduce overall Government funding, but recognition that such funding will not continue" (p. 217) to the same degree.

Nevertheless, it is evident that the Federal Government is widely involved with sport development and requires value for money across all development areas. NSOs in collaboration with SSOs share the twofold responsibility of developing sports across the spectrum from mass participation to elite level. Ultimately, governments and sporting organisations at different levels appear to work in a unified form to achieve the best sport development results. These results reinforce Elias, Cavana and Jackson's

(2002) study on stakeholder analysis that recognised that "stakeholders exist beyond the boundary of a single organisation into a partnership infrastructure" (p. 301).

It appears that at a national level less importance is placed on membership/participation. The evidence from annual reports shows the importance of membership fees to sport. Since membership/participation emerges as having the potential to financially support sports at any level, consideration should be given to reconsidering its merits at a national level. The ambiguous nature of ASC funds to NSOs and insecurity over future grants generally affect the elite level rather than mass participation. This is probably because NSOs directly address this level and filter the development of mass participation through their SSOs.

The results of this section illustrate that it is the Federal Government sport policies that set out action to advance sport development in Australia. The ASC policy directions set the agenda for the NSOs to conform to policy direction. In working closely with the NSOs the ASC set out a series of targets and NSOs core commitment is to be accountable for achieving them.

While the sport development stakeholders share the responsibility of sport development at all levels, this involvement takes place in the form of sport development practices. These practices beget sport development in Australia. The next chapter examines these practices, the role in sport development, the nature of their distinctive importance and the ways that stakeholders are involved in them. Therefore, it offers a meso-analysis of sport development.

CHAPTER 5: THE SPORT DEVELOPMENT PRACTICES

5 SPORT DEVELOPMENT PRACTICES

This chapter identifies and discusses the essential practices for the delivery of sport development. Sport development practices are the strategies, means and courses of action taken by the sport development stakeholders for successful sport development. Patterson and Rowland (1990) reinforced the impact of strategies on development by defining them as "determinants of developments and direction ... the basis for resources allocation and curriculum determinants" (p. 14). Sport practices determine who gets what, when and how. Their formulation and maintenance support the establishment and sustainability of sport development. The benefits or goals are multiple and relate to all facets of sport development and participation. In order to develop their sports, NSOs implement a variety of strategies. These strategies fall into the following five types of sport development practices: (a) Facilities, (b) Coach/Umpire and Administration/Management, (c) Player Development, (d) Promotion, and (e) Competitions/Events. These practices and the benefits they deliver to sport development are discussed next.

(a) Facilities

Sports facilities enable programs and events to take place. The role of the facilities in assisting with *player development programs* appears more prominent and pertinent than the specific initiatives aimed at the development or maintenance of sporting facilities themselves. The provision of sporting facilities has the potential to service, cater for and benefit all levels of participation and *competition/events*. Therefore, sports continue to develop their facilities, which enables players at all levels of the game to access and utilise them.

NSOs note the importance of having different types of facilities in order to, as Tennis Australia (1999/2000) summarises, "meet tournament, player development and recreational needs" (p. 32). In effect, this is consistent with literature on sport facility programming and scheduling which refers to the procedure of "planning and/or preparing programs, establishing schedules, and managing space" (LaRue, Walker, &

Krogh, 1997, p. 51). LaRue, Walker and Krogh (1997) stressed the importance of facility *changeover* which refers to the actual ability to transform a sporting facility to accommodate different activities. A study on sport facilities conducted by Westerbeek (2000) also reinforced the significance that sport should place on the various types and use of sporting facilities. In relation to the different types of facilities, NSOs discuss 'recreational' and 'training' facilities that assist the accomplishment of player development program objectives, and 'venues' that are essential for competitions and sporting events to take place. While recreation and training facilities cater for the needs of participants at all levels to play sport and train, venues cater for participants at the events and for the spectators/supporters' needs, that is, the individuals who are not necessarily participants or members of the sport, yet use the venue facilities to view sports.

1. Recreational and Training Facilities

NSOs' opinion regarding facilities is divided into two groups. In the first instance, NSOs (such as Squash Australia) recognise the importance and availability of facilities in order for participants to enjoy the sport. In the other camp are NSOs (such as Basketball Australia) that recognise the training benefits derived from the existing facilities for their athletes. The following is illustrative: "The dedicated training facility at LaSalle College provided the teams with the best training and recovery facility of any Australian team at the Olympics" (Basketball Australia, 2000, p. 16).

However, one-third of NSOs support both views. These views collectively indicate that facilities benefit all levels of sport participation. CAMS (2000) best illustrates this point by claiming: "The improved facilities at existing circuits in 2000 benefited not only the top end of the sport but all levels of circuit racing, including club and state level competition" (p. 4). Another NSO explains that "the establishment of quality facilities" is important in order "to meet both the elite level 'showcasing' and future participation growth needs of baseball" (Australian Baseball Federation, 1999/2000, p. 8).

More specifically, the NSOs that subscribed to the notion that there is a link between facilities and elite training point out that facilities support their athletes' preparation for successful performances at high-level competitions such as World Championships and the Olympic Games (*elite success*). Alternatively, the NSOs that subscribe to the importance of facilities for sports participants state that facilities may assist their *membership/participation growth*. This is best illustrated by a statement drawn from Squash Australia (2000): "The older facilities that have invested money into refurbishing have had very encouraging increases in participation. Hopefully these signs will encourage more public awareness of our sport and in turn greater participation" (p. 16).

2. Venues

Venues are the facilities where various competitions/events take place. NSOs state that the continued development of venues offers them options for running competitions. Athletics Australia (2000/01) reflects this point by arguing that "these centres, along with facilities further south in the State offer excellent options for future events" (p. 34). In another instance the AFL (2000) explains:

> After several changes by Stadium Operations Limited, the owner and operator of Colonial Stadium, the venue functioned more efficiently in the second half of the season and reinforced our view that it offers terrific facilities for supporters and in the long term, will be a major asset for the competition. (p. 24)

In fact, two-thirds of NSOs commented on the various benefits that investment in stadia development and good quality venues offers to clubs, players and sport supporters. Australian Swimming, for example, maintains that when competitors are provided with a smoothly conducted competition at a favourable venue they could perform at their peak (*elite success*). The Australian Gymnastic Federation (2001) also reports on the importance of venues to its athletes and its competitions by stating: "This new facility, specifically built for travelling sporting teams was outstanding and provided all the services, support and a fantastic environment for General Gymnastic members and the International GymFest" (p. 18). In addition, the AFL (2000) pinpoints the importance of the quality of the venues to both the "stars of the game", referring to the players, and the very "basis of the game" (p. 33), meaning the *supporters/spectators*. The following point summarises the importance of sports venues for both players and spectators: "It is important to ensure that AFL matches are played at the best possible venues with the best possible conditions for players and spectators" (AFL, 2000, p. 33).

NSOs attribute the increase in *supporter/spectator* attendances partly to venue improvements over the last decade. They express the view that rising attendances ultimately translate into gate receipts and increased TV rights (*finances*). As an illustration of the financial importance of venues to sport, Squash Australia (1999) argues that its licensed facility, Racquets South Australia, continued to grow and was "a vital source of income" (p. 21). Figure 5.1 illustrates the types and roles of the facilities in sport development procedures.

Figure 5.1: Sport Development Benefits from Facilities

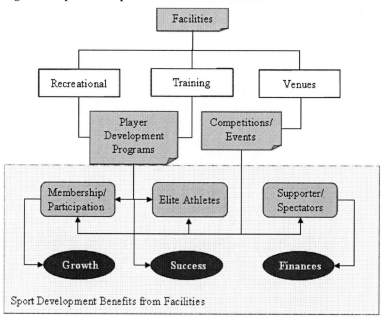

In summary, the nature of the facilities varies between recreational, training facilities and venues. Recreational and training facilities facilitate the delivery of player development programs and in particular the preparation of the elite athletes to perform successfully at the competitions in which they participate, and the increase of membership/participation numbers. Venues relate to the viability and enabling of sporting competitions/events and in particular contribute to the enhancement of elite performances (*elite success*) and increase in supporter/spectators' entertainment and therefore the sport's commercial potential and income sources (*finances*).

156

(b) Coach, Umpire and Administration/Management

The ACB (1999/2000) captures the essence of what NSOs describe as coaching programs by arguing that "coaching programs are essential in recruiting, retaining and developing cricketers. In today's competitive and professional cricket environment, coaching resources are vital in making sure Australia continues to groom stars of the future" (p. 47). Additionally, one-third of NSOs suggest finding coaches and umpires (*coach/umpire talent identification*) at grassroots level. As one of them, the AFL suggests that it is essential to take advantage of the grassroots to identify and develop umpires. Women's Hockey Australia (1999) also argues that many junior umpires are "coming through to the senior level, boosting the practical support" (p. 16). Overall, there is a view that the training of coaches, umpires, trainers and club personnel is necessary in order to, as the AFL (2000) puts it, "ensure that the game is played in a high quality environment" (p. 64).

NSOs argue that coaching development programs enrich coaches' knowledge and ability to perform their role in recruiting and skilling athletes. The Bocce Federation of Australia (2000), for instance, claims that its coaching development program "was devised to ensure that all States would have coaches capable of recruiting and skilling players in the art of the progressive and precision throws" (p. 3). Overall, there is a fundamental belief that coaching development is important for *junior talent identification* and development purposes, and for *elite success*. For example, according to the Women's Hockey Australia National Team, the Hockeyroos' results and superb performances are "a direct follow on from the forward planning and improved coaching opportunities generated by increased funding from the Federal Government for coach employment" (Women's Hockey Australia, 2000, p. 7). CAMS (2000) also stresses the importance of coaching for talent development purposes. CAMS argues that the identification of talent is one thing but coaching of talent is another. Therefore, CAMS, with the assistance of the ASC, "seek[s] suitable coaches who can develop a coaching program, map an achievable career pathway and set goals in order to achieve top end success" (p. 12).

The central issue dominating NSOs' perceptions of the main and ultimate goal of developing and supporting coaches is success, which is measured in terms of the performances of the athletes they train. The following statement from Australian Swimming (1999/2000) is representative of NSOs' views: "Our elite program has provided our swimmers and coaches with the support to succeed" (p. 17). This support includes the advancement of coaches to improve the level of their expertise. For example, Synchro Australia (1999/2000) conducts clinics where international coaches and judges give "extremely interesting and informative presentations thus providing a wonderful opportunity for Australian judges and coaches to learn about current trends in choreography and difficulty" (p. 6). As elements that contribute to the overall elite success, NSOs report that training camps provide players and coaches with a high-quality educational and motivational environment, where they are given the opportunity to 'mix', 'compete', 'exchange ideas' and to ultimately develop high levels of athlete–coach synergy.

The development of paid or volunteer officials, umpires, referees and judges has a distinct role in the growth of sport. Their contribution is considered indirect because most of their involvement relates to the running of sporting events (*operations*) and not directly to player development. Nevertheless, NSOs recognise their valuable contributions. Athletics Australia (1999/2000) stresses the importance of their role as follows: "Athletes and events benefit considerably from, and indeed rely on, their [officials, umpires and judges] continued contribution" (p. 12). As a further illustration, the Australian Softball Federation, Squash Australia and Lacrosse Australia add that these people "contribute greatly" (Lacrosse Australia, 2001, p. 4) and "ensure" (Squash Australia, 1999, p. 12) the success of events, from grassroots to international competition.

The Australian Softball Federation, CAMS, the ARL and many other NSOs agree that the smooth running of the game is 'dependent' upon the efforts of volunteer officials and they often pay 'tribute' to their contributions. In addition, the Australian Weightlifting Federation (2001) thanks all technical officers who give their time so freely to enable them "to conduct weightlifting competitions throughout Australia of such a high standard" (p. 15).

Australian Swimming (2000/01) adds that well-run competitions allow elite athletes to perform at their peak. More specifically, it argues that thanks to the technical officials and other volunteers "the competitors were provided with a smoothly conducted competition at which to perform at their peak" (p. 15). Even though almost all NSOs consider administration/management as one of their development programs, less than one-third place these programs highly in their list of development priorities within their NSO. Nevertheless, the first group of NSOs that recognises the need for administration/management programs agrees that the development of good administration and management practices are crucial to service the smooth running and operations of competitions and the successful performances (*elite success*) of the athletes. Additionally, the main function of administration and management is the provision of high quality *services* to events and all members, and assistance for successful organisational planning.

Elite successful performances are attributed not only to the athletes, coaches, judges and umpires but also to the input that the administration and management provide. NSOs point out that the success of their programs and hence the resulting performances of their athletes rely heavily on the administrative and management support of their personnel. As an example, the Australian Gymnastic Federation (1999) argues that its success is "a tribute to outstanding efforts of our gymnasts, coaches and judges and the support of the AGF administration" (p. 8). Moreover, the ARU (1999) states that the Wallabies' victory in the final of the 1999 Rugby World Cup was "the culmination of an extraordinary amount of work by players, coaches and administrators" (p. 8).

Realising the benefits that administration has to offer, sports intensify their talent search for administrators and managers from a young age (*administrator/management talent identification*). The AFL (2000) summarises this by arguing that talent "is not just sought at the athlete's level, but in coaching and administration. The link between the organisational structure and the coaching and playing staff is inextricable" (p. 10). CAMS (2000) agrees that the challenges ahead not only involve "attracting more young people to the sport as competitors but also as volunteer officials and administrators" (p. 12). For almost all NSOs, the ASC funding facilitates a degree of reliable long-term planning. In addition, the ASC grants denote better services to their members. The following examples illustrate this view. The funds available "during the pre-games period saw existing services improved and new services developed, all at no additional costs to the sailing community" (Australian Yachting Federation, 2001, p. 1). ASC grants also assisted NSOs' "ability to maintain our high customer service standards" (Australian Canoeing, 2000/01, p. 13).

Almost one-third of NSOs, including Skiing Australia, the Australian Gymnastic Federation, Diving Australia and CAMS, acknowledge the benefits that improved administration has in advancing the quality of competitions and contributing to their success (*operations*). The Australian Gymnastic Federation (2000) made the following observation on the importance of administration and management in organising, managing, and holding successful events: "Our Sports Management Committees must also be congratulated for their tireless efforts in improving the quality of competitions that they manage" (p. 32).

Figure 5.2: Sport Development Benefits from Coach, Umpire and Administration/Management Programs

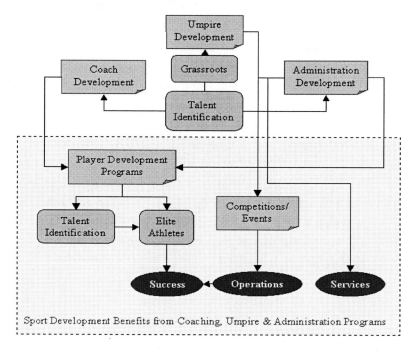

In summary, Figure 5.2 illustrates the benefits accrued by sports from coach, umpire and administration/management programs. There is a common belief that grassroots competition has the potential to supply to sporting organisations with the necessary coaching, umpire and administration talent. Coaches and managers assist with player development programs as they relate to elite athletes and strengthen their chances of being successful. Finally, umpires and managers relate directly to successful competitions/events which may assist elite performances.

(c) Player Development

Player development practices can be classified into three types of programs. Type I programs are formulated for membership/participation development needs, Type II relates to talent identification and transition to elite programs, and Type III involves specifically developed elite athlete programs. The perception of success of player development depends on the type of the program. The success of Type I programs can be measured through the numbers of individuals playing sport and the numbers participating at competitions (*membership/participation growth*). *Success* at competitions is one of the benefits received from Type II programs along with the continuous progression of participants, from being identified as talented (*talent identification*) to becoming elite athletes and taking part in higher profile competitions. Type III programs reflect elite athlete *success* and outstanding performances at a national and international level. Increased resources (*finances*) usually follow these successes.

Type I: Membership/Participation Development Programs

NSOs suggest that the major goal of their membership/participation development programs is to increase the number and the intensity of mass and junior participation (Quantity and Frequency of participation), and hence to establish overall growth. Those that represent Active Australia Providers argue that the aim of these programs is "to support sport and help clubs and organisations improve their ability to attract more participants" (Australian Baseball Federation, 1999/2000, p. 15) to the sport. Women's Hockey Australia (1999) believes that the focus is to encourage "people to be more physically active" (p. 6). Tennis Australia and its member associations also explain that their many programs are designed to encourage more people to play tennis and those who do play, to play more often.

NSOs which have managed membership/participation programs well claim that their growth efforts are in most cases rewarding. Tennis Australia, for example, maintains that the proof that its membership/participation program efforts are satisfactory is drawn from surveys conducted by Brian Sweeney and Associates and the Government. These studies confirm that tennis is one of Australia's "most popular sport[s] in terms of participation, attendance and viewership" (Tennis Australia, 1999/2000, p. 5). Athletics Australia (1999/2000), as another example, experienced similar gratifying results. It maintains that the 1999/2000 increase in registrations was "the result of a concerted program to attract more participants, which was enthusiastically supported by the clubs around the state" (p. 29).

A fundamental ingredient of the membership/participation type of player development programs is junior participants. The NSOs agree that young players are very much the focus of membership/participation player development programs. On this point, the Australian Weightlifting Federation (2001) states that the More Active Australia program encourages more people into sporting activity "through partnerships between sporting organisations, schools, business and local communities established to achieve greater numbers of participants at the grassroots level" (p. 17).

Once again, sports are compensated for their endeavours to develop youngsters by implementing player programs. For example, the Tasmanian Association of Squash argues that "increased grants to clubs for junior development related projects, have resulted in a steady increase in young players in several clubs" (Squash Australia, 2000, p. 14). Another example is drawn from the ACB (1999/2000) which suggests that the MILO programs contribute largely to the "health of grassroots cricket" (p. 44) with more and more children experiencing cricket through cricket's modified skills and games programs.

The AFL (2001) participation figures indicate that "where the AFL has decided to invest and develop a national strategy, program outcomes have been exceptional" (p. 68). The AFL Auskick program is a prime example: "In 2000, AFL Auskick registrations were up from 76,000 to more than 80,000 nationally, with huge growth recorded in NSW" (AFL, 2000, p. 6). The AFL Auskick program has dramatically increased the numbers of children involved from an early age in the AFL game. "Its adaptability to each market, reliance on community involvement and emphasis on fun" (AFL, 2000, p. 65) make it an attractive program for players and their parents. In another code, the ARL Foundation helps foster the game at junior level with school and junior league-based initiatives. The ARL (2000) states that the success of its junior development program could "be seen through increased numbers playing junior club football" (p. 8).

A small number of NSOs including Soccer Australia, Athletics Australia and Netball Australia provide information on player programs located in remote and isolated areas such as Soccer in the Outback Tours. These tours are coaching clinics that provide great opportunities to young Australians, both indigenous and non-indigenous, in remote and isolated regions. According to Soccer Australia (2000), the purpose of the Soccer in the Outback Tours is "to develop, promote and foster" (p. 7) its code of football in remote and isolated communities. This would "provide children residing in North Australia the same opportunities as other young Australians" (p. 7) to experience sports on their home fields, regardless of geographical location. Athletics Australia's indigenous program "has made the sport accessible to many new communities" (Athletics Australia, 2000/01, p. 33) and "while limited at present" (Netball Australia, 1999, p. 4) Netball will be providing "financial assistance to individual athletes, through the Indigenous Sport Scholarships Scheme" (Netball Australia, 1999, p. 4).

Finally, about one-third of NSOs suggest that successful player development programs, which lead to increased junior participants, result in an increase in competition attendance figures. This is best illustrated by the following extract: "The success of the development programme can be seen through increased numbers playing junior club football and the featuring of Victorian teams in the Australian Secondary Schools League Championships" (ARL, 2000, p. 8). Squash Australia (1999) states that in 1999 Squash ACT completed a most successful year with its junior and school development programs, and claims that these impacted positively on its "junior pennant competitions with increasing team numbers and participation in the special 1 day tournaments conducted throughout the year" (p. 19).

Type II: Talent Junior Programs

Type II programs are designed for young participants of all abilities and skill levels. However, the major concern of Type II programs is talent identification and transition of the junior members to becoming elite athletes and participating at elite-level competitions. With a focus on participation rather than competition, 11s and 12s squads[13] programs are open to all juniors, yet seek to target pre-teens who show "a natural aptitude" for sports and "who may play competitively at an older age" (Tennis Australia, 1999/2000, p. 28). The Australian Gymnastic Federation (1999) also confirms that its state programs produce "the young talent for Australian teams of today and of the future" (p. 34). Swimming is no exception; the Tip Top program supplies Australian Swimming "a wealth of talented young athletes" who are "to be the future" (Australian Swimming, 1999/2000, p. 45) of the sport.

However, Australian Swimming, along with more than half of the NSOs, argues that talent identification is not its concern; rather, the transition of the juniors to higher levels of competition. On that note, Tennis Australia (2000/01) observes that its Men's Tennis department uses a range of development strategies, including the Player Development Program, "to take players from a grassroots level onto a comprehensive journey or career path with the ultimate aim to win Davis Cup and Grand Slam events" (p. 24).

Evidently, for the transition of juniors to higher levels of performance, specifically designed programs are necessary. Orienteering Australia (2000), as another example, has a national junior training camp program in place, which is "designed to emphasise the principal [sic] of 'Total Preparation' viz that junior orienteers should lay the foundation for a long-term commitment to training and competition that is needed to become a High Performance orienteer in the long run" (p. 3). Similarly, Squash Australia's High Performance Program and State Junior and State Little Leagues are 'critical' as they provide 'valuable pathways' to the elite level program.

The ARU's (2000) Institute of Sport program has "a team in the A-grade competition, accelerating the development of the Territory's best young talents" (p. 48). The ARU

---

[13] 11s and 12s denotes the age of participants

(1999) claims that it sees the continuing development of their young players through the Institute of Sport program "with a number of the squad being selected in our senior side, the Taipans, for a tour of Sri Lanka" (p. 48). Overall, there is a common belief that in order to fulfil the need to replace older and retired athletes, sports focus on the elite junior athletes and their coaches "in an attempt to build up the depleted senior ranks" (Athletics Australia, 2000/01, p. 39).

NSOs explain that Talent Junior Development Programs ensure that young players are prepared to cope with the transition to higher levels of participation. In relation to its transition programs, Tennis Australia (1999/2000) states that they are "designed to teach young players the skills that will see them better cope with competitive stresses they will encounter in older age groups" (p. 28). Soccer Australia's (2001) High Performance Development Programs and National Training Centres aim

> to provide identified elite soccer athletes with the knowledge, experience and psychological characteristics to enable them to represent Australia, first at the junior level (U17) and youth level (U20) then later at the Olympic Games (U23) and World Cup (Senior). (p. 5)

Being well prepared will eventually result in advanced performances. On that the Australian Gymnastic Federation (1999) states that "the standard [of performances] continues to rise which is a result of a well-prepared Junior Elite Development Program" (p. 6).

NSOs unambiguously argue that successful performances are measured by competition and other sporting events results. Hence, competition outcomes are the ultimate key performance indicator. The NSOs which run training camps (e.g. the Bocce Federation of Australia) suggest that they are beneficial on the basis that the skills learned are later translated into excellent results at National Junior Championships. In a similar vein, Australian Swimming (2000/01) states that the success of the Tip Top Development Program "was displayed with fifteen gold medals, fifteen silver and eleven bronze" (p. 10). It adds that these experiences serve as a sound basis for its preparation for the Athens 2004 Olympic Games and beyond.

While player programs such as the Commonwealth Bank Cricket Academy (a program of the AIS) lead to the preparation of players for up and coming events and competitions, progress from the low to high profile and magnitude competitions occurs as athletes successfully qualify to participate at higher levels. For instance, Soccer Australia (2001) experienced the success of its national youth teams "in qualifying for their respective World Championships, with both the Under-17 and Under-20s progressing to later stages of the tournament" (p. 2).

The central issue dominating almost all NSOs' perception in relation to the success of Type I and II Player Development Programs is to build *modified* versions of their sport to meet the needs of the various groups of participants. For example, junior baseball participants enjoy a modified program called the Sizzler Pitch, Hit & Run Program. According to the Australian Baseball Federation (2000/01), the objective of this program is "to introduce the sport of baseball and softball into primary schools, allowing all students the opportunity to experience the excitement of the game" (p. 28).

Similarly, modifications are in evidence in Type I programs which make sports more fun, approachable and easy to participate in for the public. The Australian Softball Federation (2000/01) introduced the Mixed Slow Pitch Softball Competition in Queensland, which offers "an outlet for people to play softball in a casual, social environment at low cost and just for fun" (p. 41). According to Queensland Softball this is an opportunity "for significant future expansion" of softball, one which it hopes will "bring interest from the wider community" (Australian Softball Federation, 2000/01, p. 41).

Type III: Elite Development Programs

The NSOs' elite development programs' major area of concern is the development of quality elite athletes who will deliver successful performances at high-level competitions. The elite development programs provide the essential *skills* and *training* for athletes to further their careers. The ARU (2001) supports this view by arguing that the Brumbies Academy "continued to provide players with the appropriate skills and training to further their rugby careers" (p. 42). As a further illustration of this, Women's Hockey Australia (2000) claims that with the introduction of the AIS Unit, the program "gave the players the opportunity for further development and more international competition" (p. 7). In addition, the Australian Water Polo claims that elite players spending meaningful time training and playing with their clubs will lift standards.

The Australian Gymnastic Federation (1999) states that its Queensland High Performance Centre shapes "quality gymnasts whose achievements have brought great pride" (p. 32) to Queensland and Australia. Similarly, Soccer Australia contends that the AIS program continues to produce quality players, and Australian Swimming (2000/01) perceives the program as the "cornerstone for the development towards the elite" (p. 44). NSOs explicitly argue that the elite development programs account for superb results at the national and international stage. Skiing Australia (1999/2000), for example, is confident that the continuation of the elite program offers an ongoing framework for its athletes "to achieve to the best of their abilities" (p. 11). Another NSO states that its high performance program "has been most effective, culminating in Australia assuming first place in the world" (Bowls Australia, 2000/01, p. 9).

More important, there is a fundamental notion that these achievements regenerate the interest of particular stakeholders and attract further resources. The Australian Water Polo (2001), for instance, states that "the programs attracting funding allocations are the elite athlete development programs and it is these programs which will return results in the form of performances, which will maintain Australia's eminent position in world water polo" (p. 4).

In summary, Figure 5.3 illustrates the benefits derived by sports from the different types of player development programs. Type I membership/participation development programs achieve an overall growth in the volume and the intensity of the general mass participation level and emphasise increasing the numbers of junior novice participants. This is where Type II programs take over and deliver the necessary resources, coaching and support for young participants, talent identification and the development of the potential elite athletes of the country. Talented athletes are in turn benefited by the highly advanced Type III elite development programs that ensure athletes perform successfully at international and national levels. Indirectly and by means of elite athlete success, Type III programs deliver improved resources to NSOs.

Figure 5.3: Sport Development Benefits from Player Development Programs

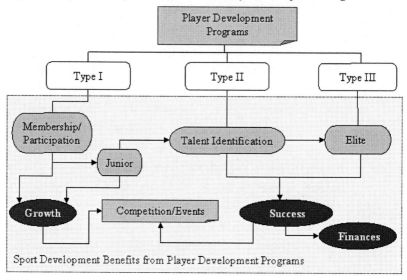

(d) Promotion

A common NSO objective is to establish their sport as what the Australian Baseball Federation (1999/2000) describes as "a vibrant sport with a strong public profile" (p. 7). Soccer Australia (2000) offers further support for promotion as one of its critical success factors to become a "progressive marketable sport with a high domestic profile" (p. 2). NSOs perceive their sports profile dependent upon mainly two issues, media exposure and sporting events or a combination of the two.

In 2000, CAMS (2001) formed a promotional group to raise the profile of the sport at all levels, and particularly "the possibility of gaining television and increased print media exposure for the Australian Off Road Championship" (p. 10). A further example is provided by Women's Hockey Australia (1999) Team Telstra Hockeyroos that saw a significant increase in the profile in 1999 "with media appearances and interest peaking around certain events. This, in turn, was beneficial to the sport as a whole" (p. 4).

While NSOs perceive sporting events and competitions as important promotional tools, they argue that the involvement and proliferation of media magnify the benefits received. While the benefits from running competitions are discussed later on, in this section attention is given to the different types of media and the benefits they bring to sport.

<u>Conventional and New Technology Media</u>

The types of media used for marketing and promotional purposes by NSOs include both conventional media and the new technology media. Conventional media could be: (a) electronic such as radio and television, which provide advertisements, programs and coverage of sporting events and competitions; or (b) print media, which include magazines, newspapers and newsletters.

The use of conventional media to increase a sports profile is illustrated by the following example of the Australian Capital Territory (ACT) Gymnastics Association. It reports that its commitment to raising the profile of gymnastics in the ACT continued during 2000 "with television advertisement displays and newspaper articles" (Australian Gymnastic Federation, 2000, p. 29). As another example, Bowls Australia (2000/01) argues that the television component of marketing its sport "has been invaluable in putting this great game 'on the map'" (p. 26).

In relation to television coverage and competitions/events, Bowls Australia (2000/01) states that the year 2000/01 was "an eventful one with the television Super Series, entering its fourth year of operation, providing an important element in the promotion of the sport here in Australia" (p. 25). The ARU (2001) argues that its tournaments are supported by a series of television commercials funded by the ARU "promoting high profile players and their favourite Super 12 moments" (p. 41). Women's Hockey Australia (1999) also promotes its team and coaches regularly by featuring "in sports related and non-sports related magazines and programs" (p. 4).

One new technology medium used for NSOs promotional purposes is the internet. The most common internet service is providing information through e-newsletters and sports websites with general information, results and flashbacks on competitions. Indeed NSOs argue that new technology media offer most of the benefits received from conventional media, in an instant and more effective way, but without replacing their importance. Soccer Australia (2000) is one of many NSOs to argue that the success or failure of its reach to the wider audiences primarily depends "on that audience's access to information, whether it be through the more conventional means of print and electronic media, or through newer technology via the Internet" (p. 10).

The influence and use of the different types of media in the marketing and promotion of sports are indisputable. The Australian Softball Federation (2000/01), for example, argues that it was able to secure a "satisfactory amount of Media exposure which went a long way to promoting Men's Softball" (p. 13). Successful marketing and promotion mean growth to the sports as a whole. This is best illustrated by Soccer Australia (2001) which notes that media relations in every aspect are "one of the major keys to the continued growth of soccer in the Australian market-place, both in corporate and community sense" (p. 9). NSO statements on media and marketing are rich enough to inform the study on the benefits received from the different types of media, the *conventional* and *new technology* media-related benefits.

1. Conventional Media

With the exception of five cases, NSOs illustrate the potential that the conventional media have in attracting new members, participants (*membership/participation growth*) and *sponsorship/TV rights* to improve their bottom line (*finances*). Bowls Australia (2000/01), for instance, states that the introduction of the series on television "has been a great success, exposing the game to a new audience and helping the drive for new members" (p. 25). Women's Hockey Australia (1999) provides a similar example as it explains that its women's team's winning performances at events help increase their exposure to the public "as many national television and radio programs, as well as printed media, created stories and exposure for the sport around the victory" (p. 4).

Squash Australia (1999) provides another example of a NSO expressing its anticipation that the marketing of its sport through the conventional media would "hopefully provide an impetus for increasing squash participation" (p. 3). CAMS (2001) explains how it works hard in producing a video which aims at becoming an effective marketing tool "to promote awareness and increased participation in the sport" (p. 12). The Australian Gymnastic Federation (2000) states that it is only through promotional initiatives like these that the entire diversity of Gymsports available can be actively promoted "with the ultimate aim of enhancing participation" (p. 24). Additionally, Squash Australia refers to the promotional influence of media on junior participants and maintains that increased promotion of junior development is a requirement for the increase in young players in several clubs.

Media did not seem to offer any direct benefits to elite athlete development with the exception of Bowls Australia's (2000/01) program. Bowls Australia states that television exposure provided further international exposure for its national team, "which has assisted with their success" (p. 26). Nevertheless, there is a common belief that elite athletes, when used by the appropriate media, assist in the promotion and the exposure of the game to the public. The Women's Hockey Australia (1999) team and coach, for example, "regularly featured in sports related and non-sports related magazines and programs, thus helping to raise the profile of the team and the sport of hockey to the Australian public" (p. 4).

In this way, sports achieve the propagation of the game not just amongst the public and participants but also amongst the most desired group of participants, juniors. One of Australian Swimming's (2000/01) marketing and promotion initiatives offered appearances for the state associations, which "provided States with the opportunity to promote the sport at the grassroots through our elite athletes" (p. 23). The only difficulty in the promotion of athletes and teams appears to be their high level of commitment, training and hectic schedule, which leaves athletes with limited time to devote to promotional initiatives. Indicatively, Women's Hockey Australia (1999) notes that the difficulties in employing Australian players for promotional purposes are "due to hectic training schedules and the AIS commitments in Perth" (p. 12).

The last issue raised by some NSOs in relation to the promotion benefits received from conventional types of media relates to the opportunity to boost their resources. To illustrate this, the AFL argues that the fact that high profile companies invest their time and resources in the AFL reflects the popularity of the sport. Bowls Australia (2000/01) maintains that the televised international exposure of its national team is a valued element of its sponsorships. It argues that the ABC network gave a long-term commitment to bowls by providing valuable free-to-air telecasts of the elite levels to a wide Australian audience. Bowls Australia maintains that the high profile that it acquires through the media increases not only its opportunities to attract sponsors but also its potential to improve its finances through television rights:

The projection of bowls nationally through some 36 hours of television is an integral part of the promotion of the game and maintains a two-pronged purpose - creating an important profile for the sport and an opportunity for sponsorship. Without television we have little to offer sponsors. Equally the FOXSPORTS coverage through pay television of some 72 hours, not only provides further exposure in a growing market, but also provides valuable income through TV rights fees. (p. 25)

2. New Technology Media

The NSOs which utilise internet technology stress the multiple benefits received. The internet is an integral part of their administrative, communications and commercial efforts. The motive for embracing technology is to "improve the area of communication and administration between Clubs, State and National office" (Australian Gymnastic Federation, 1999, p. 33) and hence reinforce the levels of intra-organisational cooperation. Basketball Australia (2000) also, in conjunction with its constituents, developed "a central online administration and communication system directly linking the national, state and local associations with the players and others involved in our sport" (p. 10).

The Australian Baseball Federation (1999/2000) has tried to establish "a culture of open and dynamic communication" (p. 8) not just throughout baseball organisations but with the broader public as well. Soccer Australia (2001) argues that the internet is "essential for the League and the clubs to connect and enhance relationships and communications with the fans" (p. 3). Similarly, the Bocce Federation of Australia aims to provide information to members, schools and researchers, and clubs. Its website was to be linked with other international bocce sites and the ASC. It also encourages the states and territories and clubs to come on line and link in to the site.

The extent of *communication* benefits received through the internet is well recognised by all NSOs that utilise it. Queensland Squash, 'armed' with funding from the state government, embarked on a mission to communicate "with its members and planning for a better future" (Squash Australia, 1999, p. 19). It argues that its communication system was greatly enhanced after it launched itself into cyberspace. Basketball Australia agrees with Queensland Squash that its website is a key communication source and the ACB (1999/2000) states that its site continues to be an important strategic communication tool "through its ability to reach so many people so quickly and in its capacity for them to provide direct feedback to the ACB" (p. 66). Additionally, the Australian Gymnastic Federation (2000) seeks close ties with its affiliated clubs through increased club communication "using both direct contact and through the increased use of information technology" (p. 35).

There is a fundamental belief that open lines of communication and the free flow of quickly accessed information help improve relationships and cooperation (solidarity) between sporting organisations and other stakeholders. The Australian Weightlifting Federation, for example, indicates that open commination and transparent policies result in improved relationships and cooperation between the Federation and its affiliated state and territory associations. Beside this, websites do exceptionally well in providing information to stakeholders such as coaches and referees. Soccer Australia (2001) maintains that Australia's geographic isolation from the major centres of world football constantly places it "behind the eight ball". "We were isolated, not just from the games that our referees need, but we were also isolated from the decision makers - from the people who select the match officials for games" (p. 7). Therefore, to succeed, NSOs argue that they have to improve communication and believe that to do so they have to make the most of the new media technology.

Whether by means of the internet or the more traditional avenues, communications are enhanced through the production and distribution of newsletters. Bowls Australia indicates that the increased focus placed on communications using a newsletter is an addition to the program resulting from the Active Australia grant. The Bocce Federation of Australia (2002) claims that the issuing of a regular National Junior Newsletter is "aimed at informing young people of developments in bocce, coaching and development tips, and other topics of interest to young people relating to sport" (p. 5). Yet again, the newsletter as another means of communication adds to the solidarity and interaction of the sporting organisations and other stakeholders and enhances their promotional and branding prospects. Bowls Australia (2000/01) recognises that "a newsletter going to every club in Australia is indeed a national newsletter and an excellent communication tool...The capacity to alter the dated image of bowls in the minds of the general community has moved with the introduction of this contemporary national newsletter" (p. 29).

173

Besides a communication tool, some NSOs view new technology media as an *administrative/management* solution that helps with running organisations efficiently (*operations*) and provides improved *services* to members. The ARU (2000), for instance, argues that tools such as the Club Website Builder, online registration and the membership database manager allow its clubs to "provide a better service to playing and non playing members while reducing the cost and time of running such organisations" (p. 27). Western Australia Swimming agrees on the more efficient servicing of members by using the internet. It claims that many forms and documents are available to be downloaded from the site as it seeks "to better serve the swimming community" (Australian Swimming, 2000/01, p. 47).

NSOs maintain that their websites are devised to link the sport community (including unions, clubs and schools) through the internet and to build a total online solution for their management and commercial benefit. Notably, NSOs explore the commercial and financial (*finances*) potential of the new technology media. As the ARU (2000) puts it, the use of internet provides "better functionality and ease of administration and the potential for revenue earning capabilities" (p. 50). This is possible because the use of new technology media has the capability to contribute to NSOs' marketing efforts and increase the popularity of sports.

The AFL (2001) observes that the network "made an invaluable contribution" (p. 26) to the game and it "played a significant role in making Australian Football the most popular national sporting competition" (p. 26). Other sports concur that the network is a valuable branding and promotional tool. The Bocce Federation of Australia (2000), for instance, believes that the site in English, Italian and French will "prove to be one of the most effective and direct ways of promoting" (p. 3) the sport. As previously mentioned, the ARU (2000) agrees and believes that the Victorian Rugby website is "both an important information and promotional tool" (p. 46).

This popularity generated by the new technology media could not go unnoticed by advertisers and sponsors. NSOs anticipate that websites will generate promotion revenue and advertising. The ARU, Soccer Australia, the ACB, the AFL and other NSOs which use the network agree on the website's commercial potential and revenue-earning capabilities, demonstrated by the following extracts: "The site's popularity has in turn attracted sponsorship from organisations" (AFL, 1999, p. 89); and "the popularity of the site drew a number of advertisers" (ACB, 1999/2000, p. 66). As an example of this, sponsors through the MILO brand "took up the opportunity to enhance promotion by adding on-line advertising to their sponsorship contract with ACB" (ACB, 1999/2000, p. 66).

More importantly, NSOs contend that the improvement of their website services and the intensified promotion of their sports may result in increased membership/participation levels. The ARU (2000), for example, argues that its latest website builds on the strengths of the previous one and increases its market share. Squash Australia (1999), as another case, in its efforts to reverse negative participation trends advanced its website and believes that the internet "may hold the key to reigniting the interest of some of the jaded players who have been leaving the sport. It is certainly believed that it will aid in our goal of increasing the participation levels of squash" (p. 20).

Various NSOs appear to use the internet and their website in unique ways to advance their market share. Athletics Australia (2000/01), for instance, used the internet to display its preferred sport and organisational image and enhance community involvement. It grasped the opportunity and managed to design a look and a feel for its site that presents athletics "as a fun, modern, and interesting community to be involved in" (p. 21). The site is designed to provide users with a "positive athletics experience" (p. 21) and will continue to be refined to "maintain its state-of-the-art look and feel" (p. 21).

Hockey is another case of the use of specifically designed websites to target junior participants. Women's Hockey explains how a brand new site www.hockeyzone.com.au was created "aiming at children and those just starting out in the sport with sections on hockey basics, how to join a club, fun and games sections and results of fixtures from the local clubs through to veteran competitions" (Women's Hockey Australia, 2000, p. 4). The ultimate aim of these services provided by the internet is to "promote the link from school to club hockey" (Women's Hockey

Australia, 2000, p. 4). Women's Hockey Australia (2000) is encouraging all states to support this site "to ensure the optimal use is made of the options available" (p. 4).

Figure 5.4 summarises the benefits sports receive from their promotional efforts. By means of new and conventional types of media, sports actively promote their profile to the public and in turn achieve membership/participation growth, elite success and improved operations, services and finances in an enhanced communication system that allows them to work in solidarity and reinforces this step.

Figure 5.4: Sport Development Benefits from Conventional and New Technology Media

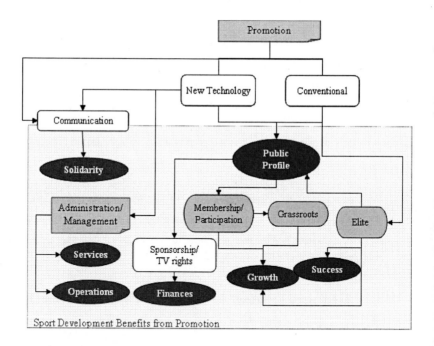

(e) Competitions/Events

One belief common to every NSO is that competitions are the foundation stone of Australia's international success. Additionally, they agree that events are essential to promoting and boosting the profile of sport and its popularity. The terms 'competitions' and 'events' are used interchangeably in this chapter.

The benefits from running sporting events and competitions are numerous and relate to a number of stakeholders, such as participants, spectators, coaches and umpires, and the growth of the sport overall. Hence, sports aim at effectively managing local, state, national or international competitions to ensure they are of benefit to their key stakeholders. NSOs' views on the key benefits derived from competitions/events can be divided into two types: (a) Type I are the sport and *player development*-related benefits received through competitions; and (b) Type II are the *promotion* benefits that events generate for sports. While the advantage of having player development pathways in place is perceived important for the *junior*, the *talented* and the *elite* athlete's successful development and performance, sport marketing and high levels of *profile* relate to general *membership/participation growth*, increasing sport *supporters/ spectators* and sports *finances*.

1. Competitions as Player Development

The vast majority of NSOs view competitions as an important component for the development of all levels of participation and the achievement of peak performance. In recognition of the first point, Basketball Australia (1999) argues that "the elite and participation ends of the sport are intricately linked" (p. 5) and, in order to capitalise on the opportunities, it concentrates on providing competitions for both ends. Additionally, the Australian Gymnastic Federation (2000) emphasises the "need for exciting, dynamic and well-managed events" (p. 32) if it is serious about growing its sport. Moreover, CAMS (2001) recognises the potential of competitions and suggests they have "enormous impact on the future of motor sport" (p. 2). In addition, in 1999 the ARU stated that the introduction of the Commonwealth Cup was going to provide a pathway and development experience for teams outside Brisbane and Sydney and that the Cup would be the standard-bearer of future development. It would differentiate them from their rival codes.

Development at any level is attainable as competitions at club, state, national or international level provide the best opportunity for participants to compete, obtain valuable experience, improve their skills and perform. SLSA and the Australian Gymnastic Federation report the opportunity that national and international competitions offer to compete at an elite level. Nevertheless, Lacrosse Australia (2001) states that it is not all about the highest profile events as "the many ancillary events also add" (p. 2) to the potential for development opportunities.

NSOs exhibit a wide diversity of benefits gained through competitions/events as player development, which when grouped assist in the *retention, skilling* and *progression* of participants. These groups of benefits are discussed here in detail.

Retention

NSOs explicitly argue that competitions provide the power to keep participants' interest levels high and give them the incentives to remain in the game. To illustrate this, Soccer Australia (2000) explains that "lack of exposure to quality competition will dull the most talented group of athletes" (p. 21). Skate Australia (2000/01) also raises a concern in relation to dropouts. It argues that its senior athletes are becoming more and more discontented with the level of competition and are leaving the sport prematurely. Therefore, its interest is to "keep the kids playing through to senior age" (p. 10).

With the same goal in mind, and in its efforts to retain participants, the ARL (2000) maintains that the scheduling of tours assists in "providing incentives for those players in the emerging states to remain in the game" (p. 2). It argues that extra competitions are introduced to give players and regions not participating in the Bundy Gold Cup "the opportunity to play additional representative football and as an incentive to stay involved in the game" (p. 7).

Moreover, some NSOs note the perceived benefit received from competitions in motivating coaches and umpires to remain in the sports and progress their careers. To stress the importance of this point, Squash Australia (1999) argues that with no career path available, there is going to be "a waning of enthusiasm from the current referees" (p. 9). It observed a decline in the number of existing referees and claimed that this was "due to the inability of being able to get enough matches to maintain the levels" (p. 9) of referee involvement.

Skilling

Competitions are perceived as crucial for acquiring valuable experience and developing participants regardless of the level of their participation. NSOs collectively note the benefits of competitions: (a) to elite athletes, by suggesting that top elite competitions help improve the general standard of play of their international players; and (b) to young and novice players, by suggesting that competitions provide essential experience.

The ARU (2001), as an example, maintains that the Australian Sevens play an important role in its development program as this competition provides "the opportunity for another stream of players to further their skills and gain international playing and travel experience" (p. 26). The ARL (2000) also makes the case that state competitions give participants "the opportunity to play at a more competitive level and to develop their rugby league skills" (p. 22).

The Australian Softball Federation (2000/01) claims that international competitions provide the opportunity for its athletes "to broaden their international experience" (p. 24). In relation to international competitions, Australian Lacrosse (2000) maintains that the development in the skill of the game its players experience is enhanced through the ongoing exposure to international competitions. They see international competitions as a chance to be exposed to and experience the level of skill which can and needs to be achieved. Australian Lacrosse (2000) states that the Baltimore World Series of 1998 "exposed many Australians to the skills which can be achieved in our sport and it is pleasing to see this development taking place" (p. 1).

The opportunity for development that athletes of all ages receive by taking part in sporting competitions/events is widely accepted by the vast majority of NSOs. For example, the Australian Baseball Federation (2000/01) states that interstate competitions give "opportunities for young baseballers to play" (p. 24), which benefits "the development of baseball in Australia" (p. 24). Nonetheless, some NSOs argue that participants are not the only ones gaining experience from competitions. Sporting events offer coach, referee and umpire development opportunities too. For example, Women's Hockey Australia (1999) in NSW supports sporting events by providing umpires and technical assistance for each of the matches. This affords "valuable development opportunities for some of our inspiring young umpires and officials" (p. 13).

Acknowledging the importance of exposing judges to international events, Synchro Australia (1999/2000) observes that "the knowledge and experience that is brought back" (p. 6) help establish a benchmark for judging in Australia. It adds that new judges need "to be encouraged and a career path to International judging be established" (p. 6), so that judging in Australia keeps up with the rest of the world. NSOs also maintain that the exposure to international events provides coaches and judges with many new experiences, the opportunity to view things from a different perspective, and great opportunities to learn and provide exposure to the international sport scene. Additionally, competitions are a good opportunity for players and coaches to interact.

Overall, events and competitions support the development of players, coaches and umpires. However, the NSOs that argue these benefits also maintain that these components of the sport as well as the competitions themselves require constant examination and re-evaluation in order to reflect the ever-changing nature of sports. The AFL (2001) noticeably believes it is important to "regularly examine key areas of the competition to ensure they reflect the changing nature of the game" (p. 34). Effectively, the constantly updated practices assist NSOs in remaining successful. This is best illustrated by the example of Basketball Australia (2001) which recognises the need to tap into world performances in order to ensure its own "rate of improvement and innovation continues to move forward" (p. 10). As a result, a major review was undertaken encompassing all of their elite programs examining all areas, the linkage between these parts and ways to improve the programs. This would assist Basketball Australia "to remain as one of the leaders in the world at the top level of basketball" (p. 10).

Progression

There is a shared understanding that competition experience is for participants and their coaches a picture of their progress in terms of "where they stand" and "where they want to go". The ARL (2000) cites the Australian Secondary Schools Rugby League as an example of an organisation which puts tours together for both the Under 15 and Under 18 players. It claims that this is a great initiative and opportunity for players, as it gives these players "something to strive for" (p. 13). Synchro Australia (1999/2000) states that working in isolation from the rest of the world and not having enough competitions holds its swimmers back. It claims that "being able to compete at the Qualifier had enabled the swimmers to have a clearer picture of where they stand and where they need to go ... the swimmers need it to use it as a constant measure to their progress" (p. 15).

The Australian Gymnastic Federation (2000) maintains that competitions provide the opportunity for gymnasts "to develop an awareness of the whole system" (p. 6) as they present them with "their goals for the future" (p. 6). Australian Lacrosse (2001) agrees that competitions enable its athletes to establish their aims for the future. Because of the intensity of competition the "skills of individual athletes continue to be set at higher levels" (p. 1). Hence, Australian Lacrosse justifies its expectations of higher standards in the future.

NSOs report that competitions are the platform for participants to step up to the next level in their ranks. As an example of this viewpoint, Netball Australia (1999) argues that its Commonwealth Bank Trophy provides "the regular on court development for our players seeking selection into the Australian Squad" (p. 5). Similarly, Australian Lacrosse and Squash Australia, among others, claim that their competitions provide athletes with the necessary experience and prepare them for higher levels of participation. Athletes benefit greatly from the experience and NSOs expect them to have "major roles to play in the future of the sport ... in Australia in future years" (Australian Lacrosse, 1999, p. 1). Squash Australia (2001) agrees that the experience gained by the participants is "invaluable in developing their squash careers in the future" (p. 15).

The NSOs emphasise the power of competitions in providing invaluable experience and ultimately preparing participants for more prestigious and challenging competitions. Australian Softball reinforces this point by arguing that its test series are played "in order to provide international experience and development opportunities" (Australian Softball Federation, 2000/01, p. 8) to its up and coming athletes. Basketball Australia (1999) also notes that the tours it organises provide "an opportunity to continue developing the team and evaluate players" (p. 9). In addition, Croquet Australia (2001) contends that events provide its athletes top-level competition that helps "improve the general standard of play" (p. 4).

Australian Swimming (2000/01) suggests that a lack of adequate competition has the effect of its swimmers "not being properly conditioned for racing in Internationals" (p. 32). Thus, sports intensify their efforts to increase athletes' experience levels in the lead-up to significant competitions. The Australian Water Polo (2001) argues that this approach helped it build its game play "in preparation for the upcoming Odysseus Cup" (p. 15) and Basketball Australia (1999) claims that "the five game Russia series, the tour of Europe (Germany and Greece) and the final series against Canada was excellent competition in preparation for the Sydney Olympics" (p. 9). Finally, Bowls Australia (2000/01) notes that the tour of England and Scotland "provided the squad members and selectors with invaluable experience in the lead-up to the selection of the 2002 Commonwealth Games team" (p. 5).

Similarly, according to CAMS (2001), many junior participants state that in motor sport events they are "learning a great deal from the driving instructors and improving their driving skills and appreciation of vehicle capabilities" (p. 14). CAMS also claims that competitions offer potential for transition to the next competitive level and that "of the 25 who attended [the 'Come and Try Day' junior development program of CAMS foundation], three immediately joined to participate in the upcoming Motorkhana Series, with another five juniors indicating strong interest to join the Club" (p. 14). The ARU (2000) argues that the importance of the Australian Rugby Shield competition could not be underestimated as it provides "a pathway for players outside Sydney, Brisbane and Canberra to higher honours" (p. 48). As a final illustration, the Australian Golf Union (1999/2000) states that the PGA Tour of Australasia provides "playing opportunities for its members" (p. 15) at Divisional Level with "progressions into higher level tournaments" (p. 15).

Elite Success and Finances

The NSOs perceive the retention, skilling and progression features of competitions/events as determinant factors for successful elite performances (*elite success*). The development of athletes' skills and experience generated by participating in competitions is converted into successful performances, which assist athletes in

182

increasing their profiles and the profile of their sports. Diving Australia claims that in 2000 it held every major international competition of the sport in Australia, thus helping to raise the profile of divers. On a similar note, Australian Swimming (2000/01) maintains that the "team's high profile, the individual athlete profile and the tradition that the swimming team has built up in the Olympic arena" (p. 48) all add up to major attention from the media, sponsors and an enthusiastic public.

In particular, two-thirds of NSOs perceive a positive relationship between elite profile and on-field success at competitions with funding received from sponsors and government sources. To demonstrate this notion, the AFL argues that one of the reasons they are able to attract corporate support can be attributed to the success of their competitions, while the ARU (1999) specifies that its "on-field success has been matched by a strong financial performance which has seen Australian Rugby Union record a net surplus" (p. 9).

Additionally, NSOs argue that successful results may generate Federal Government funding. The Australian Softball Federation (2000/01), for instance, expresses this view by stating that "the overall success of Sydney 2000 resulted in the Federal Government increasing Sport funding" (p. 9). Moreover, due to its successful performances, softball received a significant boost in government funding, which was divided between its High Performance Programs, the AIS program and Sports Development.

2. Competitions as Promotion

The marketing and promotional efforts along with the media attention and exposure sports receive from competitions/events are necessary ingredients to reap the benefits of the exposure that they offer in terms of elevating the sports and athletes' profiles and putting forward sports as a unique form of entertainment. NSOs argue that events alone are not enough to increase the *public profile* of sport and that active promotional initiatives are required for the benefits of the exposure to be gained.

Australian Canoeing (2000/01), for example, reports that effective marketing and promotion of events are required to ensure canoeing retains "its relatively high profile as an exciting and competitive sport for all age levels" (p. 4). Squash Australia (1999) argues that tournaments become the central platform for their marketing and promotional plans. The Australian Baseball Federation (2000) adds that international competitiveness promotes the sport's national teams and the baseball heroes and their successes to the public.

These influences derived from the sports competition marketing and promotional efforts result in a number of benefits that relate to participants', members', spectators' and television audiences' awareness and interest in sports, as well as to the improvement of sports finances. Overall, NSOs' views on the perceived benefits derived from competitions/events as marketing and promotional tools form three groups and are discussed here in detail.

Public Profile

NSOs believe that sporting competitions boost the profile of their game. The following examples best demonstrate this argument. The ARU (2000) claims that the aim of competition is to "raise the profile of the game" (p. 8). It continues that matches played, such as British and Irish Lions at Colonial Stadium in Victoria, create "unprecedented interest" in rugby, "giving the game a profile previously unheard of" (ARU, 2001, p. 46). Netball Australia (1999) states that the 1999 World Championships win was a major boost to the profile of the game in Australia. In addition, the underage championships and the Qantas national championships assisted "in raising the profile of the sport" (p. 5). Athletics Australia (2000/01) supports the argument and adds that the holding of an annual Telstra Grand Prix in Western Australia is perceived "as essential to the promotion of athletics" (p. 36) in Australia's most remote state. The Australian Baseball Federation is positive that the Intercontinental Cup in Sydney and the Olympic Games were a catalyst for the long-term benefit and promotion of baseball in Australia.

Squash Australia (2001) received media coverage at the 2000 World Championships that was "great promotion for the sport" (p. 15), while the Australian Water Polo (2001) had post-2000 Olympics a good year that would have been bigger had it managed its gold medal success "with active promotion around the country" (p. 7). Hence, it recognises the need to "work even harder in promoting the sport within the media and in the general public" (p. 7). The Australian Softball Federation (2000/01) also recognises the level of exposure received during the 2001 Women's Championship which "included daily articles in The West Australian newspaper, daily radio interviews and the unforgettable Channel Ten Sport Report 'live' from the Mirrabooka State Softball Centre" (p. 13). It adds that the amount of media exposure gained went a long way to promoting softball.

Additionally, the long chain of benefits received by conducting successful sporting events and the exposure given are instrumental in securing the rights to host further events and competitions that are more prestigious. Australian Canoeing reinforces the argument by stating that its successful performances secured the World Canoe Marathon Championships and Skate Australia (2000/01) argues that because of the exposure the sport received from the 2000 Oceania Championships, "Australia has been asked to host the World Speed Skating Championships in Cairns" (p. 1). Interestingly, Australian Swimming (1999/2000) explains that "it is important that Australia keep striving to host these events as it helps to justify spending money on the elite point of our development pyramid" (p. 42).

Australian Lacrosse (2001) is one amongst many NSOs to state that World Championships together with a range of other competitions provide *"the greatest-ever potential to increase the profile of lacrosse to the wider Australian community"* (p. 1). Evidently, NSOs subscribe to the notion that the successes of the national teams or athletes at prestigious events like the Olympic Games combined with planned marketing and promotional efforts increase public awareness and interest. Women's Hockey Australia (1999), for example, argues that the Festival of Hockey is "a wonderful opportunity to showcase our sport to the Australian public" (p. 2).

Media exposure, together with promotional opportunities presented by events, is in line with NSOs' strategies to increase the awareness of sport within Australia. Athletics Australia (2000/01) argues the merits of the benefits generated from the "resurgence in media coverage" (p. 19) during the Sydney 2000 Olympic Games period while the Australian Gymnastic Federation (2000) maintains that the 2000 Olympic success "has increased the awareness" (p. 20) of their sport. Nevertheless, it is up to the Federation, along with state organisations and clubs, to provide the personnel who can "nurture the enthusiasm" (p. 20). The Australian public is the target of the Australian sport marketing efforts. Increased awareness, profile and publicity attempts collectively build a pre-eminent brand or, in other words, "ensure high levels of public interest and support" (AFL, 1999, p. 16).

Consequently, sports raise their expectations regarding increased membership/ participation numbers and supporters/spectators of their sport. The Australian Gymnastic Federation (2001) expected registrations to increase substantially after the Sydney Olympic Games. It was pleased to see the number of registered gymnasts increased and argued that this could "be attributed to the exposure of the sport at the Sydney Olympic Games and increased media coverage" and "to the local promotion of gymnastics by clubs and coaches throughout the regions" (p. 30).

The Australian Weightlifting Federation (2000), in its efforts to meet the challenge of increasing its membership, planned to "tap into the enthusiasm for sport which has been generated by the Olympic Games" (p. 5). The Australian Water Polo admits that with the exposure provided by the 2000 Olympics, many younger people have turned to water polo. On the other hand, the ARU (2000), a non-Olympic sport, argues that it was the Wallabies' World Cup victory in 1999 that "enticed newcomers to the game and motivated volunteers" (p. 9).

Nevertheless, it is largely acknowledged that not all sports (Olympic or not) receive the same benefits, if any, from the Olympic Games or World Championships. For instance, Synchro Australia (2000/01), representing an Olympic sport, argues that "the predicted legacy from the Olympics in the form of increased numbers due to interest in the sport and coaching expertise from an international coach have failed to materialise" (p. 3).

Entertainment/Unpredictability

Apart from registrations, another area affected by sporting competitions and NSOs' promotional efforts are the spectators who follow the sports by either attending the events or watching television. They are influenced and attracted by the unique nature of sports to present entertainment and unpredictability of results. Numerous authors, including Chelladurai (1994) and Shilbury (1990), maintain long-established competitions and unpredictability of results as the essence of sport as entertainment, with higher levels of excellence resulting in higher entertainment value. Westerbeek

(2000) suggested that uncertainty of outcome provides the level of excitement that sport is able to offer by making competition unpredictable.

The ARU (2001) presents evidence of "the continued crowd growth, increased television audiences" (p. 41) and the capacity of the Vodafone Super 12 tournament to deliver "a closely contested competition in which less-fancied sides can defeat front-runners on any given weekend" (p. 41). In fact, sports make conscious efforts to facilitate uncertainty of results by developing policies which will "ensure a more even distribution of on-field success" (Soccer Australia, 2001, p. 3). They justify these efforts by arguing, as Soccer Australia (2001) illustrates, that "competitiveness on the field and uncertainty of results builds public interest because supporters understand their team has a chance of victory each week" (p. 3).

From the same standpoint, the South Australia Gymnastics Association is leaning towards a new look in its efforts to "make events more entertaining for a broader section of the general population" (Australian Gymnastic Federation, 1999, p. 33). These developments, it explains, are "stretching the bounds of the traditional gymnastic competition with positive responses and reactions" (Australian Gymnastic Federation, 1999, p. 33). This point reflects the NSOs' belief that in addition to the unpredictability of results, the interest of the spectators and supporters is kept alive, if not increased, by constructing events to appeal to a wider base and, more importantly, to offer high quality entertainment. As a demonstration of this, Australian Swimming (2000/01) argues that in recent years it set out to provide competitive opportunities in a professional manner to enhance the "image and reputation of the sport by ensuring public satisfaction with the entertainment provided" (p. 15). It states that "the utilisation of appropriate expertise in the event production" (p. 15) has added to its ability to entertain capacity crowds.

Finances

The marketing and promotion of successfully run sporting competitions present opportunities to boost television viewing spectators, attendance numbers and gate receipts, and to attract sponsors, advertisers, broadcasting revenue and commercial opportunities. In recognition of this, NSOs are prepared to maximise fiscal potential. To best illustrate this, Athletics Australia (2000/01) was prepared to do all possible to make the Telstra Grand Prix "both a sporting spectacle and commercial success" (p. 36). The financial gains received by boosting competition attendances are valued by many sports. Basketball Australia (1999), for example, argues that its need to increase spectator participation at international games is "a priority in easing the financial burden" (p. 6).

The previously mentioned Vodafone Super 12 tournament does not only offer unpredictability of results but its growing impact is also "reflected in the growth of the broadcast audience" (ARU, 2001, p. 41) in Australia. The ARU (2001) states that in 2001, Fox Sports' Super 12 audience grew 56 percent on the previous year, "emphasising the impact of the tournament and its value to broadcasters" (p. 41). On the one hand, membership numbers provide income in the form of fees, and event attendances provide the potential for improving sports finances by means of increasing their commercial capacity and gate takings, while on the other hand boosted TV audiences guarantee broadcasting revenue. To demonstrate the importance of this point, the AFL (2000) notes that its broadcasting revenue is the "single largest income item" (p. 27) and underpins the finances of the competition.

In summary, Figure 5.5 is a representation of the benefits gained from running sporting competitions. NSOs explain how competitions for player development help with the development and transition of the depth of playing talent, building blocks for future representative sides and the preservation of elite success by skilling and preparing athletes appropriately. NSOs illustrate how competitions provide opportunities for the talented to develop their skills and give sports the opportunity to capitalise on the host of Australian talent. Competitions provide the 'stepping-stones' for players to make the transition to elite easier.

However, with regard to examining sporting events as promotional tools and public profile generators, marketing and media exposure go a long way to promoting the sports and the athletes' performances. In turn, publicity increases and the sports' profile is elevated. This results in greater community awareness, which may result in turn in increases in membership/participation registrations (growth), supporters/spectators numbers and/or gate receipts (finances). Either way, (i.e. competitions/events as player development or as promotion) the finances of the sports may improve.

Figure 5.5: Sport Development Benefits from Competitions/Events

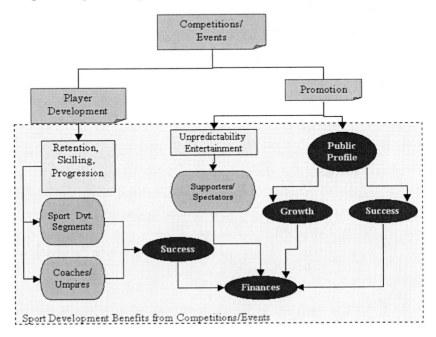

5.1 SUMMARY

This chapter examined the sport development practices and the goals and benefits that they deliver to sport development stakeholders and in particular the sporting organisations and the various sport development segments. These benefits are multiple and relate to all facets of sport development and aspects of participation. A close examination and comparison of the benefits derived from the implementation of different practices illustrate that even though the various practices target different aspects of sport development, the benefits gained and goals achieved fall into the following nine groups (see Figure 5.6):

(a) increase in membership/participation (growth)

(b) talent identification and transition to elite to achieve elite development and peak performances (talent)

(c) increase in fan and spectatorship numbers (supporters/spectators)

(d) increased community awareness and publicity of sports (public profile)

(e) financial viability and prosperity (finances)

(f) the smooth running of events/competitions (operations)

(g) the provision of improved services (services)

(h) open lines of communication and cooperation at all organisational levels (cooperation)

(i) Elite Successful Performance (success).

The relationships between the sport development stakeholders, the sport development practices and the practice benefits (goals) are illustrated in Figure 5.6. The benefits derive from stakeholders' involvement with shaping and implementing practices. The sport development practices are essential if participation, athlete, coach and umpire development and elite and organisational success are sought. Successful sport development may generate public awareness and attention that are key ingredients for stakeholders' regeneration of interest and support to sport development.

Figure 5.6: Sport Development Goals, Practices and Stakeholders

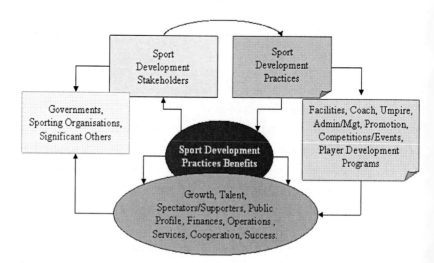

This chapter has made the links between sport development stakeholders and the sport development practices they are involved with, as well as the benefits and goals these practices deliver to the sport system. What remains to be explored in the sport development processes in Australia is the actual sport development pathways in relation to the two central codes identified (viz. the sport development stakeholders and the sport development practices). The examination of the sport development pathways will offer a complete picture of the sport development processes of the Australian sport system and a micro policy analysis. Meanwhile, the sporting organisations and the sport development segments (viz. stakeholders) reap the benefits of the practices in effect.

CHAPTER 6: THE SPORT DEVELOPMENT PATHWAYS

6 SPORT DEVELOPMENT PATHWAYS

The two previous chapters established the context and the requirements for sport development to proceed. However, so far there has been no description of the actual processes that explain how sport development takes place. This chapter presents the main categories that emerged from the analysis of data following the discovery of the factors that affect sport development (i.e. stakeholder involvement and practice implementation), the different relationships stakeholders hold and the variety of methods and practices they use in their efforts to develop sport. As theoretically deeper and more advanced links are formed, the synthesis of this section is based upon and uses all the previously discovered categories in order to inform the evolving theory. Albeit running the risk of becoming repetitive, reiterating previously discovered categories is indicative of data analysis saturation. Thus, categories such as stakeholder roles and practices are embedded in the discussion of the sport development processes.

This chapter shows that there are three distinctive sport development processes occurring within the Australian sport system: (a) the **attraction**, (b) the **retention/transition,** and (c) the **nurturing process**. These processes cater for different sport development segments and, as this section will explain, due to the three different types of sport development pathways (i.e. pathways to the **foundation**, to **talent** and to **elite athletes**) embedded within the sport development processes, these processes interrelate (see Figure 6.1). Hence, processes share an important attribute: they require pathways to allow and facilitate movement between stages.

More specifically, the three identified pathways are: (a) the pathways to link the nurturing process to the attraction process, (b) the pathways to link the attraction process to the retention/transition process, and (c) the pathways to link the retention/transition process to the nurturing process. An essential characteristic of these pathways is that they link one development process to the following process in a continuous fashion, illustrating not only participant movement but also the potential impact that each process may have on other facets of sport development. Essentially, the model shows that sport development in Australia is sequential with interrelated and interconnected processes, and that all processes are fundamental for successful sport development.

The sport development segments (a subgroup of significant other stakeholders) form the building blocks where the sport development processes take place. Hence, it is essential to recall that these segments are the members, participants of all ages and the sport supporters/spectators. An example drawn from the AFL's game development strategy shows that the sport development segments are embedded within these processes. The AFL (1999) supports the argument that game development is confined to "attracting, developing and retaining the most talented athletes" as well as "building participation and using football as a positive community influence" (p. 94).

Figure 6.1: The Overview of the Australian Sport Development Processes

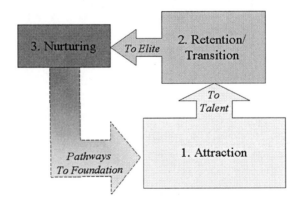

Each process and its inherent pathways engage the dynamic involvement of different stakeholders and practices. This section is divided into three parts and offers a microanalysis of the sport development processes by discussing in detail the specific role and importance of the stakeholders and the practices as they pertain to each individual process. It also covers the three development pathways as they link the three development processes and concludes that a full sport development cycle is complete only when all the pathways are in place.

6.1 THE ATTRACTION PROCESS

Attraction is the process whereby sport development practices draw new sport development segments and provide quality experiences to existing ones. This section will convey that the intent of the attraction process is to advance sport's *financial* position and through the pathways to the talented athletes offer ample *junior* participation. A stakeholder and microanalysis as it pertains to the attraction process and an exploration of the embedded pathways to talented athletes follow.

NSOs representing sports including baseball, bowls, canoeing, gymnastics, lacrosse, orienteering, rugby union, skating and softball confirm the involvement of the ASC with the *attraction process* and in particular the ASC's efforts to increase participation numbers. As previously indicated, NSOs obtain funding and policy direction from the ASC enabling them to achieve their core obligation to extend development of their game and participation in sport. NSOs maintain that the Federal Government's 2001 sport policy *Backing Australia's Sporting Ability: A More Active Australia* provides a policy direction that focuses on increasing the number of Australians playing sport. The policy sets "a clear direction for the ASC's Sport Development area to work directly with national sporting organisations to increase participation in sport" (Australian Canoeing, 2000/01, p. 10). The above includes utilising the Commission's sport development programs such as coaching, officiating, junior sport, women in sport, harassment-free sport, indigenous sport, volunteers, club management, Sportnet and research.

NSOs indicate that the ASC's development programs commit significantly more funding and effort to developing sports at the junior level rather than encouraging mass participation by building a sustainable sports infrastructure with sporting organisations at all levels. Junior sport appears to be the major focus under the new policy, with ongoing support for the Active Australia Schools Network, the development of the Olympic Youth Program and the development of a number of generic junior sport programs.

State governments through their sport departments or offices support and fund SSOs in their attraction process efforts to implement participation, talent identification and player development programs. For example, the South Australia Government, through the Office of Recreation and Sport, continuously supports squash associations through funding their development programs. In addition, owing to the participation grant from Tasmanian Government, many of squash's participation activities are made possible. Hockey NSW acknowledges the support of the NSW Department of Sport and Recreation and their major funding contribution through the sports development program "to the area of participation as well as funding through their Talent Development Unit" (Women's Hockey Australia, 1999, p. 12).

SSOs play a key role in the attraction process as they are accountable for attracting members and participation numbers overall and the NSOs are there to support them. Indicatively, Australian Swimming in partnership with its state associations points out that it is exploring ways in which to attract members in the non-elite area of its sport. The Australian Baseball Federation also is supporting its state associations by providing more hands-on and financial assistance in its attempt to arrest the falling participation rate and grow it. Similarly, Orienteering Australia assists states to explore innovative ways to encourage new membership. The Australian Weightlifting Federation (2001) is another NSO that recognises the need for stakeholders to work together to achieve increase in participation. According to its claims, this approach is going to "involve closer working relationships with the State and Territories and affiliated clubs and schools who are working at the grass roots" (p. 14).

Clubs and *associations,* similarly to SSOs, assist in the implementation of practices including training programs, competitions and promotion in order to attract individuals. They provide participation and development opportunities to the public and the local promotion of the sports. Australian Swimming (2000/01) captures the importance that clubs and associations have for sport by arguing that "the Clubs and Districts of NSW continued to be the back bone of the sport providing the opportunity for swimmers to participate and develop" (p. 43). The Australian Gymnastic Federation (2001) supports the above by noting that "it is pleasing to see the number of registered gymnasts has increased…This can be attributed to…the local promotion of gymnastics by clubs" (p. 30). The ACT Rugby Union also recognises the clubs' contribution to the growth of the sport by stating that "the high profile of the game in the region has contributed to a 15 percent growth in the team numbers. This growth would not [have] happened without our club efforts in recruiting at all levels and making sure the game is going forward" (ARU, 2000, p. 35).

NSOs point out that the chief aim of the *A More Active Australia* component of the Federal Government's policy is to significantly increase the number of people participating in sport across Australia. Support for regional and rural areas is of particular priority, with the ultimate aim of every member of every sport being able to participate in a positive and supportive environment.

This is subject to providing appropriate and adequate *facilities*. The following two examples illustrate this point. Squash Australia invested money to refurbish its older facilities and claims that this has encouraged increases in participation. On the other hand, Australian Swimming saw an increase in participation as problematic due to its substantial lack of facilities. It claims that with the exposure provided by the 2000 Sydney Olympics many young people were turning to swimming and this created a problem due primarily to the lack of pool space.

More important, at this level of participation, NSOs value the availability and implementation of *Type I player development programs*. Squash Australia, for example, maintains that the number of its senior pennant teams continues to decline at those venues which offer little more than the provision of courts for hire. NSOs explain that development programs are necessary to encourage more people to participate and to retain existing participants. They argue that participants will defect unless well-developed pathways are in place and a wide range of programs is available for all age and ability groups. As an illustration of the above, Tennis Australia (1999/2000) and its member associations continuously "expand their many programs designed to encourage more people to play tennis or those who play, to play more often" (p. 5). Athletics Australia has also intensified its activities in this area in order to significantly build membership. In addition to increased availability of Type I player programs, the ASC (2001) recognised the need to increase public *awareness* of program availability. In order to do so, the ASC's (2000/2001) $1.6 million public education awareness program created incentives for sporting organisations through Active Australia marketing to increase awareness of program availability and reinforce the health benefits associated with maintaining active lifestyles.

The NSOs' emphasis is not solely on increasing numbers but rather on providing quality experiences to existing participants and spectators that meet their needs and expectations. This is consistent with van Leeuwen, Quick and Daniel's (2002) conceptual interpretation of customer satisfaction that stresses the importance of retaining satisfied participants, members and sport spectators to ensure positive organisational outcomes. By adopting a customer-oriented approach, NSOs seek flexible options for people who wish to pursue sport for leisure and recreational purposes rather than undertaking sport as a serious pursuit. Responding to the first group of people requires a different focus. Among a number of Type I player development programs available, *modified sport* is a popular option to enhance the quality of the experience and is evidence of a more customer-focused approach.

According to Kirk and Gorely (2000), these modifications provide "clearly articulated pathways across levels of performance and across age ranges" (p. 125). They claim that the introduction of modified sport in Australia has seen many positive changes in the perceived value of sport and fair play. These include its acceptance, the opportunity to be successful and a reduced dropout from sport.

Slowpitch, for example, is a variation of softball. The NSW Softball Association supports the argument that Slowpitch offers the community an alternative to other recreational sports and the "opportunity to partake in [sport] for an extended period of time" (Australian Softball Federation, 2000/01, p. 36). Additionally, the Australian Softball Federation (2000/01) looks at alternative forms of softball events in an effort "to keep abreast with today's society and to provide a [sic] event structure aimed at the social player" (p. 38). As a result, a modified game called Flexi-Ball, which is conducted under an event-style competition as an alternative to the traditional softball structure, was developed. Similarly, other NSOs, such as Orienteering Australia, identified the need to develop lower risk experiences and a greater variety of experiences for new participants, while CAMS intends making motor sport attractive and rewarding to encourage greater involvement by a wider cross-section of the Australian community.

Sport modifications appear popular for junior development purposes too. Programs such as the MILO Cricket programs (Have A Go and Super 8s programs) are appealing to juniors, appear to be successful and are a major factor in the health of junior sport. SLSA provides individualised Surf Life Saving experiences to youth members that are tailored to their needs, and Skiing Australia launched the Inter-Schools Challenge Series to further increase participation in snow-sports. The ARU (2001) argues that the changes it introduced to its code are "designed to make Rugby a more attractive proposition for children and their parents, boosting participation" (p. 9). Another football code, in an endeavour to get more girls involved in the game, promotes "a non-contact flag belt form of the game" (ARL, 2000, p. 15). The ARL (2000) believes that these modifications are "not a sacrifice to the traditional game but a means to make more young people (including their teachers and parents) familiar and comfortable with the rudimentary skills of the game and to further promote the fun aspects of it" (p. 15).

Implementation of sport development practices in the attraction process is only possible due to the contributions of *significant others*, such as the support and works of *sport development officers* (SDOs) and the contributions of *sponsors*. Women's Hockey Australia, for example, observes that the increase it experienced at the under-age level is due to more co-ordination of coaching and greater opportunities to participate at events and play at state level. The Australian Gymnastic Federation claims that the appointment of a National Development Manager to implement the participation program has proven beneficial and Roller Skating Australia believes that its National Development Manager has the potential to assist Roller Skating and the branches to develop and implement vital participation projects that are needed to increase membership across all disciplines. The ARU (2000) expects the work SDOs have been doing in development and implementation of programs to be reflected in growth at the clubs in the coming seasons. Indicatively, the ARU (2000) argues that "nationally, 127,801 men, women and children played the game in 2000, which is the pleasing consequence of a great deal of hard work by development staff at national and state level" (p. 8).

A major focus for SDOs is junior development. CAMS (2000), for example, "work[s] closely with clubs to attract more young people and encourage clubs to appoint junior development officers to facilitate this process" (p. 12). As the following examples illustrate, sporting organisations appoint SDOs in their effort to attract and maintain young players. Bocce Australia admits that its SDO has made an outstanding contribution as a result of introducing new competitions and attracting and maintaining new players.

Conversely, the Australian Gymnastic Federation (1999) expresses a concern in relation to the numbers in its Under 17 and Under 18 divisions. It states that "while the numbers of the U/17 and U/18 divisions were up slightly on the previous year, there continues to be a significant drop-off in these age groups" (p. 6). In its effort to counter this alarming drop-off, it appointed a SDO in the hope that the officer would address this concern. Finally, Women's Hockey Australia's (2000) appointment of a full-time SDO "has led to the formation of development squads in each region involving large number of juniors" (p. 18).

The sponsor's contribution to the attraction process is widely recognised by the NSOs. Sponsorship, when available, allows NSOs to attract and increase their supporter/spectator base by reducing admission/entry fees to competitions. In some cases, sponsorship is also credited with the feasibility and continuation of certain competitions or is associated with low membership fees. Australian Canoeing (2000/01) argues that in the post-2000 Olympic climate, the sponsorship market has been difficult. However, it observes that "sport development initiatives and competition events" continue to draw sponsor support, and this provides "a level of self-sufficiency to keep our National membership and competition entry fees for canoeists, amongst the lowest for sport in the country" (p. 4).

Nevertheless, effective marketing and promotion of events and sports are required to ensure sports retain if not increase their profile as exciting and competitive for participants of all age groups. Bowling Australia notes that its sponsors' generosity is much appreciated as it provides valuable support to Bowling Australia's aim to expose its sport to the general population, hence encouraging them to participate in bowling. Squash Australia (1999), amongst other NSOs, provides an example of the way sponsorship is used to promote and develop sport. It invests a large amount of time and resources in an initiative called squashlink. The concept is venue-focused and sees squash centres nationally "becoming a group offering at the same levels of service and programs to the player" (p. 24). This initiative offers the potential for Squash Australia to grow the game through new promotional and marketing strategies. Nevertheless, these strategies require "significant financial support and therefore sponsorship is paramount to the success" (p. 24).

Sponsorship is also paramount to running Type I player development programs. NSOs argue that it would be difficult to run many of their programs which reach the wider community without the assistance that sponsorship provides. Monies derived from corporate sponsors assist sport in making significant investment in the development of their game at grassroots level. In some cases, this is facilitated and achieved by NSOs employing SDOs. The ARU (2000), for example, maintains that "on the back of major sponsorship deals with Optus and Hewlett Packard and the continued support of long-standing sponsors, the Union was able to employ another development officer" (p. 48).

One of the goals of the *Backing Australia's Sporting Ability: A More Active Australia* policy is to increase the awareness of the Active Australia brand and programs, and ultimately the interested participant numbers. NSOs recognise that this is possible by implementing *promotional* tools. The AFL (1999), for example, in its intention to "build upon existing participation and talented player strategies while increasing the funding and resources available to further boost participation in the AFL game" (p. 92), agrees that it would only achieve this by boosting its "marketing focus and capabilities, leveraging business opportunities and building the consumer association with football at all levels" (p. 92). Squash Australia (1999) hopes that its marketing efforts will "provide an impetus for increasing squash participation" (p. 3). In addition, one-third of NSOs suggest that websites provide the potential to inform existing players, renew the interest of jaded players and aid in its goal of increasing the participation levels of sport.

Participation and development are also integral to NSOs' media efforts, with Lacrosse Australia (2001) claiming that the focus of its media, marketing and promotions portfolio has moved "towards establishing a solid base for Lacrosse Australia and its members to gain the maximum benefits from hosting the forthcoming 2002 World Lacrosse Championship and associated events" (p. 3). Bowls Australia (2000/01), on the other hand, benefited from the introduction of a new series on television, as this has been a great success, by "exposing the game to a new audience and helping the drive for new members" (p. 25).

While NSOs' marketing efforts are deemed crucial for the promotion of sports to the public and have increased the levels of awareness, effective *administration/management* provides the framework to not only attract but also maintain participants within sports. One-third of NSOs argue that improved management and reporting systems are critical elements in establishing a framework to secure new clients and increase participation. The Australian Gymnastic Federation (2001), for instance, suggests that a new management structure is essential "to assist in the delivery of an improved level of service" (p. 30).

Almost all NSOs point out the importance of the quality of *service* provided in attaining and increasing membership/participation numbers. For instance, the Australian Gymnastic Federation (2001) believes that if it could continue to build on the high level of service offered at club level, it would see increasing membership numbers. It claims that the "continued updating and revision" of its programs would help in providing the customer with "quality programs and professional service" (p. 30). Similar to providing quality programs and modified sports to participants, providing quality service to members reflects once again the efforts required to keep existing participants/members satisfied.

On this, SLSA (2001) supports the argument that "whilst it is very satisfying to be able to report membership growth, it is paramount that the organization continues to develop the related support services" (p. 20). Australian Swimming (1999/2000) maintains that since Federal Government funding is not available for masters sports it has to tailor its membership fees to allow it to "continue to provide an increasing level of service" to its members, whilst at the same time it must "continue to pursue any avenue for grants that may come available" (p. 44).

Sports *events/competitions* in the attraction process act as opportunities for participants to become involved, participate and stay motivated. Additionally, NSOs recognise the potential of high profile sport events to stimulate participation and increase the membership base. The Australian Weightlifting Federation (2000), for instance, argues that it has left "no stone unturned" in its efforts to "meet the challenge of increasing our membership" (p. 5).

Realising the benefits of a wider participation and membership base, NSOs admit that, as the ARU (1999) express it, membership/participation is "the backbone of the game's social fabric and it must be nourished" (p. 10). Advances in this sport development segment provide *organisational* and *sport development*-related benefits.

In terms of the organisational benefits delivered, the larger the pool of individuals at this stage the more chances sporting organisations have to increase their pool of *volunteers* and *membership fees*. NSOs capitalising on volunteers and membership fees improve their services without added financial burdens and advance their financial revenues from membership fees (membership/participation growth has important implications for the sports organisations' finances). Membership fees paid to sport have provided a large slice of sport funding over the years.

NSOs explore all business opportunities to generate new income streams. In its efforts to identify alternative sources of revenue, Bowls Australia (2000/01) reports that even though its National Merchandising program is growing and it can generate revenue streams outside of corporate sponsorship and Federal Government funding, "Serious consideration should now be given to investigating other avenues of revenue generation from the membership base" (p. 7).

The Australian Yachting Federation (2001) declares that its membership scheme is an important revenue stream to the Federation "as reliance shifts away from government grants and sponsorship income" (p. 7). Like many other NSOs, it anticipated a reduction in Federal Government funding after the 2000 Olympics. However, with increased income from its membership program and continued endeavours to expand other sources of income, it has managed to overcome potential problems. In the process it greatly contributed towards its aim of placing the Federation in a position which ensured future viability and the success of its sport.

In recognition of the financial importance of increased membership/participation, the Western Australia Gymnastic Association (1999) states that "the continued decline in gymnastic registrations has had an impact on the Association's annual financial performance" (p. 35). The Australian Softball Federation (1999/2000) provides support for the thesis that diminishing membership brings financial woes upon sports. It recognises the need to grow "to ensure that total operating costs are divided between more members and therefore maintain, or possibly reduce, costs per head" (p. 44).

Membership/participation growth may result in reduced pressure on members by charging lower fees. The AFL (2001), for example, states that all its strategies could be realised if it continues to enhance the financial standing of the game and maximize the economic benefits for clubs, players and the football fraternity, "without imposing financial stresses on the supporters who contribute so much to the AFL game at all levels" (p. 23). In relation to keeping membership fees low, NSOs propose that as volunteers give their time and energy freely to sporting organisations this translates into financial savings and the ability to provide services that ultimately support the future viability and health of the sport. For example, the Australian Gymnastic Federation (2001) explains that "thousands of hours of volunteer work contribute significantly to the ongoing future viability of the sport, whilst maintaining relatively low fees for membership and competitions" (p. 30).

As mentioned above, the efforts of volunteers are inextricably tied to the enhancement of the delivery of sport development services. Auskick provides an example of the AFL's junior development program where family and friends are voluntarily involved in the delivery of sport development. Auskick involves both boys and girls in playing modified AFL games and activities for fun and enjoyment. While managed through the Australian Football League's Game Development Department, Auskick is *"owned and operated"* (AFL, 2001, p. 71) by parents and friends of football.

The Pathways to the Talented

The above discussion reveals the profusion of stakeholder practices in the attraction process which drive the pathways to the talented, which assist this facet of sport development to be successful in its scope to increase the number of junior athletes. Therefore, in terms of sport development benefits, the more focused the attraction of junior players within the participation base, the more chances sports have of increasing their pool of talented athletes. The membership/participation segment presents the potential to provide greater numbers of junior participants in order to advance them to the next level, the retention/transition process.

NSOs support the view that tapping into juniors is a required practice. Junior programs, such as "Tip Top" for swimming, are regarded by NSOs as exemplary in identifying, preparing and developing competitive talent. In stressing the importance of junior development programs, Australian Canoeing (2001) supports the argument that for each sport to generate high standards and performances for Olympic Games or World Championships, significant commitments must be given to athlete, coach and official development programs across Australia.

With many athletes and administrators retiring after Olympic Games or World Championships, the above task of emulating and improving upon such performances should not be taken lightly. If NSOs are to be highly regarded in the world of sport, be successful and consistently maintain their position, they need a strong domestic base. As the ARU (1999) suggests, "strengthening that base means expanding the numbers of players and raising the standard of those who get to the top" (p. 9). In a similar vein, Australian Swimming (1999/2000) argues that "success is found in the development of a new crop" (p. 42). The Australian Yachting Federation (2001) also demonstrates the above by stating that:

> To secure our dominant international position we must build a strong youth development program (YDP). Only in this way can we ensure a good flow of well-grounded young sailors likely to perform at the highest international level. Already rival nations are spending significant funds in this area. If we fail to do so, then we will quickly fall behind. The AYF have already indicated to the ASC the need to commit more resources in this area and that, in the short term, if resources are limited, senior international competitiveness may fall away. (p. 5)

A common belief among NSOs is that a wider base of membership/participation increases the penetration of sport in the community and delivers a wider base of sport followers at all levels including junior. Young players emerge from the local community. Hence, providing the wider community with the appropriate game development strategies to deepen and entrench their association with all levels of sports is essential. More important, with a wide base, NSOs believe there is more chance of capturing talented athletes. NSOs maintain that clear, well-managed and high-quality talented pathways are essential for leveraging off the juniors to attract, retain and develop the most talented youth.

Strengthening the base with a greater pool of juniors results in a superior group of young athletes coming through and presents a promising practice for future national teams. NSOs conclude that they have to continue to support development of their programs to ensure that the depth of junior athletes available to draw on for national team consideration continues to grow in both numbers and quality. For example, the ARUs' expansion in schools around Australia unearthed some wonderful future potential for the Australian Rugby Shield, a tournament that gives players in regional areas the opportunity to take the next step up to representative rugby. Generally, it is hoped that the emphasis placed on developing younger players, together with the frameworks established, will give sports greater chances for success in the future. SLSA (2000) claims certainty that "many of the outstanding young members of our organisation will make great future leaders for surf lifesaving" (p. 4).

Ample evidence reinforces the above. For instance, in 2000/01 Tasmanian junior athletes won 18 medals at the Australian All Schools and the Australian Youth Athletics Championships. Athletics Australia (2000/01) strongly believed that this was going to "provide the platform to launch greater numbers of successful senior athletes in the future" (p. 39). Netball Australia (2001), as another example, maintains that their Australian 21 and Under team's good performance "augurs well for the future of Australian Netball" (p. 4).

Similarly, the ARU (2001) emphasises that the importance placed on developing younger players gives the team "greater success in the Australian Rugby Shield in the future" (p. 46). As another case to illustrate the above, the Australian Softball Federation (2000/01) argues that "the exceptional young talent that we have in all states coming through the ranks" (p. 27) provides all the potential for future success. In addition, Australian Swimming (1999/2000) claims to be in "good shape for the future with some fantastic young and talented swimmers stamping themselves as Australian Swimming representatives of the future" (p. 45).

In summary, the attraction process caters for membership/participation growth and supporter/spectator base with a particular emphasis at the junior level. Nevertheless, the attraction process itself does not separate the talented junior from the masses. It is the stakeholder provision and implementation of the practices that operate as pathways to the talented athlete, embedded in the attraction process, that need to be shaped and implemented (see Figure 6.2).

Figure 6.2: The Attraction Process

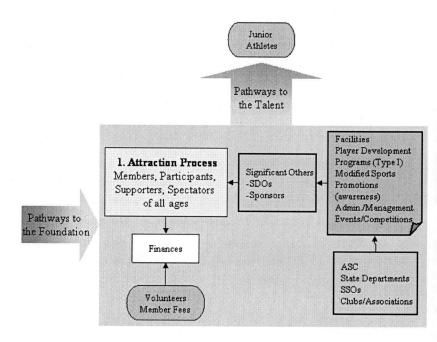

The importance of the attraction process (in sport development and in particular in the pathways to the talented) lies in the fact that it is a necessary step to the retention/transition process. Young participants provide an indication of the future prospects of sports' elite success. Young participants have the potential to shape the new generation of elite athletes, earn selection in future national teams, ensure records and maintain achievements. The pathways to the talented single out junior athletes from the masses to support the retention/transition process, where they advance to higher levels of performance. To obtain the benefits of a large junior pool, strategies aimed at facilitating junior progress to the top of the sport development processes are crucial. The retention/transition process illustrates the above journey as it caters for the junior sport enthusiasts and, more important, the most talented amongst them.

6.2 THE RETENTION/TRANSITION PROCESS

Retention/transition is the process whereby a range of policies including *Type II player development programs* and *competitions/events* are implemented to identify the talented junior athletes and to coach and train them with the ultimate aim of retaining and taking the most talented athletes through to the highest levels of the professional game. This section will suggest that the intent of the retention/transition process is to *fill the gaps* in the elite athlete ranks, and through its pathways to the elite to produce and retain high numbers of *elite athletes*. This is best illustrated by Australian Canoeing (2000/01) which maintains that this processes is where talented athletes are "identified and assisted to reach an international performance standard and an increase in the depth of skilled athletes/teams at a national level" (p. 22). Within this transition from junior to higher levels of participation, athlete retention is crucial in capitalising on and delivering most of the identified talent. A stakeholder and microanalysis as it pertains to the *retention/transition process* and an exploration of the embedded pathways to the elite follow.

NSO efforts towards talent development are significantly linked with the support of the ASC. The Australian Softball Federation (1999/2000) admits that ASC funding enables it to achieve considerable development at all levels and improve performances at the grassroots level. As a result, softball's "National Squad, and indeed the tier of athletes directly below them, is better physically prepared and more experienced in the rigours of international competition" (p. 16). With funding and assistance from the ASC through the high performance program and existing ASC talent identification programs, the state junior and state little league programs and a number of similar initiatives, NSOs foster new talent and develop career paths towards the top end of their sport.

Almost all NSOs, including the AFL, Athletics Australia, Basketball Australia, Australian Canoeing, CAMS, Skating Australia, Soccer Australia, the Australian Softball Federation, Squash Australia and the Australian Weightlifting Federation, support the argument that grassroots development and talent identification programs are essential in order to tap into as large a number as possible of young players with the potential to become elite athletes. As a demonstration of the above, Basketball Australia (2001) points out how crucial it is that the Aussie Hoops junior development program continues to be successful so that it can tap into the huge number of potential players at the primary school level and convert these into registered players at the local association level. Basketball Australia anticipate that, with the support of the ASC, Aussie Hoops would see a "redoubling of the sports focus at the grassroots level, ensuring long term benefits at the crucial coal face of basketball" (p. 12).

Another aspect of talent identification and development is the Indigenous Programs. These programs, funded by the ASC, develop, promote and foster sport in remote and isolated communities. This practice provides children residing in remote Australia with the same opportunities as other young Australians. Moreover, NSOs state that the Federal Government aims to see more sport played, particularly by school-aged children and in rural areas, "where sporting groups are often a vital factor in the cohesion of local communities" (Australian Weightlifting Federation, 2001, p. 17). Apart from the obvious social considerations for children in remote areas and provision of the same opportunities, NSOs claim that this policy has the potential to result in making the most of the junior population of this country in talent identification and avoiding the loss of potential talent located outside metropolitan areas.

Besides the Federal Government, NSOs recognise the substantial support of the *state institutes* and *academies of sport* and the subsidies that SSOs receive from *state governments/departments* to be able to afford existing, or recruit new development and talent identification staff. For example, in 2000 the Queensland Softball Association secured a grant from the Queensland Government to employ a project officer to manage its modified game program "Flexi-Ball". In 2000, and with the assistance of the South Australian Government, Athletics South Australia was able to engage a full-time development officer, a part-time Schools Field Officer and a part-time Talent Identification Coordinator. In addition to SDOs and talent identification staff, coach development is another area where state governments assist SSOs. For example, in 1999 the NSW Institute of Sport provided a wealth of support and funding for not only elite players but also coach development within NSW for Women's Hockey Australia.

The NSOs propose that *coaching* has a significant impact on talent development. In fact, there is a common belief that coaches at all levels are ultimately contributing to the development and success of elite athletes. The Australian Water Polo (2001) suggests that "the coaches are wisely building a significant base for the future" (p. 1). Similarly, the Australian Softball Federation (1999/2000) claims that "players reach the elite level because of the work of all coaches who have coached them from the time they started playing softball" (p. 20). On the whole, NSOs indicate that if coaches did not instil and encourage a love of the sport, then potential elite athletes would be lost to the sport before reaching the elite level.

Initiatives such as *training camps* reinforce talented athlete and coach synergy and development. The camps consist of practice and educational components and provide an opportunity for athletes and coaches to plan their preparation in conjunction with team coaches and NSOs personnel. In exemplification of this, as part of the Athletics Australia Olympic preparation program throughout 1999-2000, a number of national training camps were conducted for each major event group. These camps were coordinated by national event coaches in conjunction with Athletics Australia, providing development opportunities for aspiring Olympic and world junior championship competitors and their personal coaches.

NSOs maintain that retaining and advancing junior athletes to elite is far more challenging and painstaking than attracting them. The two terms 'retention' and 'transition' appear closely related because NSOs are interested in retaining juniors throughout their transition to higher levels of performance and participation. Skate Australia (2000/01), among many NSOs, poses the following question: "How do we keep the kids playing through to senior age?" (p. 7). The AFL (2000) claims that the success of its Auskick program in attracting participants is unquestionable: "however, the transition of these people to junior club football fans is a major participation issue" (p. 65). Of similar note, Synchro Australia argues that sports lost many participants at this level during the last two years in the lead-up to the Sydney Olympic Games because with the focus on the Olympics for a long period of time there was to little to offer them.

As junior participants defect, NSOs face difficulties in *filling the gaps* in the elite ranks. These gaps usually emerge as athletes retire, become unavailable or sustain injury. The NSOs support the view that these incidents pave the way for a number of younger players. The Australian Water Polo declares that it is amongst the lucky NSOs in that it has many youngsters filling the gaps left by the vacating older players from the 2000 Olympics. Women's Hockey Australia believes that although players leave its squads, there is a strong and vital basis on which to build its future.

Nevertheless, some others admit to the fear of depleted ranks. Athletics Australia, for example, argues that a large number of its athletes did not re-appear after the 2000 Olympics, which left gaps in the rankings. However, it is confident that the up and coming juniors will slowly fill these gaps. Tasmania Athletics, for instance, claims that its High Performance Program focuses on the elite junior athletes and their coaches in an attempt to build its depleted senior ranks. Australian Canoeing agrees that the international strength of its current paddlers must be balanced by the weakness of the base from which it is built. In recognition of the important role that young athletes play in filling elite athlete gaps, Soccer Australia (2001) believes that the capacity of soccer to service the National Youth Program is "critical in achieving and maintaining a world-class senior team" (p. 21).

The Australian Softball Federation, Soccer Australia and Australian Swimming are examples of the NSOs recognition of the need for a stronger focus on the development of juniors with the view to developing a squad that will continue through to senior representative level. For the above to take place, NSOs acknowledge the need for pathways that retain these participants into and beyond their teenage years. Soccer Australia (2000) perceives this process is about "enhanced growth and development based on strong formal and informal links from grassroots to the national and international levels of the game" (p. 2). The AFL, along with a great number of NSOs, expresses the opinion that linkages between levels of participation and sport providers are crucial and claims that AFL Auskick centres linked to local junior football clubs have higher retention rates.

Admittedly, for one-third of NSOs, the first step in addressing the issue of retention is to identify the reasons why people leave the sport at various stages. They report research is capable of shedding some light on questions of this nature. The AFL (2001), as a representative case faced with this problem, points out that the participation of children needs to continue as they move out of the Auskick program and into junior football. Therefore, research is needed "to develop strategies to enhance the flow of participants to school and school club ... in particular, children who make the transition from AFL Auskick into competition football need greater support in terms of resources and benefits" (p. 71). The ARL (2000) also admits that one of its challenges is to convert the players from school competitions into club competitors. In that direction, it puts strategies in place whereby "clubs can work with schools in their area and recruit players for the local competition" (p. 13).

Schools indeed appear as "lifesavers" for three-quarters of NSOs or as the ARL (2001) calls them "the feeding grounds for the growth of the sport" (p. 10), as they form their main source for talent identification. As an illustration of this point, Orienteering Australia initiated a national talent search program to identify young orienteers in schools and to provide a career pathway approved by the ASC for young coaches to help them. Similarly, the ARU (2001) continues to expand in schools around Australia, "unearthing some wonderful potential for Australian Rugby in the future" (p. 46). The ARL (2000) reinforces the argument about the multiple benefits that schools may offer by stating that:

> The Australian Secondary Schools Rugby League are to be congratulated on putting tours together for both U/15 and U/18 players. This is a great incentive and opportunity for players in the emerging states, as it gives these players something to strive for and an opportunity to be seen by NRL clubs. (p. 13)

There is mutual understanding amongst NSOs that sports can identify and retain their participants if the right inducements are provided. A popular example of an inducement provided by an ever-increasing number of NSOs is the provision of *websites*. For example, a brand new site www.hockeyzone.com.au was created by Women's Hockey Australia aimed at children and those just starting out in the sport with sections on hockey basics, how to join a club, a fun and games section and the results of fixtures from the local clubs through to veteran competitions. It is envisaged this site will promote the link from school to club hockey. Additionally, Squash Australia sees the promising advances it is making on its website and suggests it "may hold the key to reigniting the interest of some of the jaded players who have been leaving the sport" (Squash Australia, 1999, p. 20).

In order to identify, retain, develop and aid transition to higher levels of participation and performance, the core strategy appears to be sporting *competitions/events*. National competitions, international events and tournaments offer talent identification sources, development opportunities and opportunities for players to represent their country while acting as talented youth development pathways.

With regard to using competitions to unearth talent, Soccer Australia considered that the 2001 National Talent Identification Championships in Sydney would bring together a new group of players to be targeted for state national training centre programs, the AIS and the National Youth Team. The AFL expressed the same opinion that competitions provided a talent identification base for both state youth selectors and Westar clubs to coordinate their selection and development of elite players. Additionally, Bowls Australia (2000/01) has "an abundance of young fellows coming through in the Under 25 development squad" (p. 32). This group came to the fore in the Trans-Tasman series playing against much older and more experienced players. In recognition of the importance events play in talent identification, Squash Australia (1999) argues that there is an urgent need "to fully capitalise on the host of Australian talent now available" (p. 13).

Once talented athletes are identified, competitions/events help them develop their skills. The NSOs refer to competitions as the 'birthplace' of many 'superstars'. Amongst numerous examples that support this point, the ACB (1999/2000) states that "the national underage competitions are considered vital for the development of promising young cricketers" (p. 47). The AFL argues that the Under 16 and Under 18 national titles are benchmark competitions for talented, developing players in each state and territory, while development squads below the Under 16 age group provide talented players with the opportunity to develop their skills. Moreover, in 2001 Queensland Rugby Union sent three development teams to New Zealand for nine matches in an effort to develop the depth of playing talent below the Super 12 squad.

The Australian Water Polo (2001) recognises the importance of the development of its youth players, "to have these opportunities as a way of measuring themselves in an international arena" (p. 15). It notes that exposure to the pressure and intensity of elite water polo is critical in providing the building blocks for future representative sides. Similarly, the Australian Softball Federation (2000/01) suggests that test series are organised "in order to provide international experience and development opportunities for our up-coming male athletes" (p. 8).

The ARL (2000) organises tournaments as "a vital step in the development of our elite young players" (p. 1) and Australian Canoeing (2001) maintains that all tournaments and intermediate competitions held at events are crucial if NSOs want to foster young talent. The ACB (2000) confirms the above by arguing that the national underage competitions are considered vital for the development of promising young cricketers. In relation to tournaments, it believes that they display Australia's best cricketing talent and are watched by talent scouts from around the country. Australian Canoeing also believes that the Australian championships provide an excellent opportunity for Australian Canoeing to showcase the pool of potential talent while at the same time giving many athletes the opportunity to watch their peers across the various canoeing disciplines.

The development opportunities offered by competitions/events act as pathways that allow talented people to be seen and progress to higher levels. Orienteering Australia (2000) best illustrates this point by stating that competition "is needed to become a High Performance orienteer in the long run" (p. 3). All in all, the most significant aspect of the competitions at this level is their function as pathways for talented players. The ARU (1999) supports the argument that competitions/events "provide a pathway and development experience" (p. 8) for athletes and referees. It maintains that "an end of year competition involving the best of the developing states against the best of the traditional states, will provide a clear pathway that allows players to be seen and progress to higher levels if they are good enough" (p. 10). It concludes that "the Australian Rugby Shield provided the platform and the importance of this competition cannot be underestimated as it provides a pathway for players outside Sydney, Brisbane and Canberra to higher honours" (ARU, 2000 p. 48).

Australian Swimming maintains that lack of adequate competition may negatively affect its swimmers in their proper conditioning and preparation for racing in higher level competitions. Similarly, the AFL recognises that competitions provide opportunities to gain experience and the Australia Gymnastic Federation (1999) argues that competition experience gained by athletes, both in senior and junior levels, "is considered to be critical in the development of competitiveness and recognition in International competition" (p. 1).

Events and competitions are seen as 'stepping-stones' or the 'platform' that delivers the path to higher levels of participation and performance and supports the *retention/transition process*. As an example, the ARU's pathway for players in developing areas came with the creation of the Commonwealth Cup. For Skiing Australia (1999/2000), local races, continental cup and world cup events assist promising athletes to develop "to a standard where they are able to compete effectively at Junior World Championships, World Championship and Olympic events" (p. 15). Overall, NSOs indicate, as the ACB (1999/2000) describes it, that competitions aim "to provide fringe state players the opportunity to perform on a national stage at a level above club cricket and make the transition to first-class cricket easier" (p. 48).

NSOs consider the provision of a range of Type II player development programs and competitions as pathways to develop youth participants and take the most players possible from grassroots through to the highest levels of the professional game. The ARU, as one example, maintains the importance of the Australian Rugby Shield competition in providing the platform or the pathway to higher honours and, in addition, the Australian Baseball Federation (1999/2000) argues that the Australian Provincial Baseball Championships "is an excellent platform for provincial baseball and players, and one that is a critical grass root strategy for Australian baseball" (p. 15).

Closely related to the role of events and competitions is the notion of maintaining a successful *national league*. Apart from its publicity and promotional benefits, the national league is an important level of competition for young athletes to aspire to and can be a platform for international success. It is "the elite competition for Australia's rising stars" (Soccer Australia, 2001, p. 29) and the most critical part of their ongoing development. Another example, Orienteering Australia (2000) claims that the Qantas

National Orienteering League "provides not only a public image for orienteering but a focus for elite competition in Australia [and] a stepping stone for junior orienteers into elite rank" (p. 2). The NSOs view the leagues/teams as the most critical part of the ongoing development of their elite athletes. This is illustrated by the example of the Australian Water Polo (2000) that states, "the continued success of the League is and always will be closely linked to the success of our national team and our sport as a whole. It is the goal of many young players to play in the league and it is therefore a vital part of the athlete pathway" (p. 17).

The Pathways to the Elite

For the retention/transition process to be successful in producing elite junior athletes, it is imperative to effectively implement the identified practices as they pertain to the process. These practices operate as pathways to the elite and are responsible for assisting promising athletes to develop from the grassroots level, by providing a range of development programs and competitions/events as pathways. These practices put players on a journey to the highest levels of the professional game and enable them to achieve to the best of their ability. In the process they take advantage of access to some of the best facilities, coaches and support personnel available (see Figure 6.3). In short, the pathways to the elite aid the elite junior to reach the top and become successful elite athletes.

The importance of the pathways to the elite in sport development lies in the common NSO argument that the wellbeing of the game at a junior level is a precondition for elite player professional growth and development. In order for NSOs to reinforce and secure a dominant position within the sport industry, they need to build a strong youth development program. Only in this way can they ensure a good flow of well-grounded athletes "likely to perform at the highest international level" (Australian Yachting Federation, 2000, p. 5). As the Australian Weightlifting Federation (2001) best illustrates, the pathway to the elite

is a practical plan to ensure Australia's outstanding record of sporting achievement is maintained and that a new generation of Australians is given even greater opportunities to participate and improve themselves through involvement in sport. (p. 17)

Figure 6.3: The Retention/Transition Process

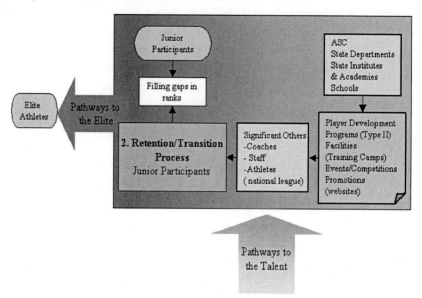

In due course, the pathways to the elite generate emerging elite athletes. Tapping talent is an area critical to securing a future for sport, replacing retiring elites and forming winning national teams to ensure continuing achievements and improved performances. The Australian Gymnastic Federation (2000) sums this as follows.

> The quality of our junior gymnasts has improved significantly in recent years. It is very encouraging for our future national team to see such a good group of young gymnasts coming through. We must continue to support further developments of our State High Performance Centre programs to ensure that the depth of gymnasts available to draw on for national team consideration continues to grow in both number and quality. (p. 6)

In summary, the attraction process discussed initially caters for membership/participation growth and offers the pathways to the talented where skilled junior athletes with the potential to become elite athletes can be singled out. The retention/transition process caters for these talented junior athletes and carries them to elite levels. Therefore, the journey to the top does not occur in a vacuum. It is the pathways to the elite level that accommodate the retention and transition of talented athletes, their development and their smooth passage to the elite level which foster long-term success.

An important aspect of the retention/transition process is that it is essential for the nurturing process. Identified and well-trained athletes are close to fulfilling their potential to successfully perform as elite athletes at the national and international level and to represent Australia. Embedded in the nurturing process are the pathways to the foundation that offer the potential to reinforce and maintain peoples' sporting interest.

6.3 THE NURTURING PROCESS

Nurturing is the process whereby Type III development programs and practices are tailored to the individual athlete, team or sport to achieve best performances on the national and international sporting stage. This section shows that the intent of the nurturing process is to not only achieve but also nurture and promote elite athlete success in Australia. The nurturing process allows sports to enjoy consistency in their elite performances and to experience the national and international success of Australia's teams/leagues. In the process, it gives the momentum for the pathways to the foundation. These pathways have the capacity to create the appropriate environment to stimulate people's (i.e. membership/participation, spectators/supporters and other stakeholders) interest in sport and motivation to actively remain involved with the industry. A stakeholder and microanalysis as it pertains to the nurturing process and an exploration of the pathways to the foundation as they are embedded in the nurturing process follow.

Apart from the previously mentioned need for coordinated efforts to attract and retain junior talented athletes to ensure the future of excellence, elite success is the result of the combined network of efforts deriving from governments and sporting organisations at all levels, practices and the athletes themselves and contributions from significant others. The following statement is typical: "The team's success is [not only] a testament to the players' talent, but also a tribute to the calibre of its management, coach and selectors" (ACB, 1999/2000, p. 6). The ARU (2001), amongst others, adds that Queensland's rugby team the Reds' success in reaching the semi finals of the Vodafone Super 12 for the third time in six years and the Under 19s' victory in the Trans Tasman

Cup "underlines the success of Queensland's coaching and development program and the impact of the Energex Reds Rugby College" (p. 44). In addition, NSOs claim that the combined efforts of the AIS, state institutes, private academies and association programs provide pathways for players to progress and be successful at the elite level.

Australian Swimming (1999/2000) notes that the most obvious example of its success is the achievement of 20 world records set by Australians. It claims that this is the result of the efforts of "long term strategies and planning of the Board, National Head Coach, National Youth Coach and volunteers and staff who have but one objective - to assist our swimmers and coaches to achieve their goals" (p. 7). The Australian Baseball Federation (1999/2000) revealed that much of its elite success "must be attributed to our program partners who include the Australian Sports Commission, the Australian Olympic Committee, the State Sport Institutes and major Go for Gold and corporate sponsors" (p. 9). Women's Hockey Australia (1999) claims that its High Performance Program continues to operate successfully with the assistance of the ASC and the AIS Senior Sports Consultant.

In examining critical success factors closely, there is a fundamental belief that the relationship between the ASC and elite success is reciprocal. NSOs maintain that support from the ASC is a prerequisite for player development programs and strategies to develop successful elite athletes while on the other hand it is clear to them that elite success is essential for further ASC support. Hall (2002) argues that situations where two (or more) organisations are dependent upon one another in accessing their resources to achieve their goals are the basis for *interdependency*. An example of this reciprocal relationship is provided by SLSA. For lifesaving in Australia, the formation of a national high performance management group has been the first step on the way to elite sporting development. The success of their Target 2000 trial program and SLSA's (2000) regaining of the world champion title in 2000

> attracted Australian Institute of Sport funding. The funding will help the implementation of high performance squad camps, a coaching network and will assist the national team's defence of their Tri-Nations Challenge champion status. (p. 14)

1. ASC funding results in Elite Success

Financial resources are critical for sports to produce top-quality players, as well as for maintaining and advancing their rankings. The principal source of funding for many NSOs is the grants they receive from the ASC to fund athlete, coach and officials programs, as well as high performance projects throughout the year. The majority of NSOs highlight the importance of this funding repeatedly. An indicative example is drawn from the Australian Weightlifting Federation (2001) which reveals:

> The amount of funding allocated to the AWF for the 2001/02 financial year is significantly higher and will ensure better conditions for our athletes in the lead up to this year's World championships. (p. 17)

Related to this view is the perception by one-fifth of NSOs that whilst there has been a distinct shift in policy towards funding broad-based participation in sport from the previous focus on high performance, the Federal Government acknowledges that to maintain the Sydney Olympic 2000 performances there must be a long-term commitment to sport funding. It has addressed this in its funding programs.

The NSOs indicate that the AIS unit of the ASC forms the 'backbone' of elite athlete development and success. They use words such as 'cornerstone' and 'pinnacle' to illustrate the importance of the ASC and the AIS to their sport. They acknowledge the AIS as a major contributor to elite development programs and in the provision of substantial support across all areas "from sports science and sports medicine to athlete welfare and support" (Australian Water Polo, 1999, p. 7). NSOs maintain that the AIS plays a vital role in the preparation of teams for major competitions and provides financial support, as well as access to first-class facilities and services. Such services may vary from intensive training centres, high performance programs and centres, coaching and officiating, state institutes and academies of sport to anti-doping and drug testing services. NSOs see the services provided by the AIS as contributing to the successful preparation and performances of elite athletes at national and international events.

They often report that their international success and progress are a direct reflection of the above support and services. The Australian Gymnastic Federation (2000), for example, admits that its Olympic results "would not have been possible without the continued financial support of the ASC and our High Performance Network" (p. 2).

Diving Australia (1999/2000) also agrees that "there would be no results or success without the support and assistance offered by the Australian Sports Commission, the Australian Olympic Committee, [and] the Australian Commonwealth Games Association" (p. 7)

Bowls Australia (2000/01) similarly supports the above argument by stating that:

> Our High Performance Program continues to bear fruit with strong performances from both the senior Australian team and the development team in all their international events. The support of the ASC has been instrumental in the development of the senior squad. (p. 7)

2. Elite Success results in ASC funding

The other side of the two-way relationship between ASC funding and elite success is best summarised by NSOs' common belief that elite success is important in maintaining Federal Government funding. NSOs provide numerous examples demonstrating that the ASC continues to recognise success with continued funding and support of their programs. An illustration of this point is provided by the Australian Baseball Federation and its claim that because of its strong 1999/2000 performances, the ASC had actually increased its levels of High Performance funding for the 2000/2001 year. Interestingly, the Australian Baseball Federation (1999/2000) concludes that "this is a creditworthy achievement and 'against the trend' of sports funding patterns in a year which saw most sports receive funding cuts" (p. 10).

Women's Hockey Australia (1999) was "thrilled" with the continued support of the ASC. It continues: "the successful performance of the national squad is duly rewarded by grants from the ASC and with this added incentive, our teams are able to travel and compete on a regular basis" (p. 2). Diving Australia (2000) reports that, following the possibility of increased funding from the Federal Government, it would be in a position to continue supporting the state institute of sport programs.

Judo Australia provides the example of Maria Pekli's Bronze medal at the 2000 Olympics that enabled it to receive additional funds for the running of Judo in Australia from the ASC. The Australian Yachting Federation (2000) demonstrates that its previous good results generated additional funding for its elite athlete programs, such as the Olympic Athlete Program. These results directly led to sailing becoming an AIS program sport for the first time from 2001. It concludes that "there can be little doubt that the results of our sailors at the Sydney 2000 Olympic Games will help to ensure that we get our share of the additional funding already committed by the federal [sic] Government" (p. 5).

In addition, Orienteering Australia (2001) suggests that these results which not only demonstrate that Australia is becoming a strong orienteering nation, but also demonstrate the two-way relationship since funding from the ASC for the sport overall are "highly dependent on our elite athletes achieving benchmark performances in world events. Performances at this level do not come without high quality support" (p. 2) such as coaches and managers.

These results support previous studies, such as Gratton's (1990), that identify elite success being closely related to the amount of resources countries and governments invest in the promotion of excellence. Nevertheless, the case appears to be different for Lacrosse Australia, where elite success can be a determining factor for Federal Government elite funding if it is supported by a high public profile and has the potential to draw mass participation.

At a state level, *state departments*, *state governments* and *state institutes of sport* are praised by NSOs for their multiple contributions. The state institutes of sport, in particular, appear to "look after" elite development. NSOs note the value and the quality of the elite development that they receive from state institutes. Indicatively, Women's Hockey Australia (2000) identifies the NSW Institute of Sport and its programs (NSWIS programs) as "the best and the most professional" (p. 20) within Australia.

In addition, state governments' and sport departments' support ranges from help in organising elite athletes and teams to travel to events and sporting competitions and covering travelling costs, to the participation in the national competition. As an example of this, Hockey Tasmania claims that it continues "to receive valuable assistance from the State Government through its Department of State Development and the Office of Sport and Recreation, which has enabled us to continue our participation in national league competition" (Women's Hockey Australia, 2000, p. 19).

Outside the government sphere, the success that elite athletes experience is a tribute to a number of significant other stakeholders or what the Australian Gymnastic Federation (1999) describes as the "outstanding efforts of our gymnast, coaches and judges and the support of the AGF administration" (p. 8). The ARU (1999) reinforces the above by stating that the Wallabies' victory in the final of the Rugby World Cup in 1999 was "the culmination of an extraordinary amount of work by players, coaches and administrators" (p. 8).

The NSOs support the argument that *coaching* reflects positively on the numbers of quality elite athletes and their on-field success. For instance, Walter Gagg, technical adviser to the FIFA President, declared that the fact that "so many of Australian footballers grace some of the best competitions in the world is a reflection of the coaching and development training offered in Australia" (Soccer Australia, 2001, p. 5). As an additional illustration, Australian Swimming (1999/2000) maintains that part of its success is "owed to the professionalism, dedication, skills and knowledge of swimming coaches across all parts of Australia" (p. 27).

Accordingly, the direct effects that coaches have on elite development and successful elite performances are widely recognised. The following examples represent the most typical statements. The Australian Softball Federation (1999/2000) argues that "elite coaches often make the difference between teams winning and losing at the highest level" (p. 20). It is the coaches that prepare athletes for their successful performances and are partially credited with the success of elite athletes. Basketball Australia (2000) argues that their Head Coach "has taken the Opals to unprecedented heights, culminating with the silver medal at the Sydney Olympics" (p. 9). It was the same coach that guided the Opals to bronze medals at the 1998 World Championships and the 1996 Olympics, and to the semi finals of OZ94, the World Championships in Sydney. Terry Mackenroth MP, Deputy Premier, Treasurer and Minister for Sport, states that "coaches are the heart and soul of Australian sport. When ever [sic] our swimmers break a world record or win Olympic gold, you can bet the coaches they've had over the years have played a major role in their success" (Australian Swimming, 2000/01, p. 42).

Similarly, Women's Hockey Australia claims that in the lead-up to the Sydney 2000 Olympics, the Women's Hockey team was widely heralded as the best prepared ever. It admits that this was because the athletes took advantage of the access they had to some of the best coaches. Overall, NSOs concur that their results have been enhanced by the work of their coaches and maintain that that these results would not be possible without their support and hard work.

Nearly one-third of NSOs maintain that there is a level of synergy between the development of coaches and that of athletes. To illustrate this, Orienteering Australia suggests that the athletes benefit from the attention of coaches and coaches learn from dealing with athletes. Skate Australia (2001) believes it is the inspiration provided by coaches to elite athletes that enables it to achieve some remarkable results. In addition, Australian Swimming (2000) stresses how important it is to foster a good working relationship between coaches and their swimmers which makes swimming in Australia the high profile sport it is today. Arguably, elite performances are the 'product' or the 'reflection' of coaching. On that note, Australian Swimming (2000/01), amongst other NSOs, maintains that its coaches did it proud "with the performances of their athletes at the Sydney Olympics and have been prepared to constantly evaluate themselves and their performances to ensure they are producing the best they possibly can on the international stage" (p. 41).

Nevertheless, there is a fundamental belief that elite success should be credited, in addition to coaches, to the *athletes* themselves, their ability, dedication, and commitment to training. The Australian Gymnastic Federation (2000) argues that successful performances "aptly reflect the quality, expertise and dedication of the High Performance Coaching staff and are a testament to the ability of the athletes" (p. 31). As a further illustration, Skate Australia provides the example of Sophie Muir who successfully won a gold medal in her first year in seniors. Additionally, the Australian Softball Federation (2000/01) notes "the desire, determination, discipline and dedication shown" (p. 27) by its athletes as an important ingredients for their success in gaining the 2000 Olympic gold medal.

In addition to the coaches' and athletes' efforts, NSOs demonstrate that the hard work of judges, officials, support staff, psychologists, members of the state and national technical and sport management committees also play an important role in the nurturing process in assisting elite success. NSOs maintain that elite success is not achieved without the professionalism and support of a dedicated team of all the above members who work hard throughout the year to support the system.

Hence, even though coaches are the 'catalyst' in elite performances, NSOs argue that the *support staff* who work behind the scenes and professional *management/administration* help athletes maintain their performances. For example, Diving Australia (1999/2000) claims that "many psychologists ... have helped our divers" (p. 31), whereas the ARU (2000) suggests that its success "can only be maximised with the professional management that currently exists at the ARU" (p. 67). Adding to this, Athletics Australia and the ACB suggest that an integral component in the success of the preparation of the teams is to keep open lines of *communication* with athletes, their families and support persons.

The numerous sport enthusiasts, including *spectators/supporters* and the community at large, with its support and uplifting spirit, have the capacity to inspire successful performances. As an example of this, the AFL (1999) suggests that the capacity to succeed "depends upon securing the support of the community at large" (p. 16). Almost half of the NSOs support the argument that besides the systematic preparation, elite athlete success is due to the "Australian spirit", which pushes the players to fight until the very end of each game.

For the NSOs that experience excellent performances at the elite level and as a reflection of this success there is an ever-increasing interest by *sponsors*. The ARU (2000) provides an example that illustrates this point. According to its estimate, its sponsorship showed an increase of 38 percent in 2000. Indications suggested that a similar growth was expected in 2001, which was "a great result reflecting the success of the Wallabies and also the professional manner in which sponsorship is managed and serviced at the ARU" (p. 66).

In fact, messages from sponsors appearing on NSOs' reports suggest that they are happy and proud to support successful athletes and teams who act as role models for young Australians. Therefore, a mutual relationship is evidenced between sponsorship and elite success, where sponsorship deals have the potential to assist with advancing performances. As the ARU (2000) suggests, its achievements in 2000 "would not have been possible without the support of Computer Associates, the team's major sponsor" (p. 35).

Furthermore, sponsors' support in the nurturing process is associated with assistance in running *competitions/events*. To illustrate this, Kellogg's Nutri Grain stepped into the breach to support the ARL's National Open Schoolboy Rugby League when the previous sponsor withdrew. As another demonstration, the ACB (1999/2000) suggests that cricket revenue drawn from sponsors also serves to "preserve and strengthen the integrity of the competition ensuring it remains the foundation stone of Australia's international success" (p. 54).

In summary, the results and rankings of the leading Australian athletes give a clear indication that, as the Australian Gymnastic Federation (1999) describes it "the pathways for National Squad athletes to follow to gain selection for international representation are appropriate" (p. 17). NSOs recognise that the practices, policies, programs and the contributions of significant others to the nurturing process are crucial in developing talented young players into outstanding athletes on the national and international stage. Steady winning performances highlight the depth of youth in sport, the effectiveness of programs undertaken and the implementation of existing practices.

The Pathways to the Foundation

Another equally important aspect of elite performances is the potential they have to fire or reignite stakeholder support and involvement with sports. That potential has three facets and is referred to as the *pathways to the foundation*. These aspects are the potential: (a) to increase media coverage and exposure of sports and athletes and generate publicity (*publicity*); (b) to enhance sports' financial conditions (*finances*); and (c) increase awareness, interest and act as an inspiration to individuals, hence boost participation (*membership/participation growth*) and increase audiences and the spectator base (*supporter/spectator base*).

The ARU (1999) summarises the three-fold action of the nurturing process as follows: "While the Rugby World Cup represented an expense to the Union, it's hoped that Wallabies' success will reap a dividend over a longer period, in terms of participation, mass audience and revenue" (p. 9). Similarly, Australian Swimming (1999/2000) has "benefited significantly both financially and publicly from these performances" (p. 34). These facets of sporting success offer the pathways to the foundation and are discussed below.

(a) Elite Success and Publicity

There is a common belief that elite success attracts the interest of media and fosters sport coverage and exposure. This intensified interest produces much desired publicity across the nation. Biskup and Pfister (1999) argued that the popularity of sporting heroes goes hand in hand with mass media and marketing strategies, and the commercialisation of sport and sportspeople.

A great number of successful performances from various sports reinforce this belief. The ARL (2000), for example, claims that the success of Melbourne Storm "created interest in the print and electronic media, whereby Rugby League now 'gets its space' in the media previously dominated by Australian Rules" (p. 8). The Australian Water Polo (2001) uses the 2000 Olympic Games to illustrate the above point and suggests that the Sydney Games success of their women's team "lingered throughout the year with many of the gold-medal team gaining articles in all the printed media while some made it to the electronic media, with one, Liz Weekes, fronting a television lifestyle show" (p. 6).

Squash Australia (1999) also maintains that Michelle Martin's achievements as a player "are well documented with her many successes gaining much needed media coverage for the sport" (p. 24). In addition, Tennis Australia (2000/01) agrees that the Australian players' on-court achievements throughout the year "equated to a consistent level of media coverage across the nation" (p. 24). Women's Hockey Australia (1999) notes that Telstra Hockeyroos enjoy a significant profile across the country for the duration of tournaments. A win of such major importance is also "a great advantage to the team and the sport of hockey, as many national television and radio programs, as well as printed media, created stories and exposure for the sport around the victory" (p. 4).

(b) Elite Success and Finances

Another aspect of the potential that positive results and elite success provide sport is an improved financial position. As a demonstration of this, the performance and style of rugby union teams such as the Waratahs versus the Reds in 2001 "drove a substantial increase in attendance at the Sydney Football Stadium and this has been critical to the improved financial position" (ARU, 2001, p. 43). In addition, hockey was "one of the top four most sought after tickets" (Women's Hockey Australia, 1999, p. 3) for the 2000 Olympic Games. According to Women's Hockey Australia (1999), this is great for the sport on an international basis and attributes to the success of the Australian Hockey Teams. Women's Hockey continues that a successful year on the pitch has culminated with publicity and a higher profile for the team, "resulting in growing interest from prospective sponsors" (p. 1).

Bowls Australia (2001) agrees that the television component of marketing its sport has been invaluable in putting bowls 'on the map'. It has provided further international exposure for bowls' national team, which assisted with its success and is a valued element of its sponsorships. Bowls maintains that it has taken a number of years to reach the level of TV coverage it now enjoys and this must be protected in the interests of the sport for the years ahead.

(c) Elite Success and Membership/Participation Growth and Supporter/Spectator Base

The third aspect of the pathways to the foundation is the NSOs' belief that elite success drives inspiration across the national, personal and junior levels. As people are inspired, elite success provides the potential for membership/participation growth and increases in supporter/spectator base. NSOs agree to what the Australian Gymnastic Federation (1999) claims, that seeing elite athletes of high quality competing proves "an outstanding success with out local Clubs and spectators" (p. 35) in terms of generating the interest and awareness of participants and spectators of all ages.

Similarly, with the success of the Women's Hockey team in Atlanta 1996 "came increased awareness", but that was dwarfed by "renewed interest" (Women's Hockey Australia, 1999, p. 2) as Sydney prepared to host the 2000 Olympic Games. These achievements, combined with other events such as the 2000 Festival of Hockey, give "a wonderful opportunity to showcase our sport to the Australian public" (Women's Hockey Australia, 1999, p. 2).

Another example of increased public interest comes from the Australian Gymnastic Federation (2000):

> The flamboyance and exuberance of Ji Wallace combined with his silver medal success made Trampolining one of the real highlights of the Olympics gymnastics program and increased the awareness of the Australian public to gymnastics and in particular Trampoline Sports. (p. 20)

There is no doubt amongst NSOs that victories and successful performances operate as pathways that "entice newcomers" and "motivate existing" members, volunteers and participants as well as supporters and spectators to continue their involvement with sport. As an illustration of the above, the Wallabies' successful World Cup campaign in 1999 meant that the ARU (2000) experienced a growth "across all age groups, including seniors, juniors, schools and social" (p. 29).

More important, there is a general belief that behind this participation and supporter base growth is the notion that elite success generates pride and inspires the nation. The Australia Gymnastic Federation is one of more than two-thirds of NSOs to suggest that athletes' achievements bring great pride to Australia and that the nation benefits from having stars that it can claim as its own. The Australia Gymnastic Federation (1999) suggests that the athletes' achievements "inspire each and every one of us to achieve the 'personal best' that become so meaningful to an individual" (p. 33). Athletics Australia (1999/2000) also illustrates this point by arguing that its aim is "to build a world class organisation that will inspire and develop personal and national pride through achieving international success" (p. 4).

On a similar note, Synchro Australia (2000/01) states that its teams could not have performed better and "certainly any Australian watching them could only be proud of their effort" (p. 21). The Australian Water Polo (2000) reinforces the above by noting that "there would not be many Australians who were not moved by the deserved and amazing conclusion to the Women's gold-medal final at the 2000 Olympic Games" (p. 1). In addition, Weightlifting Australia argues that the success of Australian athletes at the Sydney Olympic and Paralympic Games, along with the triumphs of Australian sporting teams in world competition, has been an inspiration to the nation. The Women's Hockey gold medal in the Sydney Olympics made not only "Women's Hockey and Australia very very proud!" (Women's Hockey Australia, 2000, p. 1), but their wide ranging appeal was evident and all credit to the team for "the pride they brought to everyone involved in Women's hockey" (Women's Hockey Australia, 2000, p. 3).

On a more personal level, sporting organisations and staff members also take pride when the teams, leagues or athletes perform successfully at a national and international level. As an example of this point, the manager of the Australian Synchronised Junior Teams states: "I felt very proud to be there to see the girls swim in a Junior World Championship and do so well" (Synchro Australia, 2000/01, p. 16). A further example is provided by Tasmanian Women's Hockey which was also "extremely proud" (Women's Hockey Australia, 1999, p. 16) of Bianca Langham's achievements with the Australian team in 1999.

At a junior level, elite success is an important ingredient for junior development. Soccer Australia (2000) supports the view that the growth of participants at junior level continues to exceed other competing sports as Australian youth strive to emulate the number of Australian superstars gracing the best football leagues of the world. The ARL (2000) maintains that the presence of the rugby league team Storm has created "cult heroes" "which is an important ingredient for junior growth" (p. 8) and Australian Swimming (1999/2000) agrees that the performances of its swimmers at the Sydney Olympic Games "inspire a new generation of athletes and champions" (p. 39). As another example of this, Softball Australia (2000/01) suggests that the "the exceptional young talent that we have in all states coming through the ranks ... will no doubt be inspired by what this team has achieved" (p. 27).

Studies exploring the impact of elite success to junior development (e.g. Biskup & Pfisker, 1999; Vescio, Crosswhite & Wilde, 2003) agree that the popularity of elite athletes goes hand in hand with young people's longing for someone to identify with. According to Biskup and Pfisker's (1999) study, a high percentage of boys had elite athletes as idols and saw them as role models for their strength, aggression and ability to get things done.

In contrast, female sport stars do not appear to have a role-modelling function with girls. Vescio et al. (2003) investigated the heroes of teenage girls and the degree to which teenage girls have role models in sport and physical activity. Their results challenge the idea that elite athletes are effective role models for teenage girls with the majority of them describing their role models as older, low-profile women such as family members and peers who shared a similar domain of interest rather than sports heroes. Additionally, Hidson et al.'s (1994) study on the impact of the successful New Zealand performances at the Olympic Games in Barcelona 1992 suggested that the perceived performance gap between elite performances and grassroots sport may hinder rather than inspire individuals to participate or even increase drop-out rates among less competitive people.

NSOs suggest that for the pathways to the foundation to be successful two types of elite athletes' effects on sport development are necessary. Their *direct* impact takes place when athletes are personally involved with activities and promote and coach sports, and their *indirect* impact on sport development occurs as they perform successfully as role models.

Direct Impact

Athletes are personally credited for their national and international success and as great "ambassadors" for their country. Their contribution to sport development goes beyond their achievement and medal winning performances to influence an entire nation, particularly the youth of the nation. Their role is characterised by great diversity and involves promoting, coaching and role modelling. The following example from a squash elite athlete demonstrates the various roles they may play in the sport development process.

Michelle Martin's retirement will have great impact on squash in NSW. Michelle's achievements as a player are well documented with her many successes gaining much needed media coverage for the sport. However, in her role as a person she has no peer. Her frequent nights mingling with local pennant players, attending coaching clinics, visiting country squash centres for promotion, local schools visits and generally making herself available as required within a hectic international playing schedule, separates Michelle from all others. (Squash Australia, 1999, p. 24)

Basketball Australia (2000) provides an example to support direct athlete involvement in the promotion of sport: "Shortly after the Olympic Games, members of the Opals and Boomers visited local basketball venues around Australia to promote the sport... The promotions included questions and answer sessions, autograph and photo opportunities and giveaways" (p. 13). Another example is provided by Athletics Australia which holds clinics at primary schools, led by Australian representative athletes, and provides a link for students between the elite heroes of the sport and the level of participation at which the children can be comfortably involved.

In addition to this and in order to capitalise on the positive results at the Sydney 2000 Olympic and Paralympics, Athletics Australia (2000/01) conducted a Back-to-School day promotion in October and November 2000. Some 51 athletes returned to their school and shared their athletics experience with more than 500 students. These visits "gave the students the opportunity to meet their heroes and gain a positive athletics experience" (p. 15). Nevertheless, some sports admit to experiencing difficulties in securing Australian players for promotional purposes due to hectic training schedules and their AIS commitments.

Young participants also benefit from athletes' involvement in coaching clinics. Filtering down their expertise, athletes (whether paid or volunteer) become actively involved with the sport development processes at the junior level. NSOs argue that these initiatives are successful with juniors. The Northern Territory Rugby League, for example, expressed thanks to NRL players and former players for giving up their valuable time to "help promote and develop our game throughout our regions. These visits by high profile players are always a big success with our children" (ARL, 2000, p. 9).

In 1999, Women's Hockey Australia provided a grant for an elite player to travel to the Northern Territory to coach juniors, while Athletics Australia's (2000/01) high profile athletes were involved in program–clinics (held at primary schools) to provide opportunities to connect young followers with clubs. They form "a link for students between the elite heroes of the sport and a level of participation at which the children can be comfortably involved" (p. 15). The ARL (2000) argues the benefit of elite athletes' visiting schools and coaching in promoting and developing the sport throughout the regions.

Indirect Impact

Indirectly, elite athletes with their superb performances may act as *role models*. For example, the AFL argues players as role models raise awareness and hence the popularity of the code in the community. Women's Hockey Australia (1999) agrees that its elite athletes act as role models for the hockey community and the Australian Gymnastic Federation (2000) congratulates its gymnasts on its "outstanding achievements and on being such excellent role models for gymnastics" (p. 35). In addition, the effects of role modelling are particularly related to junior and talented youth. As an example, Athletics Australia (2000/01) sponsors are proud to support the Australian athletes who are "amazing role models for young Australians as they continually demonstrate the discipline, performance and competitive spirit required to reach this elite level of sporting achievement" (p. 8).

In addition, elite athletes produce role-modelling effects not only on the young enthusiasts and the community as a whole but also on their elite peers and other talented elite athletes. The Australian Water Polo (2001) suggests that the most experienced water polo player, Nathan Thomas [the captain of the Water Polo team], "was an outstanding captain, leading by example and giving the much-needed support to the younger athletes" (p. 8). Squash Australia (1999) believes that its elite athlete Michelle Martin "has been a real role model for the AIS players" (p. 9).

6.4 SUMMARY

In summary, *nurturing* is another facet of the sport development processes whereby the finest Australia has to offer in terms of talented athletes are provided with tailored training, coaching and support services for the advancement of their abilities and performances (see Figure 6.4).

Figure 6.4: The Nurturing Process

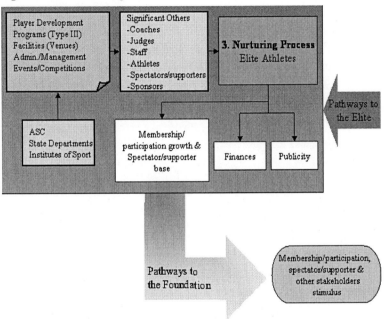

This process represents the impact or the return on investment projected by successful careers of elite athletes identified as juniors. Their success yields the environment and potential to reproduce interest among new or existing sport participants at all levels, in particular juniors, as well as sport supporters and other stakeholders. That potential is essentially the pathways to the foundation that elite athletes take as they influence others in taking up, or continuing being physically active or interested in and supporting sports.

The pathway to the foundation also has the potential to assist in drawing new members, participants and supporters to sport as well as advancing the sporting experience of the

233

existing members and supporters. Hence, even though the discussion on the sport development processes section begins with a reference to the attraction process, graphically all the sport development processes are linked, hence forming a circle where the processes constantly repeat. This function is depicted by the *Overview of the Australian Sport Development Processes* (see Figure 6.1, p. 193).

Each of the sport development processes mutually supports the others to the extent where it may be impossible for sports development to effectively proceed if one of the processes were excluded from the *Model of the Australian Sport Development Processes*. More specifically, the attraction process supports the retention/transition process by offering a pool of young athletes from which to draw elite juniors. The retention/transition process assists the nurturing process by providing the most highly refined talented athletes and the nurturing process assists the attraction process by delivering triumphant elite performances that may attract a number of stakeholders including members, participants, supporters and spectators of all ages into the sporting industry.

6.5 CONCLUSION

Chapters 4, 5 and 6 have conveyed and discussed the results of this study adopting a macro, meso and microanalysis approach. Houlihan (2000) and Girginou (2001) identify and recommend the use of a macro, meso and micro layered analysis as a holistic approach that illuminates policies in the most fruitful and informative way.

At a macro level, the sport development stakeholders' role and involvement show that for a great number of key sport development players, the Australian Government and the ASC play the most crucial part in terms of both elite and mass participation development through Federal Government sport policy deliberations. Nevertheless, a clear distinction is made between the responsibilities of the NSOs and their respective SSOs with the latter placing most of their efforts and resources into servicing the general population and in particular the junior sport enthusiasts.

At a meso level, the linkages between sport policies and their implementation through the sport development practices that are shaped and implemented by the sport development stakeholders become clear. What these practices suggest is that they are all tailored for particular participant segments to reflect the requirements, needs, and abilities of those segments. For example, player development practices offer three types of programs. Type I sport development practices concern programs formulated for membership/participation development needs, Type II relate to the retention of youth participants, talent identification and transition to elite programs, and Type III involve specifically developed elite athlete programs. The different types of sport competitions/events are another example of the specifically modified nature of sport development practices.

At a micro level, the sport development pathways cover both stakeholder involvement and particular practices as they are applicable to the different levels of sporting participation from mass participation to elite and sport spectatorship. Kirk and Gorely (2000) suggested that for sport development policies and practices to be inclusive, they need clearly articulated pathways across all levels of performance and age ranges, the use of modified sports, coach development and the stakeholders' coordinated efforts. The sport development pathways are embedded in the sport development processes that vary from the attraction of individuals to sport to their retention, transition and nurturance, and form the *Model of the Australian Sport Development Processes*. For sport policies to complete a sports development cycle, all pathways need to be in place/operate. The importance of the sport development pathways lies in the argument that the ARU (1999) summarises best, that "to achieve the twin goals of strengthening the traditional base and the developing areas, it is necessary to provide clear pathways" (p. 10).

CHAPTER 7: CONCLUSION

7 INTRODUCTION

Chapters 4, 5 and 6 conveyed the empirically constructed theory on sport development relevant to the Australian sport system. By doing so, this book examined how Federal Government sport policy affects sport development processes, explained these processes and provided an understanding of the role sport practices play in providing the required pathways for sport development in Australia. This study has realised its purpose to demonstrate that sport development does not operate in a vacuum and that the sport policy players have a significant role to play in the process. More specifically, the identified sport development stakeholders, practices and pathways are essential for successful development processes. In essence, this book is the first empirically based work to map "the different roles and responsibilities for those involved in sports development, from the lowest to the higher levels of achievement" (Bramham et al., 2001, p. 3).

7.1 CONTRIBUTION AND IMPLICATIONS

Kirk and Gorely (2000) suggested that for policy development to be "intelligent" it is essential that "it is informed by sound information and that it is research-driven" (p. 131). This book makes substantial contributions to the study of sport development and sport policy analysis in Australia. Previous research examining sport development is sparse, with even fewer studies examining sport policy in Australia. Moreover, there has been no previous research to address the sport development processes and pathways that explain sports development stakeholder involvement with sport. Similarly, there is no previous study to explore how the different sport development facets interrelate. In the absence of the aforementioned research in the field of sport development and sport policy, this study fills in a significant theoretical gap in the realm of sport management. More important, the contribution of this book is threefold as it conveys methodological, practical and theoretical considerations.

7.1.1 METHODOLOGICAL CONSIDERATIONS

Strauss and Corbin (1994) maintained that if "the phenomenon in question is a process, the method of choice for addressing the question is grounded theory" (p. 223). Additionally, Glaser (1992) argued that grounded theory is a general method that can be used successfully by researchers in many disciplines. In terms of research carried out with the aim to either expand or generate new theory, Strauss and Corbin (1998) commented that grounded theory has come to rank among the most influential and widely used modes of qualitative research. Regardless of its usefulness and popularity, the use of grounded theory in sport management has largely been neglected.

Wells (1995) suggested that grounded theory explains social phenomena and processes, the structural conditions that support the processes, the consequences of the processes and the conditions that support changes in processes. Hence, one of the objectives of this study was to assess the efficacy of grounded theory in explaining sport development processes in Australia. Using a grounded theory research approach, the study focused on contextual and procedural elements as well as the action of key players, practices and pathways associated with sport development processes – elements that have been largely omitted in previous studies of Australian sport policy and sport system.

This study utilised the coding processes and constant comparison principles of the traditional grounded theory approach. The results of this book show that the use of grounded theory is equally applicable to the field of sport management. In utilising traditional grounded theory, this study provides the first empirical analysis in relation to sport development in Australia, yields substantive theory on sport development processes and explains the pathways and relationships between the sport development facets.

7.1.2 SPORTS POLICY ANALYSIS AND MANAGERIAL CONSIDERATIONS

The results of this study offer a macro, meso and micro level analysis of sport policy and of the existing development processes and pathways that promote the mobility of participants from one level of participation to the next and foster involvement with sport. This type of examination not only provides a holistic approach to policy analysis, but also serves the traditional aims of policy analysis – to enhance the quality of policy design (Chalip, 1995; Weimer, 1993) and improve design making for public policy decisions (John, 1998). This is achieved by means of referring to the *Model of Sport Development Processes* in Australia, which allows for well-informed, research-based decisions to be made.

Policies are designed in such a way that a set of instructions from policy makers spells out the goals and the means of achieving those goals to policy implementers (Rist, 2000). Well-shaped policies deliver "coordination, cooperation and communication among all interested parties" (Kirk & Gorely, 2000, p. 131). Hence, following the results of this study, policy makers are in a better position not only to produce and design the most effective sport development policies but also to do so in a coordinated and efficient way. More important, each level of analysis offered in this book has its particular implications for the practical facets of sport management and sport development.

At a macro level, this study illustrates the role and responsibilities of the sport development stakeholders and the broader sport policy goals and requirements, explicates stakeholder interrelationships and stresses the importance of intra-organisational cooperation. By doing so, it provides government agencies, sport development officers and sport managers with a clear representation of the context within which Australian sport development takes place. This is crucial for the aforementioned group of practitioners as it allows them to make decisions based on factual research results rather conjectural estimations based solely on personal experience.

People and organisations play different roles and they are all crucial to the success of sport development. Policy makers need to be aware of the roles involved and the viewpoints of the stakeholders playing those roles. Clarifying stakeholder goals and roles assists in their relationships, coexistence and harmonious cooperation. The stakeholder analysis allows all parties involved within the sport system in Australia to understand each other's needs, requirements and interests, and act proactively to develop mutually beneficial relationships for the advancement of sport development practices. The importance of this is raised by Sautter and Leisen (1999) who claim that "if players proactively consider the interests of all other stakeholders, the industry as a whole stands to gain significant returns in the long term" (p. 326).

At the meso level, policy analysis covers all aspects of social life, and sport policy, as a fraction of the policy sphere, can be extensively vast in itself. Sports policies may concern the use of drugs, people with illness or disability, ethnic minority groups and women, urban versus rural sport policies and so forth. This study is concerned with the ASC's sport development policies. These policies, implemented by various stakeholders, take the form of sport development practices. The exploration of the existing sport development practices gives an insight into the impact of the ASC's sport development policies. Hence, at a meso level, this study offers a view of the enactment of the existing sport development policies and demonstrates that appropriate sport policy practices have the potential to operate as pathways to facilitate sport development (creating excellence and stimulating participation). Added to this, the study reinforces what Patterson and Rowland (1990) maintained that policies are the determinants of development and direction. In this study, the sport development policies and the resulting practices provide the pathways that determine sport development direction.

Stevens (2003) suggested that policies capture the essence of values and shared understandings. The crystallisation of policies through sport development practices conveys these values which contain "what to do, how to do it, and for what purposes" (Stevens, 2003, p. 622). These analyses are vital to policy developers as they ascertain and display the possibilities and limitations of the existing policies. Sport development practices reflect the coordination of the sport development stakeholders in achieving communicated development goals. A meso policy analysis exemplifies the policy goals and their compatibility. Therefore, it assists stakeholders to ensure that the achievement of one goal does not undermine achievement of the others, but rather supports them. Policy practices need to be tailored to the needs and desires of sport development segments and recognition of the peculiarities of each practice facilitates its re-evaluation and efficiency in the distribution of resources.

Murphy and Waddington (1998) suggested that the coordination of sport policies may be complex and a meso policy analysis assists in the administration of the complexities.

Additionally, the meso level analyses offered in this book may assist sport stakeholders in identifying other problems associated with the implementation of these practices.

Analysis at a micro level depicts the relationships between policy formulation at the national level and the implementation of the policy practices at all sport development levels, their outcomes and implications for the sport system. Such a rigorous appraisal of the practices and processes involved in the sport system in Australia, pertinent to its current socioeconomic, cultural and political environment, allows for the pathways embedded within each process development to emerge. Recognition of these pathways presents stakeholders with a simple means of evaluating the importance of each sport development process, identifying inefficiencies within the system and developing appropriate strategies.

Such an analysis demonstrates the dynamic nature of stakeholder involvement and policy implementation and allows researchers, policy makers and sport development practitioners and managers to explain and account for the actions of key development players and the participation practices followed by sporting organisations.

This book highlights for sport administrators and governments that the vital elements to ensure successful implementation of sport development are:

a) clear, feasible and well-communicated strategic planning developed by NSOs and SSOs;

b) an agreement on the expectations, roles and responsibilities of NSOs and SSOs;

c) stakeholder teamwork, intra-organisational cooperation and open lines of communications between all parties involved; and

d) a long-term view and continuous re-evaluation of the sport development processes to reflect the ever-changing environment in which sports operate.

7.1.3 SPORT DEVELOPMENT CONSIDERATIONS

This study makes a theoretical contribution to sport development by generating a grounded understanding of the sport development processes associated with the sport system in Australia. In doing so, it critically evaluates Australian practices and sheds light on the ambiguity surrounding the conflict between opposing assumptions about elite versus mass participation development.

The *Model of Sport Development Processes* (see Figure 7.1) depicts the three identified facets of sport development in Australia (viz., the attraction, retention/transition and nurturing of sport participants). The model conveys that the development stakeholders' involvement and roles vary within each process and that a different set of practices is necessary to reflect the needs and requirements of the sport development segment targeted. For example, the needs of the sport development segments represented in the 'attraction' processes call for sport development officers to increase awareness and facilitate development programs for mass participation whereas in the 'nurturing' process, highly qualified coaches within the institutes of sport advance elite athletes' skills.

While the level and types of stakeholder involvement and the implementation of diverse development practices are the major differentiation between processes, the model also illustrates that the three processes have something in common. In order for each process to take place, the three sport development facets require specific and effective practices to operate as pathways and facilitate the sport development processes. These pathways fall into three categories: (a) the pathways to the talented, essential to proceed to the attraction/retention process; (b) the pathways to the elite, crucial to progress to the nurturing process; and (c) the pathways to the foundation, important factors to influence the attraction process. Essentially, the pathways function as the *glue* between processes, so powerful that they make the processes interdependent.

The analyses of the key elements that support the theory on the sport development processes that follows is brief yet intricate. It is suggested that these analyses be examined with reference to Figure 7.1. The role of the theory summary that follows is threefold: (a) it points out the main differences between the new model and the sport pyramid; (b) it reveals the limitations of this book; and subsequently (c) poses questions for further research.

7.2 ANALYSES OF THE SPORT DEVELOPMENT PROCESSES MODEL

The *attraction process* is comprised of the sport members, participants, supporters and spectators regardless of the demographic and socioeconomic factors that define them. The process aims to increase awareness, maximise participation and membership and nourish large numbers of young participants. The ways the attraction process is achieved are through the various practices that sport development stakeholders set up and enforce. In the attraction process, the ASC's funds, programs and policy direction to NSOs focus on increasing mass participation and place an emphasis on junior development. State governments, through their departments for sport, and SSOs and clubs/associations, through their efforts to attract members/increase participation numbers, play a key role in the attraction process. In addition, clubs/associations provide participation and development opportunities to the public and assist in the attraction process at a local level.

The effort of these stakeholders to increase general participation and public support and involvement with sport is supported by a number of practices. These practices respond to the requirements and needs of the general public (including juniors) and in particular with reference to sport facilities, development programs, promotional efforts, everyday administration and management activities, as well as sport events and competitions which are modified/adopted to facilitate awareness, accessibility and increased opportunities for people to become involved and stay motivated and interested in consuming sport. Sport consumption can be at various levels, such as the *support* level from volunteering, the *spectator* level by attending games and competitions and watching or reading about sport, the *consumer* level by purchasing merchandise and sport products, and the *participation* level by taking part at a level commensurate with participants' age, gender, ability and skill.

What brings these practices into realisation in the attraction process is the contribution of significant other stakeholders such as development officers who assist with the implementation of programs/practices and sponsors in facilitating the smooth running of the practices. In addition, sport marketing and promotional efforts increase awareness of program availability, and organisation management assists in providing quality services.

When all necessary stakeholders and practices are in place and put into effect, a successful attraction process is established. Well-established attraction processes not only cater for large number of participants, spectators/supporters and members, they also provide the foundation for the pathways to the talented and a great pool of individuals involved with sport. This pool of individuals offers a great advantage in discovering young/junior participants to draw from and initiating the retention/transition process.

The *retention/transition process* is comprised of junior participants and it aims to capitalise on the identification of the most talented amongst them, retain them and assist them to obtain the required skills to achieve high standards of performance. As with the attraction processes, in order to achieve successful retention/transition processes, sport development stakeholders are involved through various practices to develop sport. However, these practices in the retention/transition processes reflect the requirements and needs of the new stage of sport development. Therefore, a different combination of process stakeholders similar to those in other processes is involved through new ways.

A condition for successful retention/transition is a successful attraction process. Once junior participants are detached from the attraction process through the pathways to the talented, the role of the ASC's involvement is to enable NSOs to foster new talent and develop career pathways for juniors. While schools around the country are an important source for talent identification, it is the various state institutes and academies of sport that play an important role in the retention/transition process as they assist in junior athlete skill development, physical preparation and improved performances. In addition, coaches facilitate the process by training, motivating and assisting junior athletes in skill development with the ultimate goal to be successful at the competitions in which they participate. Therefore, competitions not only present places for talent identification but also operate as the platform for higher elite levels of participation. Effectively, the practices described above lead to the pathways to the elite that aid elite juniors to become successful elite athletes.

Figure 7.1: The Model of Sport Development Processes in Australia

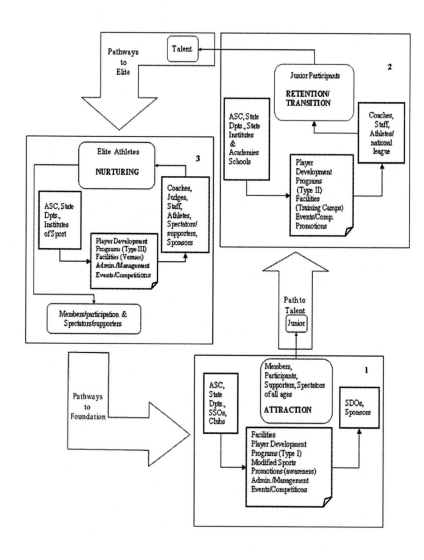

In the *nurturing processes*, coordinated efforts by sport development stakeholders are tailored to specific sports and individuals/teams. The aim is ultimately to achieve international representation of the finest athletes, success at prestigious international events and competitions and a culture of elite athletes continuing triumphant accomplishments.

To achieve this goal, the pathways to the elite that the retention/transition processes provide are crucial in order to obtain well-prepared and skilled athletes. The success of the elite athletes that form the nurturing process is not only a testament to their talent, abilities, commitment and dedication to training and competition but is also a tribute to a number of coordinated efforts from various stakeholders. More specifically, there is a reciprocal relationship between the ASC and elite success. The ASC funding and support at the elite level contribute to elite athletes' success and elite athletes' successful performances are important in maintaining ASC funding. In addition, state governments and departments as well as state institutes of sport support the nurturing process of the elite athletes in various ways that assist in maintaining the momentum of success.

Support staff such as nutritionists, physiotherapists and psychologists influence positively elite athlete performances behind the scenes. Skilled, professional, committed and knowledgeable coaches too play a most significant role in the nurturing of success. Spectator support can also make a difference between winning and losing and, finally, proud sponsors are more likely to finance successful athletes. An example of sponsor support in the nurturing process is the financial and in-kind assistance usually provided at various events/competitions.

Elite success increases the potential for: (a) sports exposure and publicity; (b) increased revenue and potential for improvement of sports finances and most importantly with regard to sport development; (c) increased awareness, interest and inspiration to boost participation and increase audiences and spectator bases. Hence, the nurturing process provides the pathways to the foundation and assists with the attraction process. With the nurturing process, a *Cycle of Sport Development Processes* is complete. Even though there is no obvious starting or finishing point in the sport development processes model, the attraction process is used to initiate the discussion for convenience.

The new model, in contrast with the traditional sport pyramid, is graphically illustrated as a circular process rather than a pyramid form, to depict the links and relationships between all levels of participation from elite to mass participation and vice versa. Hence, elite and mass participation are not seen as two ends, rather as parts of a continuous progression and sequence. Therefore, the model shows that sport development does not cease at the elite level, peak or start at the mass participation base. Rather, it recognises the potential that the elite participation level may have for the Australian public and the importance of the public in the development of elite athletes.

In his exploration of the relationship between elite versus mass participation, Buggel (1986) described two concepts. According to the first, top-class sport and mass participation activities contradict, have nothing in common and reflect two different worlds. The second, even though it features some differences between the elite and mass participation, nevertheless points to "remarkable interrelations leading to positive results for both areas" (p. 43). The model of the sport development processes in Australia portrays sport development as a continuous process and that elite and mass participation support rather than contradict each other, and work in collaboration rather in conflict. The implication of this to development policy makers is the theoretically based recognition of the extent to which elite and mass participation co-exist rather than being part of trickle-up and trickle-down effects.

Figure 7.1 shows that sport development is a much more complex and dynamic process than a static pyramid. The added benefits of the new model are that it:

(a) details the development processes that take place within each level of participation;

(b) shows how each development stage has the power to determine the next stage and is determined by/dependent on the previous one; and

(c) illustrates the different requirements of each development stage in terms of programs/practices and ways of involvement/action required by stakeholders.

While sport policies establish the direction on what to achieve, the framework depicts the results of these policies and practices. By depicting the sport development practices and pathways, the framework reflects sport development policies and may assist in identifying potential policy weaknesses or gaps in policy delivery and draws attention to the required policy corrections. Hence, the framework may assist in shaping advanced policies. The model also:

(d) explains who is involved within each development stage and in what ways;

(e) shows stakeholder-practice relationships within each level/stage; and

(f) shows the impact of this involvement on sport development.

In doing so, the framework conveys the connection between sport policy and practice as well as the impact of Federal Government policies on sport development. By implication, and mainly due to the fact that the model is a reflection of stakeholder action directed by policy goals and implemented by stakeholders, it illustrates that this is a sport policy study concerned with and explaining policy deliberation and its impact on sport.

At the outset, Figure 7.1 might give the impression that it simply depicts some well-known features of the industry, such as Federal Government involvement with sport, the role that a larger base of participants plays for talent identification purposes or the impact that elite success may have on increasing sport interest. However, as indicated in Chapter 2, the trickle-up and trickle-down effects were merely speculation since there was no evidence to support such claims. Hence, the main repercussion of the model is that it provides evidence to support the sport development processes in Australia. Furthermore, there was no evidence from this study to explain trickle-up or trickle-down effects.

The *Model of Sport Development Processes* is readily available for testing (this is explained by numerous examples for further research that follows) and provides the base for future policy considerations, planning and implementation. Interpretations regarding the usefulness of the model may be divided into two opinions. On one hand, the model arguably asserts that the sport development processes are not separate entities because they are interdependent, while on the other hand it encourages sport managers to see each sport development process as a separate entity because each development process requires and involves a different approach to development, considerations, policies, programs and initiatives, planning and management.

It is concluded that sport development is a much more dynamic process than it has been previously portrayed. Providing the right practices are in place, junior participants may assist in elite success, elite athletes have the potential to improve physical activity and interest in sports by the community, mass participation (including volunteers and spectators) facilitates the regeneration of champions, and these processes are continuous. The processes are linked to the extent that a gap in the system would be irreversibly detrimental to sport development. Equally important, these processes can only arise under the condition that the appropriate pathways are available and accessible. Stakeholders, through the formulation and implementation of sport development practices, should ensure that these pathways are developed. Besides this, as the NSOs recommend, only with all parts working together can a successful conclusion be reached.

7.3 LIMITATIONS AND FURTHER RESEARCH

According to Strauss and Corbin (1994), a substantive theory is grounded in research on one specific content area and evolves from the study of a phenomenon situated in one particular context. In contrast, formal theory pertains to a conceptual area, therefore emerging from a study of a phenomenon examined under several different types of situations.

The present study offers a substantive theory on sport development processes as they pertain to a specific rather than general context or situation, and deals with a specific area of inquiry. Therefore, it presents the potential for a formal theory with wider scope to emerge through subsequent studies. Although the study may end with the generation of a substantive theory on sport development processes in Australia as depicted by their NSOs, it provides the framework and the variables from field-based data to be subjected to further empirical testing and future research (Fielding & Lee, 1998).

Glaser (1992) argued that in grounded theory:

the research product constitutes a theoretical formulation or integrated set of conceptual hypotheses about the substantive area under study. That is all, the yield is just hypotheses! Testing or verification work on or with the theory is left to others interested in these types of research endeavor. (p. 16)

Stern (1994) and Melia (1996) suggested that grounded theory would be expected to be immediately applicable to individuals who shared the problem under study and would be expected to be testable. In addition, Hutchinson (1986) claimed that the generalisability of any theory "can be established only through verificational studies" (p. 59). She continued that the point of theory generation is to offer "a new perspective on a given situation to be tested by other research methods" (pp. 59-60).

Glaser and Strauss (1967) first presented the notion of developing higher order grounded theories by moving from substantive to formal theory. Expansion of the research focus and application of elements of a grounded theory developed in one area to other topics or populations, thereby extending the original theory, achieve the shift from substantive to formal theory. More important, grounded theory research is viewed as "the foundation for subsequent deductive studies that test out the resulting theory or interventions based on it" (Oshansky, 1996, p. 394). In summary, Glaser (1992) asserted that grounded theory provides the "bridge to seeing the same problem and processes in other areas so the researcher can further inform his theory and develop comparative substantive theory and formal theory" (p. 15).

The preceding summary of the substantive theory on the sport development process leads to the identification of two types of limitations: limitations of (a) *generic* and (b) *model*-related natures. The generic limitation relates to the *time, place* and *representation* of the study, whereas the model-related limitations reflect sport development process weaknesses. Overall, these limitations present challenges to both sport policy makers and future researchers. In the first instance, the embedded weaknesses of this study, as they are reflected on the *Model of Sport Development Processes*, may depict Federal Government sport policy gaps that need to be addressed and rectified by sport policy makers. However, these same weaknesses of the model present the potential for further research to address its limitations and examine the legitimacy of the previous claim.

7.3.1 GENERAL LIMITATIONS

Time

This book calls for a longitudinal study in order to overcome its present limitation that it reflects a point in time. The sport industry changes rapidly, with new stakeholders entering the field and becoming involved in variety of ways. In addition, innovative approaches to developing sport, constant evaluation and re-evaluation of policies, the changes of governments and of governance styles (e.g. from the traditional/delegate system to the more complex structures of today), the merging/amalgamation of sporting organisations and sport providers and ever-changing societies, needs, requirements and people's expectations all influence the way sport development processes are delivered. Hence, the *Model of Sport Development Processes* may change over time.

Place

This book is concerned with the way sport development processes occur in Australia. It is naïve to assume that the model can be generalised to reflect other sport systems. Some countries (e.g. Canada) may do similar things to Australia while others (e.g. USA) are different. Regardless of how similar or different sport development practices are in various places, the model represents the Australian environment and context and needs to be tested before any generalisations can be assumed. Additionally, it is recommended that at an international level, in order to study sport development processes, a grounded theory method should be used as a starting point rather testing the *Model of Sport Development Processes* under different contexts and situations in other countries.

Representation

This study is a reflection of the sport development processes as they pertain to the views and understanding of sporting organisations at the national level. It is therefore suggested that a study incorporating sports associations and clubs at a state and local level would be useful in providing a better representation of the sport development processes. The *Model of Sport Development Processes* is a practical guide that offers the variables to test. For instance, to further examine the attraction process in relation to the under-represented mass participation segments, according to the model, stakeholders such as the ASC, state departments, SSOs and clubs should be consulted. This could be in relation to their player development type II programs, their facilities, modified sports, events/competitions they run, the support they receive from SDOs and sponsors and the administration management that is required at this level.

Testing the *Model of Sport Development Processes* under different contexts and situations across Australia will assist sport managers in comprehending the ways the model may be challenged and modified to better reflect the sport development system. Subsequently, as suggested by Strauss and Corbin (1994), from a study of the phenomenon examined under several different types of situations, a formal theory on sport development processes will emerge.

7.3.2 MODEL-RELATED LIMITATIONS

Attraction Process

The *Model of Sport Development Processes* illustrates the existing sport development processes and the sport development system in Australia to an unprecedented extent. While the sport system has the potential to attract a large number of individuals such as volunteers, members, participants of all ages and sport supporters/spectators, it evidently places an emphasis on the development of junior athletes and their transition to elite.

With the exception of the junior segment, the participation of the general population and the supporter/spectator needs and development appear to be the least fully portrayed by or receive least attention in the *Model of the Sport Development Process*. Nevertheless, this book suggests that there are a number of practices and stakeholders actively involved with general participation and sport supporters. This suggests that the sport system in Australia under-represents health and fitness membership/participation pathways as well as commercial pathways for spectators/supporters. The fact that junior athletes are removed from the attraction process and are led to the retention/transition process though the pathways to the talented supports the argument that an emphasis is placed on talent identification and elite development.

It is suggested that the membership/participation and spectators/supporters segments follow different development pathways to junior players, which the current sport system does not actively portray to the extent that it does for junior development. Therefore, there is a need for the pathways as they pertain to the aforementioned segments (e.g. commercial pathways for supporters/spectators, and general fitness and health pathways for senior participants) to be identified, clarified and understood. An understanding of these processes will offer a comprehensive depiction of all aspects of sport development in Australia. This will enhance sport stakeholders' understanding and implementation of the right polices for membership/participation and supporters/spectators, as effective as the policies in place for the junior level. Additionally, for the same reasons, the development of coaches, umpires and managers/administrators is inseparable from successful sport development practices and it is essential that it is further investigated.

Retention/transition Process

This study focused on the Federal Government's involvement with sport. The ASC has no influence on physical education in schools and the physical education and skill development components of participation. The provision for physical education in schools falls within the responsibilities of state departments of education. Therefore, the curriculum for physical education and skill acquisition in schools is a state government issue. This suggests that the retention/transition process does not indicate the place and role of physical education in the development of movement skills for future sport participation opportunities. Hence, a complementary study on the retention/transition process that addresses the issue of physical education in schools would be a fundamental addition to the process.

Nurturing Process

Similar to the lack within the retention/transition process, a lack of stakeholder representation is evident within the nurturing process. This poses another limitation to the study. With an emphasis on governments and institutes of sport, the roles of a large and ever-increasing number of sport scientists (such as physiologists and physiotherapists, biomechanics, nutritionists and psychologists) who work for the success of elite athletes in a variety of ways, usually behind the scenes, are largely omitted. Hence, it is recommended that the nurturing process is further explored by investigating the impact of all support staff in the overall process and elite success.

To conclude, this book investigated an area that has been largely neglected and has successfully fulfilled its aim to examine how the Federal Government's sport policy impacts on sport development processes at a national level in order to understand the role of sport policies in providing the required pathways for sport development in Australia. In doing so, this study used a grounded theory method which has only partially been used in the field of sport management previously. In the process, it has opened up a rich and fertile research agenda to be conducted in the area of sport development.

REFERENCE LIST

Annells, M. (1996). Grounded theory method: Philosophical perspectives, paradigm of inquiry, and postmodernism. *Qualitative Health Research, 6*(3), 379-393.

Armstrong, T. (1985). *Sport as public policy.* University of Queensland, Unpublished Masters Thesis.

Armstrong, T. (1987). A debate in sports history-sport and recreation policy: Will she be right? *Sporting Traditions, 3*(2), 162-172.

Armstrong, T. (1988). *Gold Lust: Federal sports policy since 1975.* Macquire University, Unpublished PhD Thesis.

Australian Labor Party. (2003). *History,* Available on line at www.alp.org.au.

Australian Sports Commission. (1989). *Australian Sports Commission Act 1989, No 12 of 1989 - Sect 6*: Available on line at www.austlii.edu.au/au/legis/cth/num_act/asca1989347/s6.html.

Australian Sports Commission. (1994). *Review of Funding Programs.* Canberra: Office of the Minister for the Environment, Sport and Territories.

Australian Sports Commission. (1996). *Annual Report 1995/96.* Canberra: Author.

Australian Sports Commission. (1997). *A guide to the Australian Sports Commission's grants, programmes, and services to National Sporting Organisations.* Canberra: Author.

Australian Sports Commission. (1999a). *The Australian Sports Commission: Beyond 2000.* Canberra: Author.

Australian Sports Commission. (1999b). *Annual Report 1998-1999.* Canberra: Author.

Australian Sports Commission. (2000a). *Media Release: A new direction for Australian sport.* Author. Available on line at http://www.ausport.gov.au/fulltext/2000/ascmedia/20000511.html.

Australian Sports Commission. (2000b). *Media Release: Building stronger community sport.* Author. Available on line at http://www.ausport.gov.au/fulltext/2000/ascmedia/20000511d.html.

Australian Sports Commission. (2000c). *Annual Report 1999-2000.* Canberra: Author.

Australian Sports Commission. (2001). *Annual Report 2000-2001.* Canberra: Author.

Australian Sports Commission. (2002a). *Strategic Plan 2002-2005.* Canberra: Author.

Australian Sports Commission. (2002b). *Annual Report 2001/02*. Canberra: Author.

Australian Sports Commission. (2002c). *Australian Sports Directory 2002*. Canberra: Author.

Australian Sports Commission. (2003a). *ASC Structure 2002*. Retrieved August, 2003, from http://www.ausport.gov.au/asc/structure.htm

Australian Sports Commission. (2003b). *Overview: The Australian Sports Commission at a glance*. Author. Available on line at http://www.ausport.gov.au/asc/overview.htm.

Australian Sports Commission. (2003c). *Media Centre: ASC Fact Sheets*. Author. Available on line at http://www.ausport.gov.au/asc/media/factasc.htm.

Australian Sports Commission. (2003d). *Governance: Principles of best practice*. Canberra: Author.

Australian Sports Institute Study Group. (1975). *Report of the Australian Sports Institute Study Group to the Minister for Tourism and Recreation; A. Coles*. Canberra: AGPS.

Babchuk, W. (1997). *Glaser or Strauss? Grounded theory and adult education*. Paper presented at the Midwest Research-To-Practice Conference in Adult, Continuity and Community Education, Michigan.

Baka, R. (1976). Canadian Federal Government policy. *Canadian Association for Health, Physical Education and Recreation Journal, 42*, 52-60.

Baka, R. S. (1986). Australian Government involvement in sport: A delayed, electric approach. In G. Redmond (Ed.), *Olympic Scientific Congress* (Vol. 7, pp. 27-32). Champaign, IL: Human Kinetics.

Bedecki, T. (1979). Models for national involvement with sport. In R. Howell, Howell, M.L., Toohey, D.P., & Toohey, D.M. (Ed.), *Methodology in comparative physical education and sport* (pp. 136-146). Champaign, IL: Stipes.

Benoliel, J. Q. (1996). Grounded theory and nursing knowledge. *Qualitative Health Research, 6*(3), 406-428.

Biskup, C., & Pfister, G. (1999). I would like to be like her/him: Are athletes role-models for boys and girls? *European Physical Education Review, 5*(3), 199-218.

Bloomfield, J. (1974). *The role, scope and development of recreation in Australia*. Canberra: Department of Tourism and Recreation.

Booth, D. (1995). Sports policy in Australia. *Australian Quarterly, 67*(1), 1-10.

Bramham, P. (2001). Sports policy. In K. Hylton, Bramham, P., Jackson, D., & Nesti M. (Ed.), *Sports development: Policy, process and practice* (pp. 7-36). London: Routledge.

Bramham, P., Hylton, K., Jackson, D., & Nesti M. (2001). Introduction. In K. Hylton, Bramham, P., Jackson, D., & Nesti M. (Ed.), *Sport development: Policy, process and practice* (pp. 1-6). London: Routeldge.

Brett, J. (1997). The Liberal Party. In D. P. Woodward, A. & Summers, J. (Ed.), *Government, politics, power & policy in Australia* (6th ed., pp. 148-166). Melbourne: Longman.

Brink, P. J. (1989). Issues in reliability and validity. In J. M. Morse (Ed.), *Qualitative nursing research: A contemporary dialogue* (pp. 151-167). Rockville, MD: Aspen.

Brown, L. B. (1973). *Ideology*. Harmondsworth: Penguin Books.

Brown, M. (2000). Future sport. *Sport, 19*(2), 20-22.

Brown, S. (2003). *Amalgamation: A guide for recreation and sporting organisations*. South Australia: Office for Recreation & Sport.

Bryman, A. (1988). *Quantity and quality in social research*. London: Unwin Hyman.

Bryman, A. (1992). *Research methods and organization studies* (Vol. 20). London: Routledge.

Buggel, E. (1986). Mass-Sport activities and Top-Class athletics: Unity or Contradiction? In G. Redmond (Ed.), *Olympic Scientific Congress 1984* (Vol. 7, pp. 43-49). Eugene: Human Kinetics.

Burden, T. (1998). *Social policy and welfare: A clear guide*. London: Pluto.

Byrne, M. (2001). Grounded theory as a qualitative research methodology. *AORN Journal, 73*(6), 1155-1156.

Cashman, R. (1995). *Paradise of sport: The rise of organised sport in Australia*. Melbourne: Oxford University Press.

Chalip, L. (1991). Sport and the state: The case of the United States of America. In F. Landry, Landry, M., & Yerles, M., (Ed.), *Sport: The Third Millennium* (pp. 243-250). Quebec, Canada: Les Presses De l'Universite Laval.

Chalip, L. (1995). Policy analysis in sport management. *Journal of Sport Management, 9*, 1-13.

Chalip, L. (1996a). Critical policy analysis: The illustrative case of New Zealand sport policy development. *Journal of Sport Management, 10*(3), 310-324.

Chalip, L. (1996b). Introduction: Thinking about national sport policies. In L. Chalip, Johnson, A., & Stachura, L. (Ed.), *National sport policies: An international handbook* (pp. vii-xiv). Westport: Greenwood Press.

Chalip, L., & Johnson, A. (1996). Sports policy in the United States. In L. Chalip, Johnson, A., & Stachura, L. (Ed.), *National sport policies: An international handbook* (pp. 404-430). Westport: Greenwood.

Chalip, L., Johnson, A., & Stachura, L. (Ed.). (1996). *National sport policies*. Westport: Greenwood.

Charmaz, K. (2000). Grounded theory: Objectivist and constructivist methods. In N. K. Denzin & Lincoln, Y. S. (Ed.), *Handbook of qualitative research* (2nd ed.). Thousand Oaks, Calif: Sage.

Chelladurai, P. (1994). Sport Management: Defining the field. *European Journal for Sport Management, 1*(1), 7-21.

Clumpner, R. A. (1986). Pragmatic coercion: The role of government in sport in the United States. In G. Redmond (Ed.), *Olympic Scientific Congress* (Vol. 7, pp. 5-12). Champaign, IL: Human Kinetics.

Collins, M. F. (1991). Sport and the state: The case of the United Kingdom. In F. Landry, Landry, M., & Yerles, M. (Ed.), *Sport: The Third Millennium* (pp. 261-268). Quebec: Les Preses De L'Universite Laval.

Confederation of Australian Motor Sport. (2000). *Annual Report*. Caulfield East: Author.

Confederation of Australian Sport. (1999). *A whole new ball game: Sports 2000 Task Force*. ACT: Author.

Cooke, G. (1986). The Leeds sports development scheme. *Coaching Focus, 3,* 14-15.

Cooke, G. (1996). Sport and politics: A history of Government funding. *Sport, 16*(1), 17.

Creswell, J. W. (1998). *Qualitative inquiry and research design: Choosing among five traditions*. Thousand Oaks, Calif.: Sage.

Cuskelly, G., McIntyre, N., & Boag, A. (1998). A longitudinal study if the development of organizational commitment amongst volunteer sport administrators. *Journal of Sport Management, 12*(3), 181-202.

Cutcliffe, J. R. (2000). Methodological issues in grounded theory. *Journal of Advanced Nursing, 31*(6), 1476-1484.

DaCosta, L. P. (1996). The state versus free enterprise in sports policy. In L. Chalip, Johnson, A., & Stachura, L. (Ed.), *National sport policies: An international handbook*. Greenwood: Westport.

Davis, G., Wanna, J., Warhurst, J., & Weller, P. (1988). *Public policy in Australia*. Sydney: Allen & Unwin.

Denzin, N. K., & Lincoln, Y. S. (2000). *The handbook of qualitative research*. Thousand Oaks, Calif.: Sage.

Department of Industry Science & Resources. (1999). *Shaping Up: A Review of Commonwealth involvement in sport and recreation in Australia*. Canberra: Author.

Department of Industry Science & Resources. (2001). *Backing Australia's sporting ability: A More Active Australia*. Canberra: Author.

Dick, B. (2000). Grounded theory: A thumbnail sketch, *Resource papers in action research*. Available on line at
http://www.scu.edu.au/schools/gcm/ar/arp/grounded.html.

Di Gioacchino, D., Ginebri, S. & Sabani, L. (2004). *The role of organized interest groups in policy making*. New York: Palgrave Macmillan.

Donnelly, P. (1991). Sport and the state in socialist countries. In F. Landry, Landry, M., & Yerles, M. (Ed.), *Sport: The Third Millennium* (pp. 303-310). Quebec, Canada: Les Presses De l'Universite Laval.

Douglas, S. A. (1978). Policy issues in sport and athletics. *Policy Journal Studies, 7*(1), 137-151.

Dubnick, M. J., & Bardes, B. A. (1983). *Thinking about public policy: A problem-solving approach*. New York: Wiley.

Dye, T. R. (1976). *Policy analysis: What governments do, why they do it, and what difference it makes*: University of Alabama Press.

Dye, T. R. (1987). *Understanding public policy* (6th ed.). Englewood Cliffs, N.J.: Prentice-Hall.

Eady, J. (1993). *Practical sports development*. London: Pitman.

Eaves, Y. D. (2001). A synthesis technique for grounded theory data analysis. *Methodological Issues in Nursing Research, 35*(5), 654-663.

Edwards, M. (2000). *Social policy, public policy: From problems to practice*. St Leonards: NSW: Allen & Unwin.

Eisenhardt, K. M. (1989). Building theories from case studies. *Academy of Management Review, 14*(4), 532-551.

Elias, A. A., Cavana, R.Y., & Jackson, L.S. (2002). Stakeholder analysis for the R&D project management. *R&D Management, 32*(4), 301-310.

Farmer, P., & Arnaudon, S. (1996). Australian sport policy. In L. Chalip, Johnson, A., & Stachura, L. (Ed.), *National sport policies: An international handbook* (pp. 1-22). Westport: Greenwood Press.

Fielding, N., & Lee, R. (1998). *Computer analysis and qualitative research*. London: Sage.

Flick, U. (1998). *An introduction to qualitative research*. London: Sage.

Forward, R. (1974). *Public policy in Australia*. Melbourne: Cheshire.

Girginou, V. (2001). Strategic relations and sport policy making: The case of Aerobic Union and School Sports Federation Bulgaria. *Journal of Sport Management, 15*, 173-194.

Gittins, R. (2000). Sporting policies set to mine gold. *Sydney Morning Herald*, p. 21.

Giulianotti, R. (2002). Supporters, followers, fans, and flaneurs. *Journal of Sport & Social Issues, 26*(1), 25-46.

Glaser, B. (1978). *Theoretical sensitivity: Advances in the methodology of grounded theory*. Mill Valley, Calif.: Sociology Press.

Glaser, B. (1992). *Emergence vs. Forcing: Basics of grounded theory analysis*. Mill Valley, Calif.: Sociology Press.

Glaser, B., & Strauss A. (1967). *The discovery of grounded theory: Strategies for qualitative research*. Chicago: Aldine.

Goulding, C. (2002). *Grounded theory: A practical guide for management, business and market researchers*. London: Sage.

Goward, P. (2000). *We are going to show the world*. National Press Club, Canberra.

Grattan, M. (2001). Grassroots sport targeted as $547m kicked into play. *Sydney Morning Herald*.

Gratton, C. (1990). The production of Olympic champions: International comparisons. *Sport in Society Policy, Politics and Culture*, 50-64.

Gratton, C., & Taylor, P. (2000). *Economics of sport and recreation*. New York: Spoon Press.

Grbich, C. (1998). *Qualitative research in health: An introduction*. St Leonards, NSW: Allen & Unwin.

Green, C. B. (2001). Leveraging subculture and identity. *Sport Management Review, 4*(1), 1-19.

Green, M., & Oakley, B. (2001). Elite sport development systems and playing to win: Uniformity and diversity in international approaches. *Leisure Studies, 20,* 247-267.

Haig, B. D. (1996). Grounded theory as scientific method. *Philosophy of Education,* Available on line at:

http://www.ed.uiuc.edu/EPS/PES-yearbook/95_docs/haig.html.

Hall, R.H. (2002). *Organizations: Structures, processes, and outcomes* (8th ed.). New Jersey: Prentice Hall.

Hall, W. A., & Callery P. (2001). Enhancing the rigor of grounded theory: Incorporating reflexivity and relationality. *Qualitative Health Research, 11*(2), 257-272.

Ham, C., & Hill, M. (1984). *The policy process in the modern capitalist state.* Brighton: Wheatsheaf Books.

Hassard, J. (1990). Multiple paradigms and organisational analysis: A case study. *Organisational Studies, 12*(2), 275-299.

Haynes, S. (1998). Post 2000. *Sport, 18*(4), 3.

Heah, M. (2003). Tips on being a good coach. *Malaysian New Straits Time-Management Times, 7-5-03.*

Heclo, H. (1983). Policy analysis. *British Journal of Political Science, 21*(2), 83-108.

Henry, I., & Chao Lee, P. (2004). Governance and ethics in sport. In S. Beech J. & Chadwick (Ed.), *The business of sport management.* Essex: Prentice Hall.

Henry, I. P. (2001). *The politics of leisure policy.* New York: Palgrave.

Henry, I. P., & Nassis, P. (1999). Political clientism and sports policy in Greece. *International Review for the Sociology of Sport, 34*(1), 43-58.

Hidson, A., Gidlow, B., & Peebles, C. (1994). The 'trickle-down' effect of top-level sport: Myth or reality? A case-study of the Olympics. *Australian Journal of Leisure and Recreation, 4*(1), 16-31.

Hill, M. (2000). *Understanding social policy.* Malden, Mass.: Blackwell.

Hodder, I. (2000). The interpretation of documents and material culture. In N. K. Denzin, & Lincoln, Y. S. (Ed.), *Handbook of qualitative research* (pp. 703-715). Thousand Oaks, CA: Sage.

Hogan, K., & Norton, K. (2000). The 'price' of Olympic gold. *Journal of Science and Medicine in Sport, 3*(2), 203-218.

Hogwood, B. W., & Gunn, L.A. (1984). *Policy analysis for the real world*. New York: Oxford University Press.

Hollway, S. (2002). Vital volunteers. *Australasian Leisure Management, Dec 2001/Jan 2002*, 58-59.

Hong, F. (1997). Commercialism and sport in China: Present situation and future expectations. *Journal of Sport Management, 11*, 343-354.

Houlihan, B. (1990). The politics of sports policy in Britain: The examples of football hooliganism and drug abuse. *Leisure Studies, 9*, 55-69.

Houlihan, B. (1991). *The government and politics of sport*. London: Routledge.

Houlihan, B. (1997a). *Sport, policy, and politics: A comparative analysis*. London: Routledge.

Houlihan, B. (1997b). Sport national identity and public policy. *Nations and Nationalism, 3*(1), 113-137.

Houlihan, B. (2000). Sporting excellence, schools and sports development: The politics of crowded policy spaces. *European Physical Education Review, 6*(2), 171-193.

Houlihan, B., & White, A. (2002). *The politics of sport development: Development of sport or development through sport?* London: Routledge.

House of Representatives (Standing Committee on Finance and Public Administration). (1989). *Going for gold: The first report on an inquiry into sports funding and administration*. Canberra: The Committee.

Hutchinson, S. A. (1986). Education and grounded theory. *Journal of Thought, 21*(3), 50-68.

Hylton, K., Bramham, P., Jackson, D., & Nesti M. (Ed.). (2001). *Sports development: Policy, process and practice*. London: Routledge.

Irwin, R. L., Lachowetz, T., Cornwell, B.T, & Clark, J.S. (2003). Cause-related sport sponsorship: An assessment of spectator beliefs, attitudes, and behavioral intentions. *Sport Marketing Quarterly, 12*(3), 131-139.

Jarvie, G. (1987). Politics and leisure. In G. Jarvie (Ed.), *Contributions to the politics of leisure* (pp. 16-24). London: Leisure Studies Association.

Jobling, I. F. (1991). Sport and the state: The case of Australia and New Zealand. In F. Landry, Landry, M., & Yerles, M. (Ed.), *Sport: The Third Millennium* (pp. 251-260). Quebec, Canada: Les Presses De l'Universite Laval.

John, P. (1998). *Analysing public policy*. Ebbw Vale: Creative Print and Design.

Johnson, T. A. (1978). Public sports policy. *American Behavioral Scientist, 21*(3), 319-344.

Johnson, T. A., & Frey, J. (Ed.). (1985). *Government and sport: The public policy issues.* New Jersey: Rowman & Allaheld.

Kendall, J. (1999). Axial coding and the grounded theory controversy. *Western Journal of Nursing Research, 21*(6), 743-756.

Kirk, D., & Gorely, T. (2000). Challenging thinking about the relationship between school physical education and sport performance. *European Physical Education Review, 6*(2), 119-134.

Krueger, R. (1994). *Focus groups: A practical guide for applied research* (2nd ed.). London: Sage.

Landry, F., Landry, M., & Yerles, M. (1991). *Sport - The Third Millennium.* Paper presented at the International Symposium, Quebec, Canada.

Larson, M., & Wikstroem, E. (2001). Organising events: Managing conflict and consensus in a political market square. *Event Management: An International Journal, 7*(1), 51-65.

LaRue, R. J., Walker, M.L. & Krogh, D.B. (1997). Programming and scheduling. In M. L. Walker, & Stotlar, D.K. (Ed.), *Sport facility management.* Boston: Jones and Bartlett Publishers.

Leach, R. (1993). *Political ideologies: An Australian introduction* (2nd ed.). South Melbourne: Macmillan.

Leeds, M., & von Allmen, P. (2004). *The economies of sport* (2nd ed.). Boston, MA: Pearson Addison Wesley.

Levine, N. (1974). Why do countries win medals? Some structural correlates of Olympic Games success: 1972. *Sociology and Social Research, 28*(4), 353-360.

Liberal Party of Australia. (2003). *Liberal Party in Australia, NSW Division.* Available on line at www.nsw.liberal.org.au: Author

Lynch, R., & Veal, A.J. (1996). *Australian Leisure.* South Melbourne: Longman.

Macintosh, D. (1996). Sport and government in Canada. In L. Chalip, Johnson, A., & Stachura, L. (Ed.), *National sport policies: An international handbook* (pp. 39-66). Greenwood: Westport.

Macintosh, D., Bedecki, T., & Franks, C.E.S. (1987). *Sport and politics in Canada: Federal Government involvement since 1961.* Canada: McGill-Queen's University Press.

Macintosh, D., Franks, C.E.S., & Bedecki, T. (1986). Canadian government involvement in sport: Some consequences and issues. In G. Redmond (Ed.), *Olympic Scientific Congress* (Vol. 7, pp. 21-16). Champaign, IL: Human Kinetics.

Mahony, D. F., & Howard, D.R. (2001). Sport business in the next decade: A general overview of expected trends. *Journal of Sport Management, 15*(4), 275-296.

McDonald, D., & Tungatt, M. (1992). *National demonstrations projects; major lessons and issues for sports development*. London: Sports Council.

McDonald, I. (1995). Sport for All - 'RIP'. A political critique of the relationship between national sport policy and local authority sports development in London. In S. Fleming, Talbot, M., & Tomlinson, A. (Ed.), *Policy and politics in sport, physical education and leisure* (pp. 71-94). Eastbourne: Leisure Studies Association.

McKay, J. (1986). Hegemony, the state and Australian sport. In G. Laurence, & Rowe, D. (Ed.), *Power play: The commercialisation of Australian sport* (pp. 115-135). Sydney: Hale & Iremonger.

McKay, J. (1990). Sport, leisure and social inequality in Australia. In D. Rowe, & Laurence, G. (Ed.), *Sport and Leisure: Trends in Australian popular culture* (pp. 125-160). Sydney: Harcourt Brace Jovanovich.

McKay, J. (1991). *No pain, no gain? Sport and Australian culture*. New York: Prentice Hall.

McKay, J., Laurence, G., Miller, T., & Rowe, D. (1993). Globalization and Australian sport. *Sport Science Review, 2*(1), 10-28.

Melia, K. M. (1996). Rediscovering grounded theory. *Qualitative Health Research, 6*(3), 368-378.

Mewett, P. (2000). Sport. In R. P. Jureidini, M. (Ed.), *Sociology: Australian connections* (pp. 403-425). Melbourne: Allen & Unwin.

Minichiello, V., Aroni, R., Timewell, E., & Alexander, L. (1995). *In-depth interviewing: Principles, Techniques, Analysis* (2nd ed.). Sydney: Longman.

Mishra, R. (1990). *The welfare state in capitalist society: Policies of retrenchment and maintenance in Europe, North America and Australia* (Vol. 5). London: Harvester Wheatsheaf.

Mitchell, R., Agle, B., & Wood, D. (1997). Toward a theory of stakeholder identification and salience: Defining the who and what really counts. *Academy of Management Review, 22*(4), 853-886.

Morse, J. M. (1999). Qualitative generalizability. *Qualitative Health Research, 9*(1), 5-6.

Morse, J. M. (2000). Theoretical congestion. *Qualitative Health Research, 10*(6), 715-716.

Morse, J. M. (2002). Theory innocent or theory smart? *Qualitative Health Research, 12*(3), 295-296.

Mullin, B. (1985). Characteristics of sport marketing. In G. Lewis, & Appenzellar, H. (Ed.), *Successful sport management*. Charlottesville: Michie Co.

Murphy, P., & Waddington, I. (1998). Sport for all: Some public health policy issues and problems. *Critical Public Health, 8*(3), 193-205.

Nixon II, H. L., & Frey, J.H. (1996). *A sociology of sport*. Belmont: Wadsworth Pub. Co.

Oakley, B., & Green, M. (2001). Still playing the game at arm's length? The selective re-investment in British sport, 1995-2000. *Managing Leisure, 6*(2), 74-94.

O'Faircheallaigh, C., Wanna, J., & Weller, P. (1999). *Public sector management in Australia: New challenges, new directions*. South Yarra, Vic.: Macmillan.

Ogle, S. (Ed.). (1997). *International perspectives on public policy and the development of sport for young people*. London: Routledge.

Olafson, G. A., & Brown-John, C.L. (1986). *Canadian international sport policy: A public policy analysis*. Paper presented at the Olympic Scientific Congress, Champaign, IL.

Olin, K. (1981). Structure of sport policy in Finland. *International Review of Sport Sociology, 3*(16), 87-96.

Oshansky, E. F. (1996). Theoretical issues in building a grounded theory: Application of an example of a program of research on infertility. *Qualitative Health Research, 6*(3), 394-404.

Pandit, N. R. (1996). The creation of theory: A recent application of the grounded theory method. *The Qualitative Report, 2*(4), Available on line at: http://www.nova.edu/ssss/QR/QR2-4/pandit.html.

Patterson, J., & Rowland, G. (1990). Teacher involvement in the policy process: The key to a future for the physical and health education profession.

Patton, M. Q. (1990). *Qualitative evaluation and research methods* (2ⁿᵈ ed.). Newbury Park, Calif: Sage.

Perry, C. (2000). A structured approach to presenting a thesis: Notes for students and their supervisors. MCB University Press, Literati club. Available on line at http://www.literaticlub.co.uk/wrtiting/theses.html.

Pettavino, P. J., & Pye G.M. (1996). Sport in Cuba. In L. Chalip, Johnson, A., & Stachura, L. (Ed.), *National sport policies: An international handbook* (pp. 116-138). Westport: Greenwood.

Pfeffer, J. & Salancik, G.R. (1987). *The external control of organizations: A resource dependence perspective.* New York: Harper & Row.

Phillips, S. (2002). *How hockey avoided merger meltdown.* Canberra: Australian Sport Commission.

Pitter, R. (1996). The state and sport development in Alberta: A struggle for public status. *Sociology of Sport Journal, 13*, 31-50.

Puig, N. (1996). Sport policy in Spain. In L. Chalip, Johnson, A., & Stachura, L. (Ed.), *National sport policies: An international handbook* (pp. 346-369). Greenwood: Westport.

Qualitative Solutions & Research. (2003). Available on line at www.scolari.com.

Richards, T. J., & Richards, L. (1994). Using computers in qualitative research. In N. K. Denzin, & Lincoln, Y. S. (Ed.), *Handbook of qualitative research* (pp. 445-462). Thousand Oaks, CA: Sage.

Riess, S. A. (1998). Historical perspectives on sport and public policy. *Policy Studies Review, 15*(1), 3-16.

Riordan, J. (1986). Politics of elite sport in East and West. In G. Redmond (Ed.), *Olympic Scientific Congress* (Vol. 7, pp. 35-41). Champaign, IL: Human Kinetics.

Riordan, J. (1993). Sport in Capitalist and Socialist countries: A Western perspective. In E. G. Dunning, Maguire, J. A., & Pearton, R. E. (Ed.), *The sports process: A comparative and developmental approach* (pp. 245-264). Kingswood, SA: Human Kinetics.

Riordan, J. (1995). From Communist forum to Capitalist market East European sport in transition. *European Physical Education Review, 1*(1), 15-26.

Rist, R. (2000). Influencing the policy process with qualitative research. In N. K. Denzin, & Lincoln, Y. S., (Ed.), *The handbook of qualitative research* (pp. 1001-1017). Thousand Oaks: Sage.

Rodichenko, V. (1991). Sport and the state: The case of the USSR with references to GDR, Cuba and China. In F. Landry, Landry, M., & Yerles, M., (Ed.), *Sport: The Third Millennium* (pp. 281-286). Quebec, Canada: Les Presses De l'Universite Laval.

Ryan, C. (2002). *Athletics Australia overhaul boosts performance*. Canberra: Australian Sport Commission.

Sautter, E. T., & Leisen, B. (1999). Managing stakeholders. *Annals of Tourism Research, 26*(2), 312-328.

Schraeder, M., & Self, D.R. (2003). Enhancing the success of mergers and acquisitions: An organizational culture perspective. *Management Decision, 41*(5), 511-522.

Seiter, M. (1983). Making public policy work at physical education. *Journal of Physical Education, Recreation & Dance, 54*(7), 49-51.

Semotiuk, D. (1981). Motives for National government involvement in sport. *International Journal of Physical Education, xviii*(1), 23-28.

Semotiuk, D. (1987). A debate in sports history: Commonwealth government initiatives in amateur sport in Australia 1972-1985. *Sporting Traditions, 3*(2), 152-162.

Shilbury, D. (1990). Managing corporate sport and the Australian sport system. *The ACHPER National Journal, Spring*, 9-12.

Shilbury, D. (1999). The gateway. *Sports Australia, 2*(4), 108-112.

Shilbury, D. (2000). Considering future sport delivery systems. *Sport Management Review, 3*(2), 199-221.

Shilbury, D., & Deane, J. (2001). *Sport management in Australia: An organisational overview*. Melbourne, Vic: Strategic Sport Management.

Shilbury, D., & Deane, J. (1995). *Sport management in Australia: An organisational overview*. Burwood, Vic: Bowater School of Management and Marketing Deakin University.

Shin-pyo, K., MacAloon, J., & DaMatta, R. (1988). The Olympics and east/west and south/north cultural exchange. In K. Shin-pyo, MacAloon, J., & DaMatta, R. (Ed.). Hanyang University: The Institute for Ethnological Studies.

Silverman, D. (2000). Analyzing talk and text. In N. K. Denzin, & Lincoln, Y. S. (Ed.), *Handbook of qualitative research* (pp. 821-834). Thousand Oaks: CA: Sage.

Slack, T. (1997). *Understanding sport organizations: The application of organizational theory*. Champaign, IL.: Human Kinetics.

Smith, A. (2000). Active Australia? [Radio National (Director)], *The Sports Factor*. Sydney: ABC.

Smith, A., & Stewart, B. (2001). "Beyond number crunching": Applying qualitative techniques in sport marketing research. *The Qualitative Report, 6*(2), Available on line at http://www.nova.edu/ssss/QR/QR6-2/smith.html.

Sotiriadou, K., & Quick, S. (2003). Sport for 'some'. In S. Colyer, & Lobo F., (Ed.), *Leisure futures, leisure cultures: Selection of papers from the 5th ANZALS and 3rd Women in Leisure International Conferences, 2001* (pp. 105-116). Perth, Australia: Praxis Education.

Soulliere, D., Britt, D. W., & Maines, D.R. (2001). Conceptual modeling as a toolbox for grounded theorists. *Sociological Quarterly, 42*(2), 253-270.

Sport Business. (2000). Administering sporting success. *Sport Business, 15*.

Sport Canada. (2002). *The Canadian Sport Policy*: Author. Available on line at http://www.pch.gc.ca/progs/sc/pol/pcs-csp/2003/polsport_e.pdf

Sport Canada. (2003). *Sport Canada Mission Statement*: Author. Available on line at http://www.pch.gc.ca/progs/sc/mission/index_e.cfm.

Sport England. (1999). *Best value through sport*. Wetherby: Author.

Sport England. (2000). *More people, more places, more medals*. Wetherby: Author.

Sport England. (2003). *Sport England*: Author: Available on line at http://www.sportengland.org/.

Stern, P. N. (1994). Eroding grounded theory. In J. M. Morse (Ed.), *Critical Issues in Qualitative Research Methods* (pp. 212-223). London: Sage.

Stevens, L. P. (2003). Reading first: A critical policy analysis. *The Reading Teacher, 56*(7), 662-668.

Stewart, B. (1985). *Australian sport: A profile*. Canberra: Australian Government Publishing Service.

Stewart-Weeks, M. (1997). The third wave: Developing a post-2000 sport policy framework. *Sport, 17*(1), 6-12.

Strauss, A., & Corbin, J. (1998). *Basics of qualitative research: Techniques and procedures for developing grounded theory* (2nd ed.). Thousand Oaks: Sage.

Strauss, A., & Corbin, J. (1990). *Basics of qualitative research: Grounded theory procedures and techniques*. Newbury Park, Calif: Sage.

Strauss, A., & Corbin, J. (1994). Grounded theory methodology: An overview. In N. K. Denzin, & Lincoln, Y. S. (Ed.), *Handbook of qualitative research* (pp. 273-285). Thousand Oaks: CA: Sage.

Strigas, A., & Jackson, E.N. (2003). The importance of motivational factors and demographic attributes at the design, marketing, and implementation of successful volunteer recruitment programs: What sport and recreation professionals should investigate first. *Research Quarterly for Exercise and Sport, 74*(1), 24.

Suisheng, Z. (1999). Liberalization of China and the prospects for democracy. Available on line at
http://www.cnn.com/SPECIALS/1999/china.50/50.beyond/democracy.zhao/.

Sweany, K. (2000). What price Olympic success? *Australian Leisure Management, 22*(42-43).

Sweany, K. (2001). Where do we go from here? *Australian Leisure Management, February/March* (25), 4.

Tak, S. H., Nield, M., & Becker, H. (1999). Use of computer software program for qualitative analyses - Part 2: Advantages and Disadvantages. *Western Journal of Nursing Research, 21*(3), 436-439.

Talbot, L. (1995). *Principles and practice of nursing research*. St. Louis: Mosby.

Tesch, R. (1991). Software for qualitative researchers: Analysis needs and program capabilities. In N. Fielding, G. & Lee, R.M (Ed.), *Using computers in qualitative research* (pp. 16-37). London: Sage.

Thoma, J. S., & Chalip, L. (1996). *Sport governance in the global community*. Morgantown: Fitness Information Technology.

Turner, B. A. (1981). Some practical aspects of qualitative data analysis: One way of organising the cognitive processes associated with the generation of grounded theory. *Quality and Quantity, 15*, 225-247.

Vamplew, W., Moore, K., O'Hara, J., Cashman, R., & Jobling, I. (Ed.). (1994). *The Oxford companion to Australian sport*. Melbourne: Oxford University.

Van Leeuwen, L., Quick, S., & Daniel, K. (2002). The sport spectator satisfaction model: A conceptual framework for understanding the satisfaction of spectators. *Sport Management Review, 5*(2), 99-128.

VanderZwaag, H. J. (1998). *Policy development in sport management*. Westport, Conn.: Praeger.

Veal, A. J. (1987). *Leisure and the future.* London: Allen & Unwin.

Veal, A. J. (1994). *Leisure policy and planning.* Essex: Longman.

Veal, A. J. (1998). Leisure studies, pluralism and social democracy. *Leisure Studies, 17,* 249-267.

Veal, A. J. (2002). *Leisure and tourism policy and planning* (2nd ed.). New York: CABI.

Vescio, J., Crosswhite, J.J., & Wilde, K. (2003). Role models and heroes in the lives of teenage girls. In S. Colyer, & Lobo F. (Ed.), *Leisure futures, leisure cultures: Selection of papers from the 5th ANZALS and 3rd Women in Leisure International Conferences, 2001* (pp. 31-38). Perth, Australia: Praxis Education.

Warhurst, J. (1997). The Labor Party. In D. P. Woodward, A. & Summers, J. (Ed.), *Government, politics, power & policy in Australia* (pp. 167-187). Sth. Melbourne: Longman.

Watt, D. C. (1998). *Sports management and administration.* London: Routledge.

Webb, P., Rowland, G., & Fasano C. (1990). Development of sport policy and programs in sporting organisations: Theoretical and practical considerations. *The ACHPER National Journal, 129*(Spring), 5-8.

Weimer, D. L. (1993). The current state of design craft: Borrowing, tinkering, and problem solving. *Public Administration Review, 53*(2), 110-120.

Wells, K. (1995). The strategy of grounded theory: Possibilities and problems. *Social Work Research, 19*(1), 33.

Westerbeek, H. (2000). The influence of frequency of attendance and age on 'place' - Specific dimensions of service quality at Australian Rules Football Matches. *Sport Marketing Quarterly, 9*(4), 194-202.

Westerbeek, H., Shilbury, D., & Deane, J. (1995). The Australian sport system, its history and an organisational overview. *European Journal for Sport Management, 2*(1), 42-58.

Wilson, H., & Hutchinson, S. (1996). Methodologic mistakes in grounded theory. *Nursing Research, 45*(2), 122-124.

Wilson, J. (1988). *Politics and leisure.* London: Allen & Unwin.

Wimpenny, P., & Gass, J. (2000). Interviewing in phenomenology and grounded theory: is there a difference? *Journal of Advanced Nursing, 31*(6), 1485-1492.

Woodman, L. (1988). Sport development: Systems, trends and issues. *Sports Coach, 11*(4), 29-38.

Xiangjun, C., & Brownell, S.E. (1996). The People's Republic of China. In L. Chalip, Johnson, A., & Stachura, L. (Ed.), *National sports policies: An international handbook* (pp. 67-88). Greenwood: Westport.

Yin, R. K. (1989). *Case study research: Design and methods.* Beverly Hills, Calif: Sage.

Yin, R. K. (1994). *Case study: Design and methods.* Thousand Oaks, Calif: Sage.

Ying, T., & Roberts, K. (1995). Sport policy in the People's Republic of China. In S. Fleming, Talbot, M., & Tomlison, A. (Ed.), *Policy and politics in sport, physical education and leisure* (pp. 109-125). Eastbourne: Leisure Studies Association.

Zilberman, V. (1996). East European Countries' transition to Western model of sport organization: Major trends reflecting changes. *ICHPER-SD, xxxii*(3), 32-36.

APPENDIX 1: THE GROUNDED THEORY DEBATE

1. The Coding Debate

A series of publications articulating the grounded theory processes followed the initial 1967 publication. These include the Glaser (1978) *'Theoretical Sensitivity: Advances in the Methodology of Grounded Theory'*, Strauss and Corbin (1990) *'Basics of Qualitative Research'*, and Glaser (1992) *'Emergence vs Forcing: Basics of Grounded Theory Analysis'*. In fact, it was the first publication of *'Basics of Qualitative Research'* by Anslem Strauss cooriginator of grounded theory and Julie Corbin (1990) which attempted to outline the processes involved in the generation of in-depth, dense grounded theories for grounded theory researchers, and in particular beginners, that ignited the grounded theory debate in the early 1990s.

According to Wimpenny and Gass (2000) the major disagreements between Glaser and Strauss are reflected on Glaser (1992) *'Emergence vs. Forcing: Basics of Grounded Theory Analysis'*. His arguments have stimulated considerable debate relative to the merits of the two positions of grounded theory research (Benoliel, 1996).

Kendall (1999) asserted that both Glaser (1978, 1992) and Strauss and Corbin (1990) employ and perceive coding procedures essential for transforming data into "theoretical constructions of social processes" (p. 746). Glaser calls for *substantive* (open) and *theoretical coding* by means of *saturation* and *constant comparison* of concepts. Strauss and Corbin incorporate open coding yet differentiate by replacing theoretical coding with *axial* and *selective coding*, and the use of a *coding paradigm*, as elements that offer a more structured approach to grounded theory. These changes suggested by Strauss and Corbin (1990) are at the centre of grounded theory debate and have been criticised by Glaser (1992) for deviating from the original method.

Strauss and Corbin (1990) stated that conceptualising data "becomes the first step in analysis' (p. 63). By breaking down and conceptualising they mean "taking apart a single observation, sentence, or paragraph, and giving each discrete incident, idea, or event a name, which indicates something that stands for or represents a phenomenon" (Glaser, 1992, p. 40). Glaser on the other hand stated the opposite. By breaking down and conceptualising the data:

> We do mean comparing incident to incident and/or to concepts as the analyst goes through his data. We look for patterns so that a pattern of many similar incidents can be given a conceptual name as a category, and dissimilar incidents can be given a name as a property of a category, and the compared incidents can be seen as interchangeable indices of the same concept. And when we get interchangeable indices we get saturation. (1992, p. 40)

Grounded theory calls for saturation of categories by *constant comparison* of concepts rather using a preconceived paradigm model (Glaser, 1992). While the aforementioned traditional grounded theory coding and analysis processes are detailed in the data Coding and Analysis Section (3.6), a brief illustration of Strauss and Corbin's (1990) tenets of grounded theory follows in order to explicate the major differences.

Strauss and Corbin's (1990) grounded theory coding procedures involve the identification of categories, subcategories, *properties* and *dimensions*, and then the articulation of the *coding paradigm*. Categories are composed of subcategories called properties, which reflect the characteristics of each category. Properties represent multiple perspectives about the categories (Creswell, 1998), and define the how, when, where, why and so on of a category (Strauss & Corbin, 1998), in an effort to "give a category specificity through definition of its particular characteristics" (Strauss & Corbin, 1998, p. 116). Properties in turn are *dimensionalised.* Category dimensions represent the "range along which general properties of a category vary, giving specification to a category and variation to the theory" (Strauss & Corbin, 1998, p. 101). To clarify, whereas "properties are the general or specific characteristics or attributes of a category, dimensions represent the location of a property along a continuum or range" (Strauss & Corbin, 1998, p. 117).

Strauss and Corbin (1998) maintained that while *open coding* fractures the data into concepts and categories, as well as properties and dimensions, *axial coding* is the analytic process that follows open coding, and the "act of relating categories to subcategories along the lines of their properties and dimensions" (p. 124). Pandit (1996) summarised the procedure of axial coding as the process where the researcher

272

reconstructs data in new ways by making connections between a category and its properties and their dimensions. *Selective coding*, being the last coding process, involves the identification of the *core category*. Pandit (1996) argued that the core category is defined as the phenomenon, which according to Glaser (1992) articulates "how participants process their main concern or problem" (p. 64). At this stage, the research uses the core category to develop a *coding paradigm*.

According to Strauss and Corbin (1990) after the identification of the phenomenon, other categories are then related to this core category using the paradigm. The coding paradigm involves the following elements: *causal conditions, phenomenon, context, intervening conditions, action/interaction strategies and consequences* (Strauss & Corbin, 1990). The causal conditions of the schema are the events that lead to the development of the phenomenon. Context refers to the particular set of conditions and intervening conditions, the broader set of conditions, in which the phenomenon is couched. Action/interaction strategies refer to the actions and responses that occur as the result of the phenomenon and finally, the outcomes, both intended and unintended, of these actions and responses are referred to as consequences (Pandit, 1996).

Melia (1996) found the work of Strauss and Corbin (1990) rather formulaic and not helpful to have "such a plethora of categories, subcategories, as well as properties and dimensions, and the appearance of so many rules" (Melia, 1996, p. 375). Glaser (1992) argued that:

> Strauss' method of labelling and then grouping is totally unnecessary, laborious, and tedious and is a waste of time. Using the constant comparison method gets the analyst to the desired "conceptual power" quickly, with ease and joy. Categories emerge upon comparison and properties emerge upon more comparison. And that is all there is to it. (p. 43)

Even though Strauss and Corbin's (1990) approach has been criticised for being procedural due to the number of steps they outline (Bonoliel, 1996; Melia, 1996), their version of grounded theory has been recommended for providing novice researchers with direction in carrying out grounded theory analysis (Kendall, 1999; Melia, 1996).

2 The Debate on Theory Emergence

The second subject of controversy, as an expected consequence of the use of the coding paradigm, is the matter of theory *emergence*. Kendall (1999) described emergence as the "process by which codes and categories of the theory fit the data, not the process of fitting the data to predetermined codes and categories" (p. 746). In other words, rather than embarking upon research with preconceived notions of how data is to be interpreted, the grounded theory researcher allows concepts and hypotheses to emerge from collected data to continue to influence the ongoing data collection process and the sampling technique.

According to Stern (1994), Glaser insists on allowing the theory to emerge, whereas Strauss prefers a method that is tightly prescriptive. Even though this procedural and mechanistic approach is easier to follow by novice researchers, it has the potential to interfere with theory emergence. Glaser (1992) argued that what is presented in Strauss and Corbin's (1990) book is not grounded theory but full *conceptual description*. In conceptual description, it is argued that Strauss is forcing the data and theory, rather than allowing emergence (Wilson & Hutchinson, 1996) and "a preconceived and verificational approach to qualitative data analysis" (Melia, 1996, p. 371) is used. Subsequently, Glaser (1992) presented his corrected version of generating grounded theory emphasising emergence (Wilson & Hutchinson, 1996).

While Glaser argued that Strauss and Corbin had developed another method, that is conceptual description by means of using a preconceived model, Bonoliel (1996) and Melia (1996) shared the perspective that methods must be re-examined, revised and further explicated and improved in terms of clarity for knowledge generation to take place. They do not share Glaser's perspective that Strauss and Corbin have deviated from grounded theory. In addition, they maintain that methodologies are refined over time and this is what happened with grounded theory. As such, the previously mentioned publications set out new boundaries for grounded theory, raised critical evaluations of the method under investigation and presented the future potential of grounded theory.

Even though the debate about the current status of grounded theory has been growing (Eaves, 2001), grounded theory "has a dominant position in the analysis of non-numeric data" (Fielding & Lee, 1998, p. 39), and may be the most widely employed interpretive framework in the social sciences (Denzin & Lincoln, 2000). It should also be emphasised that regardless of Glaser's aforementioned criticism, Strauss and Corbin's (1990) work has been widely utilised by researchers especially in qualitative health and nursing research and aspects of grounded theory such as open coding, supported by both cooriginators, are pertinent to this study.

APPENDIX 2: NSO INVITATION TO PARTICIPATE TO THE STUDY

Popi Sotiriadou/Doctoral student
School of Leisure, Sport & Tourism
University of Technology, Sydney
PO Box 222, Lindfield NSW 2070
Phone: 02 9514 5412
Fax: 02 9514 5195
E-mail: popi.sotiriadou@uts.edu.au

«Date»

«SPORT»
«Company»
«Title» «FirstName» «LastName»
«City» «State» «PostalCode»

Dear «Title» «FirstName» «LastName»,

You are invited to participate in a research study that investigates the impact of Federal Government involvement on sport. This research is being done as part of my program as a doctoral student at the University of Technology, Sydney and is being conducted with the knowledge of the ASC.

At the moment I am engaged in the exploratory phase of the research. I would very much appreciate it if you would forward me copies of your annual reports 1999 forward (one postage paid envelope is provided). These documents are necessary to construct the study's primary source of data.

In order to contribute to the sport management field, this project has a number of benefits to offer to your organisation, as well as the development of sport as a whole.

PRIMARY BENEFITS FROM THE RESEARCH:

- It will provide quality organisational and managerial data, which will support coaching, conditioning and recruitment. This will in turn bolster performance of individuals and teams on every level of participation.
- It will provide a useful framework to sport policy makers to develop and implement appropriate and effective strategies to assess sport inequities with respect to elite versus grassroots participation.

I am writing to you in the hope that you will see the value of my project and wish to support it. In essence, in return for your cooperation with my research, I would like to offer you a considerable amount of sport management research and data to assist your organisation. Upon request, your organisation will receive: a) a summary report of the results, as they pertain to your organisation only and b) copies of anonymous aggregated data.

If you have any questions on this research please feel free to contact me on 9514 5412 or my advisor Dr. Shayne Quick on 9514 3575.

Thank you for your assistance.

Yours sincerely,

Popi Sotiriadou
E-mail: popi.sotiriadou@uts.edu.au
Phone: (02) 9514 5412
Fax: (02) 9514 5195
Mob: 0418 22 16 15

Dr. Shayne Quick
E-mail: shayne.quick@uts.edu.au
Phone: (02) 9514 3575
Fax: (02) 9514 5195

APPENDIX 3: REFERENCE LIST OF NSO ANNUAL REPORTS

Athletics Australia. (2000). *Annual Report 1999-2000*. Melbourne, VIC: Author.

Athletics Australia. (2001). *Annual Report 2000-01*. Melbourne, VIC: Author.

Australian Baseball. (2000). *1999-2000 Annual Report*. Southport Business Centre, QLD: Australian Baseball Federation Inc.

Australian Baseball. (2001). *2000-2001 Annual Report*. Southport Business Centre, QLD: Australian Baseball Federation Inc.

Australian Baseball. (2002). *2001-2002 Annual Report*. Southport Business Centre, QLD: Australian Baseball Federation Inc.

Australian Canoeing. (2001). *2000/2001 Annual Report*. Ultimo, NSW: Author.

Australian Cricket Board. (2000). *Annual Report 1999-2000*. Jolimont, VIC: Author.

Australian Cricket Board. (2001). *2000-2001 Annual Report*. Jolimont, VIC: Author.

Australian Football League. (1999). *103rd Annual Report 1999*. Melbourne, VIC: Author.

Australian Football League. (2000). *104th Annual Report 2000*. Melbourne, VIC: Author.

Australian Football League. (2001). *105th Annual Report 2001*. Melbourne, VIC: Author.

Australian Rugby League. (2000). *17th Annual Report of the Australian Rugby League*. Sydney, NSW: Author.

Australian Rugby League. (2001). *18th Annual Report of the Australian Rugby League*. Sydney, NSW: Author.

Australian Rugby Union. (1999). *Annual Report 1999*. North Sydney, NSW: Author.

Australian Rugby Union. (2000). *Annual Report 2000*. North Sydney, NSW: Author.

Australian Rugby Union. (2001). *Annual Report 2001*. North Sydney, NSW: Author.

Australian Swimming. (2000). *Australian Swimming 91st Annual Report*. Belconnen, ACT: Author.

Australian Swimming. (2001). *92nd Annual Report 2000/2001*. Belconnen, ACT: Author.

Australian Water Polo Inc. (1999). *Annual Report 1999*. Sandford, TAS: Author.

Australian Water Polo Inc. (2000). *Annual Report 2000*. Sandford, TAS: Author.

Australian Water Polo Inc. (2001). *Annual Report 2001*. Sandford, TAS: Author.

Australian Weightlifting Federation. (2000). *2000 Annual Report*. Hawthorn, VIC: Author.

Australian Weightlifting Federation. (2001). *2001 Annual Report*. Hawthorn, VIC: Author.

Australian Wrestling Union Inc. (2002). *Australian Wrestling Union Reports*. Kenwall, NSW: Author.

Australian Yachting Federation. (2000). *Annual General Meeting Annual Report & Ancillary Meetings*. Kirribilli, NSW: Author.

Basketball Australia. (1999). *Annual Report '99*. Bondi Junction, NSW: Australian Basketball Federation Incorporated.

Basketball Australia. (2000). *Annual Report 2000*. Bondi Junction, NSW: Author.

Basketball Australia. (2001). *Annual Report 2001*. Bondi Junction, NSW: Author.

Bocce Federation of Australia. (2000). *Annual Report*. Kew East, VIC: Author.

Bocce Federation of Australia. (2001). *Annual Report*. Kew East, VIC: Author.

Bocce Federation of Australia. (2002). *Annual Report*. Kew East, VIC: Author.

Bowls Australia. (2001). *Annual Report 2000/2001*. Hawthorn West, VIC: Author.

Confederation of Australian Sport Limited. (2000). *2000 Annual Report*. Malvern East, VIC: Author.

Confederation of Australian Sport Limited. (2001). *2001 Annual Report*. Malvern East, VIC: Author.

Croquet Australia. (1999). *AGM 1999 Report*. Applecross, WA: Australian Croquet Association Inc.

Croquet Australia. (2000). *AGM 2000 Report*. Applecross, WA: Australian Croquet Association Inc.

Croquet Australia. (2001). *2001 Annual Report of the Australian Croquet Association Inc*. Applecross, WA: Australian Croquet Association Inc.

Diving Australia. (2000). *Annual Report 1999/2000*. Carina, QLD: Diving Australia Inc.

Gymnastics Australia. (1999). *Annual Report 1999*. Hawthorn East, VIC: Australian Gymnastic Federation Inc.

Gymnastics Australia. (2000). *Annual Report 2000*. Surrey Hills, VIC: Australian Gymnastic Federation Inc.

Gymnastics Australia. (2001). *Annual Report 2001*. Surrey Hills, VIC: Australian Gymnastic Federation Inc.

Judo Federation of Australia Inc. (2001). *Annual Report 2001*. Ultimo, NSW: Author.

Lacrosse Australia. (1999). *1999 Annual Report*. Aberfoyle Park, SA: Australian Lacrosse Limited.

Lacrosse Australia. (2000). *2000 Annual Report*. Aberfoyle Park, SA: Australian Lacrosse Limited.

Lacrosse Australia. (2001). *2001 Annual Report*. Aberfoyle Park, SA: Australian Lacrosse Federation Limited.

Netball Australia. (1999). *1999 Annual Report*. Harris Park, NSW: Author.

Netball Australia. (2000). *2000 Annual Report*. Harris Park, NSW: Author.

Netball Australia. (2001). *Netball Australia 2001*. Harris Park, NSW: Author.

Orienteering Australia Inc. (2001). *Annual Report 2001*. Glebe, NSW: Author.

Orienteering Federation of Australia Inc. (1999). *Annual Report 1999*. Glebe, NSW: Author.

Orienteering Federation of Australia Inc. (2000). *Annual Report 2000*. Glebe, NSW: Author.

Professional Golfers' Association of Australia Limited. (2000). *Annual Report 1999/2000*. Crows Nest, NSW: Author.

Roller Sports Australia. (2001). *Annual Report*. Cairns, QLD: Author.

Skiing Australia. (2000). *Skiing Australia Annual Report 1999/2000*. Melbourne, VIC: Skiing Australia Limited.

Soccer Australia. (2000). *Soccer Australia Annual Report 2000*. Sydney, NSW: Author.

Soccer Australia. (2001). *Annual Report 2001*. Sydney, NSW: Author.

Softball Australia. (2000). *1999/2000 Yearbook (16th edition)*. Box Hill, VIC: Australian Softball Federation Inc.

Softball Australia. (2001). *2000/2001 Year Book (17th edition)*. Box Hill, VIC: Australian Softball Federation Inc.

Squash Australia Ltd. (1999). *1999 Annual Report*. Milton, QLD: Author.

Squash Australia Ltd. (2000). *2000 Annual Report*. Milton, QLD: Author.

Squash Australia Ltd. (2001). *2001 Annual Report*. Milton, QLD: Author.

Surf Life Saving Australia. (2000). *2000 Annual Report*. Brighton Le Sands, NSW: Author.

Surf Life Saving Australia. (2001). *Annual Report 2001*. Brighton Le Sands, NSW: Author.

Synchro Australia. (2000). *Annual Report 1999-2000*. Nunawading, VIC: Synchronised Swimming Australia Inc.

Synchro Australia. (2001a). *Annual Report 2000-2001*. Nunawading, VIC: Synchronised Swimming Australia Inc.

Synchro Australia. (2001b). *Annual Report 2001-2002*. Nunawading, VIC: Synchronised Swimming Australia Inc.

Taekwondo Australia Inc. (2001). *Annual Report*. Eight Mile Plains, QLD: Author.

Taekwondo Australia Inc. (2002). *Annual Report 2002*. Eight Mile Plains, QLD: Author.

Tennis Australia. (2000). *1999-2000 Annual Report*. Melbourne, VIC: Author.

Tennis Australia. (2001). *Annual Report 2000-2001*. Melbourne, VIC: Author.

The Equestrian Federation of Australia. (2001). *2001 Reports*. Eastwood, SA: Author.

Women's Hockey Australia. (1999). *1999 Annual Report*. Surry Hills, NSW: Author.

Women's Hockey Australia. (2000). *2000 Annual Report*. Surry Hills, NSW: Author.

VDM publishing house ltd.

Scientific Publishing House

offers

free of charge publication

of current academic research papers, Bachelor´s Theses, Master's Theses, Dissertations or Scientific Monographs

If you have written a thesis which satisfies high content as well as formal demands, and you are interested in a remunerated publication of your work, please send an e-mail with some initial information about yourself and your work to *info@vdm-publishing-house.com.*

Our editorial office will get in touch with you shortly.

VDM Publishing House Ltd.
Meldrum Court 17.
Beau Bassin
Mauritius
www.vdm-publishing-house.com